LAST WORDS

LAST WORDS

VARIATIONS ON A THEME IN CULTURAL HISTORY

Karl S. Guthke

REVISED, EXPANDED, AND TRANSLATED BY THE AUTHOR

PRINCETON UNIVERSITY PRESS

PRINCETON, NEW JERSEY

Frontispiece:
Rubens, *The Dying Seneca*.
Courtesy of the Bayr.
Staatsgemäldesammlungen, Munich

*Library of Congress Cataloging-in-
Publication Data*

Guthke, Karl S.
Last words : variations on a theme
in cultural history / Karl S. Guthke
p.   cm.
Includes bibliographical references
and index.
ISBN 0-691-05688-9

Originally published as *Letzte Worte*
by C. H. Beck Verlag, 1990.

This book has been composed in
Linotron Palatino

Princeton University Press books are
printed on acid-free paper, and meet
the guidelines for permanence and
durability of the Committee on
Production Guidelines for Book
Longevity of the Council on Library
Resources

Printed in the United States of
America

10 9 8 7 6 5 4 3 2 1

Contents

Preface vii

A Note on the English Version ix

1 LAST WORDS IN Forms and Meaning of
 EVERYDAY CULTURE a Convention in Life
    and Letters 3

2 WHY THE INTEREST IN Completion, Immortal-
 LAST WORDS? ity, Mystique 48

3 PORK-PIE OR FATHER- The Last Words as
 LAND: AUTHENTIC OR Artifact and "Inherited
 BEN TROVATO? Mythology" 67

4 GUIDANCE, ENTERTAIN- Anthologies of Last
 MENT, AND FRISSON Words 98

5 AN INTELLECTUAL Landmarks in Un-
 HISTORY OF LAST WORDS? charted Terrain 155

Notes 191

Select Bibliography 229

Index 236

Preface

Death, as *the* taboo of our time, arouses secret interest. The "last words" of the dying stand on the border of that taboo region. Interest in them is less inhibited, having grown for centuries before death itself became a forbidden topic. As a result, last words have been a familiar concept in the world of our experience, an institution in fact; paying attention to them is a well-established tradition. Accordingly, such words of the final moment, such exit lines, meet certain expectations. What expectations? Why? How? The last words of the famous and the not-so-famous have become so commonplace in our everyday life that we forget to ask such questions—until we are made conscious of them by a film or novel or play, a newspaper story, a biography, a hit song, or one of those anthologies of last words which have become ever more popular in recent years.

How does one come upon such a subject? To commemorate the bicentenary of the death of the Swiss scientist and writer Albrecht von Haller (whose remarkably bad looks are flatteringly portrayed on the 500-franc note), I was asked several years ago to deliver an address in Berne, his hometown. It was only natural to start with the circumstances of his death. One source stated that Haller, whose works include edifying Christian apologetics, had passed on with an appropriate confession of faith on his lips; another source claimed the opposite, that Haller had—in so many words—died the unbeliever he was rumored to have been. Yet a third reported that the great empiricist physiologist felt his own pulse and whispered with his last breath: "It's beating...beating...beating—it's stopped." Was Haller's lifelong intellectual conflict played out on his very deathbed? A biographer commented that "for a long time there was widespread and heated discussion" about which source was right. To be sure, a fourth "last word" turned up in due course, one which should have satisfied all parties: "I am calm."[1] Still, the fundamental question had been posed, and it was a challenge: Was one faced here with a feature of cultural history that might be worth pondering? One that might be able to tell us something about ourselves, as members of the human species or as individuals? A few years before his death, the Swiss dramatist Friedrich Dürrenmatt discovered a fifth version of Haller's last words in a note written by the pastor officiating at the deathbed: "My God! I am dying!" When Dürrenmatt reported the find in his acceptance speech for the Schiller Prize of the State of Baden-Württemberg in 1986, he not only furnished yet another example of the vitality of the institution—of the widespread cultural convention of paying attention to last words—then and now, he also confessed in a more personal vein: "Haller, feeling his own pulse while dying, has become a symbol of my writing."[2] And why does the audience smile so knowingly at the scene in Robert Bresson's film *Le Diable probablement* in which the protagonist has himself shot in the back in the Père Lachaise cemetery in mid-sentence, commenting that the bullet is interrupting his last word?

My interest in this at first esoteric and then no longer so esoteric subject refused to be shaken off. As Thomas Mann noted in *The Genesis of a Novel*: "There is something almost comical about the ability and willingness to find references to one's own passionate preoccupation in whatever one reads, and the truth is that pertinent things run into one from all directions, they are played into one's hands virtually in the manner of a procurer."

Over the years many people have humored my fascination with last words with "procuring" indulgence or a kind of sportsmanship bordering on complicity. I think of them with gratitude; almost every page of this book harbors happy memories of this sort. And when I heard "You should go on with it. It's dilettantish," I knew to whom I should dedicate this book.

Parts of *Last Words* were written in 1987 during my Fellowship at the Institute of Advanced Studies in the Humanities at the University of Edinburgh, thanks to its director, Professor Peter Jones, who, no stay-at-home himself, saw academic possibilities in this somewhat adventurous expedition into rarely traveled territories. I should also like to thank my assistant Doris Sperber for her patience, for her help with explorations in libraries, and for the good spirits with which she has allowed herself to be caught up in my interest in this subject.

K.S.G.

A Note on the English Version

Last Words is a translation of *Letzte Worte* (1990), extensively revised and significantly enlarged. I undertook it during my stay in a mountaintop village in the Vaucluse beneath Mont Ventoux, with friends interrupting my routine with excursions throughout Provence, which generated the good cheer I hope is evident on some of the following pages. The section on Shakespeare's use of last words in Chapter I replaces a discussion of dying speeches in German drama of the age of Goethe. Once again, many people, humorously tolerant of seeming scholarly eccentricity, have aided and abetted my project with suggestions for additions of all kinds—colleagues, friends, associates, students; above all, the ever-resourceful and enterprising members of Harvard's Signet Society, and the stimulatingly conspiratorial group that made my Freshman Seminars on Last Words in the fall of 1990 and 1991 an unusually happy teaching experience. Further new material was unearthed during my Fellowship in the summer of 1991 at the Herzog-August-Bibliothek Research Center, Wolfenbüttel. Special thanks are due to Daniel Sharfstein for valuable references to last words in popular culture, and to Justin Levitt for calling my attention to the works of art mentioned in the following pages.

Translations of quotations are my own, unless noted otherwise. Earlier versions of some sections were published in *The Harvard Library Bulletin* (1988), *Fictions of Culture*, ed. Steven Taubeneck (Frankfurt, 1991), and *Jahrbuch der Deutschen Shakespeare-Gesellschaft West* (1992).

I am most grateful to Robert C. Sprung for the critical care with which he reviewed my translation. To Rainer Gruenter I am indebted for the postcard reproduced on page 82.

K.S.G.

LAST WORDS

1

LAST WORDS IN EVERYDAY CULTURE

Forms and Meaning of a Convention in Life and Letters

✜

"The unexamined life is not worth living." Such has been the conventional wisdom of the educated ever since Plato reported the words of Socrates in the *Apology* (38 B). Goethe, the unfailing oracle of worldly wisdom in German-speaking lands, equated the unexamined life with that of an oyster,[1] which generally enjoys a lesser reputation with writers than with gourmets; Hume and Holberg come to mind. Samuel Johnson thought a life without reflection was fit for oxen.[2] But whether oyster or ox, the opposite is man as a being conscious of himself. This "eccentric" ability of man to reflect on himself forms the foundation for the anthropology of, among others, Helmuth Plessner, who, from this point of view, also went on to define man as the only form of life capable of laughing and weeping.[3]

By definition, reflection on one's own self is realized only retrospectively. Such retrospection, such self-examination, takes one form when we are young, another when we are middle-aged, and yet a different one when we are old. But, according to Walter Benjamin's much-quoted essay on narra-

tion, it is only at the very end that human life gains "communicable" or "transmissable" form as well as "that authority
. . . which even the poorest soul has over the survivors when
it comes time for him to die."[4] This final, self-validating articulation of consciousness in extremis is commonly known as
"the last word" or "the dying word."

The last word's special rank is more than hinted at in Hugo
von Hofmannsthal's *Death and the Fool*, in which the protagonist is troubled by the realization that it is only the approach
of death that may teach us "to see life not through a veil, but
clearly and in its entirety."[5] Accordingly, we associate truth
and wisdom with last words. We are alerted to this fact by the
Renaissance proverb, often paraphrased by Shakespeare, to
the effect that nobody would die with a lie on his lips (because
it could offer no earthly gain and would gamble away the
grace of God),[6] or the quotations familiar to every Frenchman:
"He who has only a moment to live has no longer anything to
hide" (Quinault), and "Wisdom is on the lips of those who are
about to die" (Lamartine).[7]

Last words in this sense are an element of culture, particularly in the Western world, or an "institution" (D. J. Enright)
that has been accorded particular attention, even reverence,
for centuries. "The tongues of dying men / Enforce attention,
like deep harmony" (*Richard II*, II.1.5–6). At the very least, last
words have been a well-established concept, a familiar theme
in our culture. But how is this theme defined more precisely?
What are its facets? What questions does it raise and what
problems are implied in it? What insights does it permit? Let
us first look at a few cases: the last words of some famous
persons (or what passes for their last words and as such has
entered our literary folklore).

When Oscar Wilde lay dying in the Hôtel d'Alsace in Paris,
his last words were, "I am dying, as I have lived, beyond my
means." How fitting. When the nurse attending Henrik Ibsen
at his last illness whispered to bystanders that he seemed a

little better, Ibsen retorted "on the contrary" and died. What could be more in character? Franz Kafka's last coherent remark was to his friend and physician, Robert Klopstock, who had promised him morphine, "Kill me, or else you are a murderer." Could anything be more typical of the master and victim of paradox? Goethe muttered something about opening the shutter so that "more light" might come in before he fell silent in the green Biedermeier armchair in his bedroom from which, in earlier years, he had on occasion made profounder pronouncements. It has been thought for generations that this epitome of the Enlightenment could not have chosen a more appropriate exit line. "But the peasants," said Tolstoy as the end was approaching in the house of the Astapovo stationmaster, "how do peasants die?" One might have guessed it. Diderot's final gem is authoritatively reported to have been, "The first step toward philosophy is incredulity." Consistent to the end. Gustav Mahler's heart stopped after a final word which is food for thought and argument for both historians of music and others: "Who will now look after Schönberg?" Exiled King Umberto II of Italy expired on 18 March 1983 in Geneva with just one word on his lips, according to an eight-line item in *Newsweek*: "Italia";[8] while kings of Sweden tend to murmur "Sweden" when the curtain falls, according to usually well informed Swedish sources. Brendan Behan, much like a character in one of his plays, is said to have used his final breath to thank the nun who was wiping his feverish forehead: "Thank you, Sister! May all your sons be bishops." The last words heard from Cecil Rhodes, at the height of his imperial achievement, were: "So little done, so much to do." Suitable for framing. Heinrich Heine, predictably, checked out with a witticism: "God will forgive me; that's his job." On his deathbed, Frederick William I of Prussia, father of a flute-playing son, listened to the hymn "Naked I came into the world, naked I shall leave it" and died claiming a royal exception to the human rule: "No, not quite naked, I shall have my uniform on." What else could the soldier-king have said? Edith Sitwell's last words were in reply to being asked how she felt: "I am dying, but otherwise quite well." How Edith could Dame Edith be. Gainsborough's thought, as the final darkness closed in on him: "We are all going to heaven, and Van Dyck is of the company." Who else? First things last.[9] And finally, a popular magazine reported a few years ago that Conrad Hilton, in reply to the question whether he had one last message to the world, solemnly intoned, "Leave the shower curtain on the *inside* of the tub," and passed away.

This random roll call of quality ghosts could be continued indefinitely, were it not for consideration of the reader. For the last words of hundreds and perhaps thousands of people—famous, infamous, and obscure—are known and anthologized, quoted and misquoted, until they become bon mots known by everyone including the dying—who sometimes have an unblushing way of quoting each other without attribution (which would never be forgiven in closer-to-life scholarship).[10] For example, at least six persons, when asked on their deathbeds to renounce the devil, are reported to have replied: "This is no time for making enemies."[11]

It seems safe to conclude from all this what one already knows instinctively: particular importance is, and has always been, attached to last words. Indeed, they have been treasured since time immemorial in cultural communities that otherwise have little in common. As a result, last words have survived where other, perhaps more significant, words have not; in some instances, they have become proverbial.

Dying words have a better than usual chance to survive. There are reasons, reasons rooted very deep in human nature, why men pay particular attention to them and preserve them. They answer an expectation. The interest, because so natural, is older than anyone can say. It is and has been for uncounted centuries the daily stuff of legends and biographies and histories and ballads, has pointed many a moral and adorned many a tale. Peoples far distant in time, place and customs have joined in the feeling that the utterance which is never to be followed by any other is by that very fact significant. Sometimes we remember nothing else, nothing of Nathan Hale or Captain Lawrence except their last words. Those who have never read Goethe in prose or verse can still tell you that he said on his death-bed, "More light!"[12]

The process in which such dying words become common property even today is observed with a keen eye, and not without irony, by Carlos Fuentes in his novel *The Old Gringo*: "Try always to get yourself killed—that was the last thing General Frutos García said before he died in 1964 in his home in Mexico City, and his words became famous among the anecdotes told by the men who had fought in the Revolution."[13] To most readers, incidentally, this is probably one of the many cases in which death is more memorable than the life preceding it, or indeed is the only reminder that there ever was such a life.

Last words, then, seem to have a status all of their own in life and literature in the Western world (we shall go no further afield for the time being, although there appears to be a similar convention in Japan, for example). This status, guaranteed by the irrevocability of the final utterance, is highlighted perhaps by the way we use such phrases as "to have the last word," or "the last word on . . ." (makeup, or life insurance); in the German idiom, a person who pledges to speak "no dying word" (*kein Sterbenswort*) will be silent even under the greatest pressure to tell the truth. The special status of last words also tends to provide inspiration for a characteristic brand of jokes: the *Edinburgh University Library Guide* no. 42, on *Dissertation and Report Writing* (1986), reminds its students that professors whisper "Verify your references" just before they are gathered to their academic fathers (p. 14); the gentleman of the old school in the electric chair, when asked if he has any final thoughts, regrets that he cannot offer his seat to a lady, etc. Indeed, the collective imagination tends to invent such anecdotal last words in cases in which no last utterance of the sort is actually recorded—as in the macabre story about the suicide of the Viennese critic and historian Egon Friedell: jumping out the window of his apartment a step ahead of the Gestapo, he is said to have shouted: "Watch out, please!" On the day of his suicide in 1972, French novelist Henri de Montherlant, according to a sophisticated travel-guide to Paris, had dinner in his customary restaurant; when the waiter, as always, brought him his decaffeinated coffee, he instructed him: "Today I'll have a real coffee."[14]

Some people, however, do apparently make an effort to die with words that lend themselves to such anecdotes, be it Laurence Olivier, whom *Encounter* reports to have expired with a theatrical reference to *Hamlet*,[15] or the otherwise-unknown killer of a Louisiana State trooper, who said, referring to his victim's family, "I hope they're happy."[16] In any case, last-word jokes, often in the form of cartoons—Gene Shalit's *Laughing Matters*[17] reprints one from *Playboy* about someone editing and reediting his "really and truly" last words—are not below the standards of the *New Yorker* (General Wolfe trying to think of the right last word; a man at the side of a hospital bed directing, "Call in the family, Nurse McIntire. I think he's about to process his last words"[18]); nor beneath the *New York Review of Books* (which put Goethe's last words about more light back into their original, nonsymbolic context[19]); nor the scholarly journal *Genre* (Mirabeau to Count Lamarck: "Connoisseur of beautiful deaths, are you content?" and the historian Frederick Jackson Turner: "Tell Max [Ferrand, his agent] I am sorry that I haven't finished my book"[20]). In their way, such jokes too point to the fact that last words are cultural heirlooms.

The belief, alluded to by Socrates in the *Apology* (39C), that the words of the dying have *magical* powers and that the dying are distinguished by the gift of *prophecy* is now considered limited to "primitive" societies.[21] But "civilized" society still expects significant persons to die with significant words. Novelist and biographer Wolfgang Hildesheimer, committed to the view that the whole truth of a life will escape the searching glance even of the most painstaking biographer, noted bitterly in his *Mozart*: "The last hours and the death of genius . . . must provide at least some undisputed beauty for reverent generations to come; they must also have the stuff of tradition, 'last words,' last gestures."[22] Rilke's alleged last words—"Aber die Höllen!"—which supposedly took back the message of his poetry and his life, were the subject of a notorious and protracted controversy.[23]

In the past, the expectation associated with last words was even greater than it is today. For example, Puritan "conduct books"—handbooks of holy living and dying popular in the sixteenth, seventeenth, and eighteenth centuries—were quite explicit about the duty of the dying not to depart from this world without words designed to leave an impression on the survivors.[24] And throughout the nineteenth century, if novels and biographies are any guides at all, the formal deathbed scene, with family and friends in attendance, complete with last words and not infrequently theatrical, was a sine qua non of the final hours and, hence, part and parcel of virtually everybody's life experience—and eagerly sought after at that. Failure to speak a last word caused great disappointment, as private notes and letters document.[25] There was, in fact, a virtual cult of deathbed scenes and of last words. "In those days," one reads in Willa Cather's *Death Comes for the Archbishop*,

> even in European countries, death had a solemn social importance. It was not regarded as a moment when certain bodily organs ceased to function, but as a dramatic climax, a moment when the soul made its entrance into the next world, passing

in full consciousness through a lowly door to an unimaginable scene. . . . The "Last Words" of great men, Napoleon, Lord Byron, were still printed in gift books, and the dying murmurs of every common man and woman were listened for and treasured by their neighbours and kinfolk. These sayings, no matter how unimportant, were given oracular significance and pondered by those who must one day go the same road.[26]

The death of the Anglican divine William Marsh (1775–1864) is an illuminating case in point: "In their eagerness to catch [his] last testament his family installed his eldest daughter in the sick room, unseen by him, to record his conversation, whereupon he recovered and the entire process had to be repeated over a year later."[27]

"In those days" one could therefore give incomparable weight to someone's or even one's own convictions by passing them off as utterances of the last moment, as did, for instance, a certain "M. H.," whose pious meditations appeared as *Death-Bed Thoughts*, despite the fact that she survived to publish them at the insistence of "some dear and intimate friends."[28]

Even in the twentieth century, this convention has not lost its power. The Mexican revolutionary Pancho Villa, assassinated on his ranch in Chihuahua in 1923, died imploring a journalist: "Don't let it end like this. Tell them I said something." Whether authentic or not, this often-cited remark pointedly plays up the collective fascination with last words. William Saroyan, in his essay "Last Words of the Great," describes his own thrill at discovering this phenomenon:

> When I was 10 or 11 years old I found an old almanac in the barn of the rented house at 2226 San Benito Avenue in Fresno, half gone, but I studied every page that was still in place. And all I remember is the feature entitled Last Words of the Great. I was so impressed by what people had said at death that I felt absolutely exhilarated by the promise that someday I would die, and say my last words.[29]

Last Words. It is a curious experience to explore this little-known yet nearby territory whose natives we all are, though we may lack the love of dilettantism that gets us far into its interior. Nearly everybody knows at least a few quotable last words, as one can easily find out by being a capital bore and asking anybody one meets at a conference or cocktail party. Julius Caesar's proverbial "Et tu, Brute" may come up, or Archimedes' "Don't disturb my circles," or the words of re-cantation, expected impatiently by some bystanders and others, that David Hume did *not* speak on his deathbed, or Queen Elizabeth's "All my possessions for a moment of time" (and she may have had as many dresses as Imelda Marcos had shoes), or Captain Lawrence's "Don't give up the ship." Another good bet is Gertrude Stein's expectedly sibylline "In that case, what is the question?" after her earlier "What is the answer?"—directed to Alice B. Toklas—remained unanswered. Schiller might come to mind with his eminently appropriate exit line, "Judex" (judge), or Lessing's choice of lottery ticket number fifty-two as he had just turned fifty-two, etc. And what did Voltaire "really" say with his final breath? Michel Foucault, death already casting its shadow over him, devoted one of his last lectures at the Collège de France to a searching analysis of Socrates' famous last words.

Finality commands attention; last words, unlike all others, cannot be taken back. "The most trivial sentence becomes significant when nothing in the world or in oneself is strong enough any longer for another one to follow. Everybody agrees that he who has not said all has said nothing," says a French anthologist of last words.[30] Roland Barthes agrees: "What counts is the last throw of the dice. . . . Victory is his who captures that small animal that gives omnipotence: the last word. . . . Who is a hero? He who has the last word. Who has ever seen a hero who did not speak before he died?"[31] Therefore, it seems, last words are worth listening to, worth preserving, and worth citing in the media—even if the intended audience cannot be expected to know anything about the subject. For example, the dying words of Hapsburg Emperor Francis I, "Don't change a thing," uttered in 1835, were said to be an instructive warning with a view to the possible decline of the American Empire in a recent *Newsweek* article.[32] The official Scottish exhibition commemorating the four hundredth anniversary of the death of Mary Stuart was announced throughout the country in 1987 by a gorgeous poster bearing as a motto words which were the dying utterance of King James V of Scotland—a fact deemed unnecessary to explain to the Scots, or to the English for that matter.

At the very least, last words have a sort of curiosity value, which proves irresistible even to the *New Yorker* and the *New York Times*. Both found it intriguingly newsworthy that French President Doumer "spent the last conscious moments of his life wondering how an automobile got into the charity book sale at the Maison Rothschild, where his assassination occurred."[33] Rather more macabre, and in worse taste, is the present-day habit of newspapers of revealing the last taped words of flight captains of crashed planes, no matter how insignificant. "Pilots reportedly talked of stewardess, not snow, before crash," runs the headline of one such news story in the *Boston Globe*.[34] And, on a Boston Harbor cruise, one may hear a bobbing buoy explained as a marker of the site of Nick's Mate Island, which sank into the sea after the mate was hanged there for the murder of Captain Nick; his last words under the gallows had predicted that if he were in fact hanged, the little island would go under.

Such attention paid to last words, whether they are highly revealing or bizarrely random, is a well-established convention in our society. No wonder *The Lazy Man's Guide to Death and Dying* by E. J. Gold advises not to say anything at all when the bell tolls.[35] This attention to last words (which, as Nietzsche thought it necessary to remind his philistine contemporaries, has its direct antecedents in the literature and historiography of antiquity as well as in the Old Testament)[36] is so ingrained that if a news magazine dedicates only half a dozen lines or so to the death or the anniversary of the death of a celebrity, the last words will often be included. Front-page or, at any rate, lengthier and more-than-routine obituaries in the daily press would, of course, be incomplete without the piquant detail of the dying utterance, even in the arguably less-than-world-shaking case of crooner Rudy Vallee—and no matter how trivial the last words themselves.[37] On the other hand, there is the case of Leonard Bernstein, whose last words—"What's this?"—*Newsweek* not implausibly considered a veritable signet of his "investigating, questioning" mind in its two-page obituary.[38] And the same news magazine is properly alert to the folkloric quality of the convention when it reports in a two-sentence notice that a former governor of Guam shot himself at a downtown intersection flanked by a placard alluding to one of the most famous American last words: "I regret that I only have one life to give to my island."[39]

Obituaries in the media featuring last words are not just a convention of the present. As early as 1921, H. L. Mencken made fun of the practice in a letter to Theodore Dreiser, who had humorously informed him of his own passing. If he were to write an obituary for the *New York Times*, Mencken wrote, he would have to know Dreiser's last words. Rumor had it, he continued jokingly, that Dreiser had planned to say "Shakespeare, I come!" but now one heard that he had called for a "Seidel Helles." Mencken takes this as his cue for reminding Dreiser that Walt Whitman had for years practiced high-minded last words (ben trovato according to authoritative biographies), only to die with the expression of a rather more elementary human need.[40]

Last words of the newsworthy even cast their mythical spell over the 1988 Democratic primary campaign when the much publicized bloodstains on Jesse Jackson's shirt suggested, in the words of New York mayor Koch, that Jackson was "the last man to speak with" Martin Luther King—a story deemed significant enough for the *Christian Science Monitor*.[41] The implication appears to be that Jackson must also have been the only one to hear King's last words, qualifying him to inherit his mantle. But fame was not a prerequisite to having one's last words recorded in the media even in the late 1980s. On 16 March 1988, the *Boston Globe* reported that a New Hampshire villager revealed on his deathbed the murderer of his daughter-in-law's first husband—it was his own son, which elevated the last word to the status of what is known as poignant family drama (p. 19). Similarly, *Newsweek* noted that when a 78-year-old Bible teacher was stabbed with a 12-inch butcher knife by a teenager in Gary, Indiana, she "recited the Lord's Prayer as she died."[42] By contrast, a political cliché was revived when the German newspaper *Die Zeit* quoted a survivor of Hitler's camps as remembering: "In Sachsenhausen, Soviet inmates died with Stalin's name on their lips."[43] Finally, the magazine *Nursing* recorded the last sentence of a twelve-year-old boy dying of leukemia as the high point of an uplifting human-interest story: "I'll remember you when I get to heaven," he said to a nurse.[44]

But to return from the obscure to the more prominent: When a panel of noted men of letters, W. H. Auden, Aldous Huxley, and others, were interviewed on the BBC Brains Trust program in the 1950s, David Daiches, one of the participants, recalls that the question designed to get to the heart of the matter was what their last words would be if this were the occasion for them. After all, life and literature have taught us that truths concealed throughout a long life will be revealed in the hour of death. Goethe, in an entry in his *Italian Journey* dated 18 November 1786, tells of the dramatic case of the classicist painter Raffael Mengs who confessed *in articulo mortis* that a supposedly antique fresco was really his own work, unleashing a heated controversy. And a documentary on Picasso reveals in its concluding seconds that the painter's last words were (supposedly): "Painting remains to be invented." In films, ranging from *Jules et Jim* to *Broadcast News* and *Breaking Away*, from John Huston's *The List of Adrian Messenger* and Michael Curtiz's *Angels with Dirty Faces* to Woody Allen's *Love and Death* and *Bananas*, there is a veritable cult of last words—one that is beautifully parodied in Robert Bresson's *Le Diable probablement* (see Preface). And there is at least one film on the theme of the search for the meaning of a last word ("Maybe he told us all about himself on his deathbed"): *Citizen Kane*, which not only encapsulates its message in the protagonist's last word, but beyond that, has made this last word into a sort of shorthand symbol, among cognoscenti, of what makes life worth living.[45] "Rosebud" has become part of the folklore of the educated.

Even advertising has discovered the power of last words, as in a commercial for Tombstone Pizza or the ad for a book about Madame Roland, the heroine of the French Revolution, in *Merkur* of January 1989 (p. 65). And of course cartoons ("Bugs Bunny") and comic strips have long discovered the hidden charm of last words: Garry Trudeau's "Doonesbury," for example,[46] Jim Davis's *Garfield Stepping Out*,[47] and Matt Groening's book *Work Is Hell* (which contains the piece, "What Will You Say on Your Deathbed?").[48] Not to be outdone, an educational coloring book, *Liber Romanus Pingendus: A Coloring Book of Rome*,[49] features the last words of Emperor Vespasian, while the Lufthansa in-flight magazine *Bordbuch* offers those of Emperor Maximilian: "Viva México." What else?[50]

Just how much last words have become part of our everyday cultural heritage and our popular mythologies may also be gathered from the curious fact that "What were Mexican revolutionary Pancho Villa's dying words?" appears as the question of the day for 16 October 1987 in the popular *Workman Page-A-Day* "365 Trivia Calendar." Needless to add, *Trivial Pursuit*, the fun-for-the-entire-family game of choice, also thrives on the fact that last words are part of our cultural literacy. There is even, as Clifton Fadiman discovered in the early 1950s, "a world-wide fraternity of collectors of Last Words," for which he thought there was more to be said than for philatelists.[51] The London *Times Literary Supplement* thought nothing of hosting a competition designed to test readers' knowledge of last words of the famous,[52] while another respectable newspaper had a "contest" for the most appropriate "totally imaginary last words of famous real people, living or dead, in 25 words or less";[53] among the winners and attesting to the moderate sophistication of the enterprise: Descartes, "I think I'm dead, therefore . . ."). In England during the 1930s and even during the years of the blitz, the admittedly not lowbrow *New Statesman* tried to cheer up its readers by running similar competitions. One assignment was to invent fitting exit lines for an odd lot of figures such as Nero, Shakespeare, Mozart, Rimbaud, Charlie Chaplin, Cassandra, A. E. Housman, Picasso, Narcissus, Lot's wife, Richard Wagner, Dreyfus, Ribbentrop, Hemingway, Catherine the Great, Proust, Einstein, etc.—regardless of whether they had in fact left last words or had unconscionably neglected to do so. The prize-winning answers with their sophisticated allusions, quotations, and references were generally witty and sometimes thought-provoking; above all, however, they throw a revealing light on the rich educational heritage of the participants, as does, one may assume, the large number of responses. This is equally true of the prize contest held by the *New Statesman* in 1942, which asked for appropriate last words of animals; this, one would like to think, in the animal-loving British tradition of erecting monuments to horses and dogs just as matter-of-factly as to conquerors and statesmen. One result was that well-known last words of the European tradition were given to animals, with the dying ant sighing: "So little done, so much to do," and the moth expiring with "Mehr Licht!"[54] The *New York Times* played a similarly highbrow game, limited to imaginary last words of musicians; for example, Richard Wagner: "Ah, what lovely embossed wallpaper . . . is it paid for?"[55] In Germany, Hans Blumenberg—philosopher and intellectual historian turned pop-philosopher at the height of his fame—has recently put the not-entirely unimportant matter of how certain philosophers died or might have died on the agenda by focusing on the genre of "imaginary anecdotes":

> I would like to know what will be reported about Heidegger's death and "last words" in the next millennium, and would have no reservations about a contest for suggestions to be offered for passing on to posterity.
> I would like to know through some personal indiscretion, but I don't. The question would be: What can a man who was as preoccupied with existential analysis as with the inquiry into the "essence of reasons" ["Grund"] have had to say at the end? In the most favorable case of evidence: What must he have said? Possibly: *No reason ["Grund"] for concern any longer.*[56]

All these serious jokers had been preceded by Mark Twain as early as 1869. In an essay entitled "Last Words of Great Men" he had lambasted the entire "institution" of last words by inventing amusingly fitting deathbed utterances for (mostly) important people. But, of course, in doing so he only succeeded in reaffirming indirectly the significance and vitality of the convention itself (see below pp. 26–27). To mention only one piece of evidence from Mark Twain's own country: to this day, "Last Words" is a bona fide subject category in the Library of Congress classification system, which has been adopted by most public libraries throughout North America.

To continue this necessarily haphazard *tour d'horizon* of the many manifestations of our culture's fascination with last words, there is at least one "dictionary" and also a large number of anthologies of last words,[57] some of them kept handy in university library reference collections somewhere between

Who Was Who and the *Encyclopedia Britannica*. Also, several commonly used dictionaries of quotations contain sections entitled "Last Words,"[58] and some biographical reference works and encyclopedias will include last words as well; for example, Chalmers's *Biographical Dictionary*, *The Dictionary of National Biography*, *The Everyman Encyclopedia*, and the *New Encyclopedia Brittanica*. Some people must want to check such facts regularly, as reference librarians will indeed confirm.[59] And no reference library would be complete without Joseph Nathan Kane's *Facts About the Presidents* which, naturally, contains a "Last Words" section between "Assassinations" and "Burial Sites."[60]

Sacha Guitry even assembled a collection of last words of the famous on a long-playing record entitled "Leur dernier quart d'heure" (Pathe Marconi, n.d.). The American "alternative" writer Antler did the same for poetry: he wrote a long poem studded with dozens of last words, most of which are part of American, but not exclusively American, highbrow folklore, with the poem itself thematizing the institution.[61] Alois Brandstetter attempts the same, with a keen eye for the satiric possibilities, in his "Letzte Worte."[62] Similarly playful citations of famous exit lines, again with a flattering appeal to the cognoscenti, startle the unsuspecting reader in academic novels such as Robertson Davies's *Papers of Samuel Marchbanks*[63] and Umberto Eco's *Foucault's Pendulum*.[64] A more popular case is Hemingway's *Across the River and into the Trees*; the title alludes to the words of Stonewall Jackson, spoken "on the occasion of his unfortunate death." Hemingway's protagonist, Colonel Cantwell, explicitly cites them in the concluding chapter, thus indicating that he is counting on his own imminent death, which turns out to be no false alarm; in fact, it has been overshadowing the events throughout the novel bearing the ominously revealing title. In all such cases of literary allusion, it is taken for granted that the utterance of the final moment enjoys a status of special significance and that

familiarity with at least some of the "historical" last words is part of a liberal arts education. But it remained for Julian Barnes to bring the phenomenon truly into the late-twentieth century: in his novel *Staring at the Sun*, the protagonist uses his personal computer to call up "the last words of the famous"—which allows the author to indulge in a fascinatingly whimsical reverie about the charm and the pitfalls of our ingrained habit of paying serious attention to curtain lines.[65] Understandably, "Last Words" is guaranteed to be an attention-getting book title, as it has been for a collection of sermons or of newspaper articles, a novel, a comedy, an interview, a bunch of stories, or the autobiography of a dancer.[66]

Not infrequently, the fascination with the end takes on rather strange forms. In Italy, according to an anonymous essay on "Last Words" in *Every Saturday*, "the sayings of the departed on their death-beds are sometimes written on scrolls, and hung in their parish church." [67] And why did ordinary people go to see public executions? The 1985 Michelin guide to London instructs the tourist: "From the Tower or Newgate the condemned were drawn through the streets on hurdles to be hanged (and sometimes drawn and quartered too) before the great crowds who gathered to hear the last words" (p. 99). Last words were indeed an important part of public executions for centuries. But this does not mean that the present-day sightseer has to miss out entirely on these specialized thrills. In Elizabethan England and later, hundreds, perhaps thousands, of broadsides and pamphlets, chapbooks, and even ballads were printed and reprinted that reported the last words (usually, but not always, carefully prepared and conforming to a formula allowing for little spontaneity or originality) spoken by traitors and highwaymen, pirates and murderers, royalty and dissenting ministers literally under the gallows or in front of the executioner's block.[68] As a rule, they are entitled "The Last Words . . . " or "The Last Speech . . . " or "The Death and Dying Words. . . . "

In France there were apparently no such pamphlets or broadsides in which individual criminals erected their own monuments. Nor did the German-speaking territories have a convention corresponding to that of the English, though one does come across an errant title like *[Hyazinth] Bayers letzte Worte vor und während dem Hingange zur Richtstätte*, by Johannes Chrysostomus Sacher.[69]

In English-speaking countries, as early as the seventeenth century, we find entire collections of dying speeches of the executed, be they Scottish Covenanters or English state prisoners of various kinds; in Germany and in France such anthologies existed as well, but they are much rarer.[70] Sometimes, to be sure, public disputes arose about what was *really* said in the last speech, as in the case of the traitor Thomas Wentworth, who was executed in 1641.[71] With luck, one may even chance upon a book like *The Tragical History of Jetzer . . . with an Epistle, wherein are some Soft and Gentle Reflections upon the Lying Dying-Speeches of the Jesuites lately Executed at Tyburn* by William Waller,[72] a book whose very title refers to the assumption underlying the institution of last words; namely, that what a person says in the expectation of imminent death is to be considered infinitely more weighty than virtually anything that was said before this moment of truth. Finally, if proof were needed of the immense popularity of the gruesome charm of the genre of "The Death and Last Speech of . . . " writing, one might mention two broadside parodies that are representative of several others of this type: *The Last Speech and Dying Words of the Bank of Ireland. Which was Executed at College Green on Saturday the 9th Inst.* (1721) and *The Last Speech, Confession, and Dying Words, of a Queen Ann's Guinea, Who was Tried, and Condemned, on a Late Act of Parliament, for Being Too Light; and Executed by the Unmerciful Hands of a Butcher, in Salisbury market* (1774?).

Such parodies do not, of course, signal the demise of the genre of last words. Later in the century in France, the generally less-formal dying remarks of some victims of the Revolution and its aftermath, their words said on the way to the guillotine, became common knowledge—indeed, part of the national folklore or the collective memory: Marie Antoinette's "Pardonnez-moi, monsieur," for example, as she stepped on the executioner's foot.[73] Similarly, the last words of heretics, patriots, and soldiers dying on the battlefield have become part of our popular mythologies: Nathan Hale's dying words, "I only regret that I have but one life to lose for my country," have for some time been familiar to American children; most Canadians have known, and still know, in our days of multiculturalism, what General Wolfe said somewhat chauvinistically as he died of the wound received in the Battle of Quebec ("I die happy," after being told that the French were fleeing). And until the late-nineteenth century, pamphlets entitled *Last Words of . . .* and *Dernières Paroles de . . .* continued to commemorate deceased (rather than executed) figures of public life such as George Washington, Queen Caroline of Great Britain (d. 1821), Pope Paul V; politicians like Gaspard de Coligny (Duke of Châtillon), Mirabeau, Jean-Jacques de Barillon; military men such as Marshal Fabert; or, again, Robert W. Logan, a missionary in Micronesia. The catalogues of the Bibliothèque Nationale, the British Library, and the Library of Congress will yield many more such pamphlets. Also, as such and similar catalogues reveal, the related genre of bulletin-like booklets catching the eye by their very titles, which promise accounts of "the last days," "the last hours," "the last moments," or "the last farewell" of well-known persons, flourished in several languages well into the nineteenth century. Among the more famous names are, in random order, Byron, Beatrice Cenci, Louis II of Bavaria, Frederick the Great, the Great Elector, Louis XVI, George Sand, but also the executioner of King Charles I of England as well as a village pastor, a stone mason, and a child murderess. Last words are usually featured in those pamphlets that have been accessible to me.

At the present time, this particular pamphlet genre seems to be extinct. Its place has been taken by more substantial books, anthologies, and death chronicles in the manner of John Gunther's *Death Be Not Proud* (1949) and Simone de Beauvoir's *Une Mort très douce* (1964), or by literary works such as Hermann Broch's *The Death of Virgil* (1945), W. S. Burrough's *The Last Words of Dutch Schultz* (1969), and Bernard-Henri Lévy's *Les Derniers Jours de Charles Baudelaire* (1988). But, in a way, the more sensational and topical tradition persists: Even in the second half of the twentieth century, it is not uncommon to ask criminals on their way to the electric chair or the gallows for their last words—and to write books about what they have to say, under titles such as *Death Row Chaplain* and *By the Neck*.[74]

❖ ❖

Biographies—straddling the fine line between literature and science in that they combine factual and "mythical" truths[75]—frequently start out with the death of their subject; and even when they do not, they often seem to have been written all along with at least one eye on the end or, more specifically, on the dying word, which is felt to give a summary of the life and to throw into relief its real significance (and this not only in the case of saints' lives). Some seasoned biographers have in fact stated that this is the only way to practice their craft, for "very often death-bed words mirror the life-long outlook of a person and are therefore more revealing than entire autobiographies," as the publisher's blurb in Herbert Nette's anthology reminds us. All the greater the astonishment of modern critics that earlier biographers (supposedly) failed to exploit this gold mine.[76] Lytton Strachey, on the other hand, "frank" even about himself, admitted that he had conceived his biography of Queen Victoria from the deathbed scene, and the book does actually read much like a prologue to its deservedly famous last page—

which Strachey had in fact put on paper before he wrote any other part of the book.[77] This conclusion alone validates *Queen Victoria* as a superb example of what Strachey called, in the preface to *Eminent Victorians*, "the most delicate and humane of all the branches of the art of writing" (even though it also corroborates Oscar Wilde's remark that it is usually Judas who turns biographer). Samuel Johnson must have had in mind a remotely similar view of the significance of the ending when he quipped to Boswell that Gilbert Burnet's biography of the Earl of Rochester, which makes great play of the deathbed repentance and conversion of the notorious and ingenious sinner, was "a good *Death*: there is not much *Life*."[78] In Lytton Strachey's case, by the way, this biographical cult of the death scene and the last word was strangely ironic, as he himself died saying: "If this is dying, I don't think much of it."[79] This has not, of course, stopped later biographers from continuing the tradition of using the last word as a meaningful cue, a telling detail, or even a structuring principle of the overall composition.

Like eighteenth- and nineteenth-century biographies with their heavier reliance on didactic intent, twentieth-century lives rarely fail to play up the utterance that is followed by no other. A fine recent example is A. N. Wilson's *Tolstoy*. Here the final remark, "How do peasants die?" is modulated throughout the book in a particularly meaningful way as the leitmotif of the life of the peasant-aristocrat.[80] In a more heavy-handed manner, Gerhart Pohl calls the last word into service in his 1953 memoir, *Gerhart Hauptmann and Silesia*:

On the third of June, Gerhart Hauptmann's last words were spoken. They were not a final testament of the great poet; they were not an appeal to the world; they were not words of love for his dearly loved wife. Instead, they formed a question that is shocking and that greatly shames mankind, because the situation made it plausible: "Am—I—still—in—my—own—house?"

One of the greatest German poets, and certainly Silesia's
greatest, died in the awareness that he was in danger of being
driven from his own home.[81]

A superb example, on the other hand, is Van Wyck
Brooks's biographical portrait of John Butler Yeats, the poet's
father, which concludes with this paragraph:

> When, many years later, in Dublin, I met the painter Jack B.
> Yeats and spoke of his father's courage in crossing the ocean to
> start life anew at three score years and ten, he said, "As you
> mention courage, how about this? Once my father's eyes gave
> out momentarily and he believed that he was going blind. But,
> saying nothing about this, he called for my sister Lily and
> began dictating a novel to her. If he was no longer to be able to
> see to paint, he would turn himself into a writer and the
> sooner the better." In fact, without ceasing to paint, he became
> a writer, and all in the natural course of things; but what force
> of life the story represented, the force that kept him in his ad-
> venturous exile so buoyant and so bountiful and, as he said, so
> cheerful and full of hope. This was the man whose last words,
> addressed to a friend, in the middle of the night, were,—as he
> lay dying in his room in New York,—"Remember, you have
> promised me a sitting in the morning."[82]

It is not hard to see the intellectual horizon of such biographical attention to the verbal conclusion of a life. "The less
people believe in theology, the more do they believe in
human experience," the biographer Harold Nicolson has remarked, adding that it is for this reason that the present-day
reader asks for that "detail" that bears the stamp of the *sigillum veri*.[83] Yet biographical theory is still faced with the task of
refining this insight with a view to the revealing nature of the
last word; the formula familiar from both antiquity and saints'
lives, "As in life, so in death," while relevant, is a bit crude.
"His Death was of a piece with his Life," Addison said about
Thomas More in the *Spectator*, after a pointed reference to

Epaminondas's claim that it is only death that provides the measure of a person.[84] Modern biographers do not generally go further than that, regardless of whether they feel that the exit line confirms the known or reveals the unknown.[85]

As an aside, it might be mentioned that Harvard University's institution of honoring late professors with a "Memorial Minute" has finessed the biographical convention by reporting the deceased's "last joke," though fortunately, for those of us who might someday want to compete, not in all cases.[86]

One may go a step further and suspect that biographers are not the only ones convinced of the telling nature of final words. Sometimes even their subjects share this view and cooperate by making the last moment count, writing their obituary on the deathbed as it were, or at least trying to, as did Queen Elisabeth of Romania: "'You are supposed—to say—beautiful things—and you can't,' the old woman rasped out with her last conscious breath before she fell into a coma and died."[87] The problem of the American writer Charles Wertenbaker was the opposite: "I'm running out of last words," his wife reports him to have said after various, failed suicide attempts.[88] Others succeeded rather better. Emperor Julian the Apostate is reported to have staged his death in imitation of Socrates; and Henry Huntington managed his own farewell to life quite adroitly, if the story is remembered correctly by A.S.W. Rosenbach, a dealer in rare books and manuscripts who sold Huntington many of the treasures now in the Huntington Library; also present was Sir Joseph Duveen, the art dealer who had obtained many major works for Huntington. Huntington, Rosenbach reported to Arthur A. Houghton Jr., lay with his arms outstretched. He looked at Rosenbach, then at Duveen. "Do you know what I feel like?" he asked Rosenbach. "What, Mr. Huntington?" "Christ between the two thieves," said Huntington, and died.[89]

Some, in other words, try hard to die with a memorable last word. Why? In order to live up to the expectations of posterity; or perhaps to verbally make up for a life they consider less memorable than what is yet to come; or, again, the hope may be to transform their ideal identity into an artifact—the self-made man on the deathbed. One might want to think of this as a secular variation on the sinner's deathbed recantation (which, for all its seriousness, was a popular genre well into the eighteenth century): ending a less than beautiful life with a beautiful line that will survive.[90]

Of course, there are no guarantees, and a dying word may instead "take back" whatever was beautiful about the life it concludes. This rather exceptional view is taken by the novelist B. Traven: "The last word of a dying person—" he noted in his radical journal *The Brickburner* (*Der Ziegelbrenner*), writing under his earlier pseudonym Ret Marut,

> don't make a fuss about it, and don't hold it in awe on any account. For the last word is no longer the dying person's own; half of it is a breath from a different condition which has nothing to do with you and your life. No one has ever understood the last word of a dying person. And no one has ever heard it. Nonetheless it has wreaked more havoc than the words of the living. And be careful not to hear the last word of persons you like and esteem! It may topple the wisdom of their entire lives with a single syllable, leaving you at a loss. The last word of a dying person is even less important than that of a man who is dead drunk.[91]

Mark Twain may have had something like this in mind when he expressed the hope that "our great men" would cease to come up with those typical, supposedly weighty but really "flat" exit lines; he suggested that the survivors should instead concentrate on the next-to-last words of the great and not-so-great that might be more "satisfactory":

> A distinguished man should be as particular about his last words as he is about his last breath. He should write them out on a slip of paper and take the judgment of his friends on them. He should never leave such a thing to the last hour of

his life, and trust to an intellectual spirit at the last moment to enable him to say something smart with his latest gasp and launch into eternity with grandeur. No—a man is apt to be too much fagged and exhausted, both in body and mind, at such a time, to be reliable; and maybe the very thing he wants to say, he cannot think of to save him; and besides there are his weeping friends bothering around; and worse than all as likely as not he may have to deliver his last gasp before he is expecting to. A man cannot always expect to think of a natty thing to say under such circumstances, and so it is pure egotistic ostentation to put it off. There is hardly a case on record where a man came to his last moment unprepared and said a good thing—hardly a case where a man trusted to that last moment and did not make a solemn botch of it and go out of the world feeling absurd. . . .

I do wish our great men would quit saying these flat things just at the moment they die. Let us have their next-to-the-last words for a while, and see if we cannot patch up from them something that will be more satisfactory. The public does not wish to be outraged in this way all the time.[92]

Mark Twain's iconoclastic reaction—just like his parody in *A Tramp Abroad*, where last words are prepared with great care before a duel[93]—of course only succeeds in pointing to the undeniable and unchangeable fact that in our civilization it is the last word and not the next-to-last word that carries weight; that it is the last word which is surrounded by the aura of the significant, that is treated with the awe and reverence that a "Last Will and Testament" will *not* necessarily enjoy, even if it does account for the best bed, as Shakespeare's does not. It is a curious fact that the supremacy of last words is recognized even in the law courts of some countries—or possibly "of all nations," if Chambers's *Encyclopedia* is correctly informed,[94] and the *Oxford Companion to Law* (1980) suggests it might be. In Anglo-Saxon countries, at any rate, the so-called "dying declaration" enjoys a special evidential status, vastly superior to *in vino veritas*. Such a dying declaration is defined as

> a verbal or written statement made by a dying person, which although not made on oath or in the presence of the accused, is admissible in evidence on an indictment for murder or manslaughter of that person, provided the person making it had a belief, without hope of recovery, that he was about to die shortly.

Thus the succinct definition found in the *Oxford Companion* (p. 386).

The American last word on this, or one of them, is the textbook *McCormick on Evidence*, which in its third edition (1984) devotes seven very large pages to this particular exception to the exclusion of hearsay, pages that also instruct the reader how to tell whether the "declarant" was conscious of imminent death and how to assess the precise "weight" of his declaration (ch. 28). A dying person is not presumed to lie— "Nemo moriturus praesumitur mentiri," as the maxim of common law has it[95]—the underlying assumptions being that there is no earthly motive for telling anything but the truth, and that one will soon face the judgment of one's Maker, who will exert retributive justice on those who die with a lie on their lips. Law courts today are becoming aware, however, of just how questionable, how ideologically biased, this assumption is.

Paradoxically, even pictorial art thrives on the theme of the last word: Rubens's "Death of Seneca" may come to mind, where an attentive scribe is taking down the sage's final utterances as his life is trickling away from his opened vein; or David's "Death of Socrates," in which the philosopher's raised index finger, as he returns the cup of hemlock to an attendant, indicates that it is his last words that focus the intense attention of the disciples surrounding him. Other examples are Le Brun's "Death of Cato," Benjamin West's "Death of General Wolfe," and Goya's "Nada. Ello dirá" in *Los Desastres de la guerra*, originally titled "Nothing. Those were his very words."

❖ ❖ ❖

Literature, not unexpectedly, has made the widest possible use of last words—this high-brow folklore that surrounds us everywhere. Many seventeenth-century German poems, for example, are really versifications of the late-medieval and early-modern Christian instructions on how to die "well"; that is, of the many and popular *artes moriendi* according to which the words spoken at the very last moment counted infinitely more than all others, as they determined the destination—heaven or hell—of the soul about to depart.[96] Sixteenth-century Everyman plays thrived on the same tradition.[97] Elizabethan drama, too, developed certain conventions of the magnificent dying speech; these, however, reflect not only the teaching of the artes moriendi concerning the supreme horror of dying suddenly, unprepared, and the blessing of dying reconciled with one's Maker, but also the Renaissance desire to achieve immortal fame, last but not least at the moment of death and, needless to say, through last words destined to survive, passed on from generation to generation.[98] And the convention continued, with certain metamorphoses.

Without memorable deathbed speeches revealing a noble heart, some literary genres would be incomplete: the nineteenth-century novel, and to some extent its predecessors in the eighteenth century, from Rousseau and Richardson to Dickens, Thackeray, Hawthorne, Hugo, Zola, and Fontane; sentimentalist middle-class tragedy in the manner of George Lillo and Gotthold Ephraim Lessing; and, of course, opera. But in other and more recent literary genres, too, it seems,

one cannot die without saying something significant. Even
the detective thriller, no doubt taking its cue from real-life
cases reported in the media, is not above using the victim's or
a witness's last utterance as the decisive clue leading to the
resolution of the case—Agatha Christie's *Why Didn't They Ask
Evans?* (1934), for example, with the title containing the crucial
last words; Bill Pronzini's *Dead Fall* (1986), which came out in
1989 in German as *Die letzten Worte* (*The Last Words*); or Reginald Hill's *Exit Lines* (1984), which sports the extra feature of
mottoes for each chapter that are themselves the well-known
last words of major players in world history and literature.
Arthur Conan Doyle, predictably, had provided a model with
such stories as "The Adventure of the Speckled Band" and
"The Adventure of the Lion's Mane."

   To continue in this literary vein, a multitude of poems thematize the last word, beginning with those popular seven-
teenth- and eighteenth-century English ballads on the executions and final speeches of notorious criminals, which have
their movingly fake echo in Chatterton's "The Dethe of Syr
Charles Bawdin." Numerous also are the first-person poems
that themselves purport to be such a farewell to life, the voice
being either that of the lyrical self or a persona identified by
name or function—"Last Words" by Sylvia Plath or Owen
Meredith or Carl Dennis or Greg Johnson on the one hand,
W. S. Landor's "Dying Speech of an old Philosopher," George
Meredith's "The Last Words of Juggling Jerry," or Robert
Cooperman's "Thomas Alva Edison's Last Words" on the
other, to provide an odd assortment of samples. The anonymous poem "Last Words of a Dying Soldier" ("Letzte Worte
eines sterbenden Soldaten," published in Nisky in 1870) may
not be everyone's favorite, but it has few equals in that it is
introduced by the statement: "An Austrian officer, who lost
both his feet from a cannonball in the battle of Breslau on 5
December 1757, wrote the following verses on the battlefield

with his own blood." Other, less bloody literary genres may choose a similar thematic focus. One might think of works as different as Edgar Allan Poe's "The Facts in the Case of M. Valdemar," Dürrenmatt's *Der Meteor*, Ionesco's *Le Roi se meurt*, Beckett's *Malone Dies*, or Christa Wolf's *Kassandra*; an especially gripping example is Graham Greene's 1988 story "The Last Word," published in his eponymous collection of short stories, which turned out to be his final book.[99]

Polemics and didactic tracts find the subject of last words equally irresistible; this is what Voltaire's warning against Christianity, "Les dernières paroles d'Épictète à son fils" (1768), and Sade's "Dialogue entre un prêtre et un moribond" (1782) have in common with the prohibitionist pamphlet *Death-Scene of an Inebriate*[100] and *The Dying Sailor: Or, the Victim of Parental Neglect*;[101] or, for that matter, with the anonymous monument of the noble savage, *The Dying Words of Ockanickon*.[102]

Another subgenre in its own right is constituted by those literary works (lyrical, narrative, or dramatic) that endeavor to encapsulate the emotional intensity of the last moments of historical figures; apart from those already mentioned in a different context, they include Juan León Mera's *Últimos momentos de Bolívar*,[103] Leone Fortis's *Le ultime ore di Camoens*,[104] and Peretti's *Ultimi momenti del Padre Ugo Bassi, fucilato dagli Austriaci in Bologna*.[105] At the other end of the intellectual spectrum, it might be mentioned (if with an academic blush), there is the hit that was probably the longest-lived in the annals of carnival, Teutonic style: Willy Millowitsch's "'Schnaps!' Das war sein letztes Wort, / Dann trugen ihn die Englein fort" ("'Schnaps!' he said, and without delay / The angels carried him away"). And Paul McCartney drew inspiration from Picasso's parting remark—as reported in *Time* magazine: "Drink to me; drink to my health. You know I can't drink any more"—to compose his song "Picasso's Last Words."[106]

The literary techniques and devices employing last words are too numerous to even hint at here. After the dying speeches of Homer's heroes, the last words of Dido in the *Aeneid* are among the most popular examples in classical literature (during the Renaissance, they were set to music more frequently than the last words of Jesus on the cross).[107] And in the third cultural sphere of the Western world, Old Icelandic sagas stylized the pointedly "cool" last words of expiring warriors into an art form all their own, which has resulted in the curious fact that some figures are known only or primarily for their last words—Atli Asmundson in the Grettir Saga, for example, is stabbed with a spear, and dies saying: "These broad lances—they are coming into fashion."[108] In modern literature, the famous last words of Ibsen's *Ghosts* may come to mind (the victim of hereditary alcoholism stuttering "The sun, the sun"—where the sun is symbolical, how could it not be?), or the falsification of last words for maximum political impact in Orwell's *Animal Farm*.[109] One might think of Robert Burns's parody of the convention in his poem "The Death and Dying Words of Poor Mailie, the Author's only Pet Yowe," Ionesco's spoof of the same convention in *The Chairs*, or Bernard Malamud's college novel *A New Life* in which the chairman of the English Department, suffering a stroke on his daily walk, cannot get beyond "The mystery of the infin—"; a helpful, non-tenured colleague suggests "infinite,"—which revives the "old grammarian" to the point of being able to correct sternly: "infinitive," whereupon he passes into silence.[110] Others may recall Harold Pinter's or Joe Orton's witticisms à propos "last sacred words" in *The Homecoming* and *Loot*;[111] Ezra Pound's grotesquerie about the paternity of a dying sailor ("I am not your fader but your moder," *Canto* XII); or, reaching back into the furthest recesses of childhood, Captain Hook's premature dying speech in *Peter Pan*, "lest when dying there may be no time for it" (act 5). In *The Razor's Edge*, Somerset Maugham has the social climber Elliott Templeton live his entire life toward the climax at which, dying, he is in a position to turn down a long-hoped-for invitation from a lady of the Haute Volée, "owing to a previous engagement with his Blessed Lord." "He gave a faint, ghostly chuckle," the narrator comments, "' . . . The old bitch,' he said. These were the last words he spoke."[112]

More often than not, such startling last words are to be found at the very end of a literary work, as its crowning *clou*. This technique is evidenced in works as disparate as Erich Segal's *Love Story*—"'Thanks, Ollie.' Those were her last words"—and Kafka's *Hunger Artist*, who does not eat, he confides to the circus guard with his last ounce of energy, "'because I could not find the food I like . . .' Those were the last words."[113] In Kafka's story, if not in Segal's, the word of the last conscious moment is the word of truth—a cliché, of course, but infinitely enriched by surprise and thematic implications. Similarly, Patrick White, the Australian Nobel Laureate, who late in life admitted to having "always been fascinated by last words,"[114] teases an unexpected nuance out of the age-old convention in his novel *The Twyborn Affair*, where Monsieur Vatatzes expires saying to Madame Vatatzes: "I have had from you, dear boy, the only happiness I've ever known"[115]—in a flash, we know "all" about the protagonist. Nabokov gives the technique a quirky twist when in *Speak, Memory* he manages to sketch a "complete" character vignette of Aunt Pasha by reporting virtually nothing but her death: "She died in 1910. [Her] last words were: 'That's interesting. Now I understand. Everything is water.'"[116] And the protagonist of Ralph Ellison's *Invisible Man*, a black man trying to make it in a white-dominated world, is continually haunted by the challenging legacy of his grandfather's dying words ("I want you to keep up the good fight. . ."), which at the same time unobtrusively give the book its cohesive, leitmotivic structure or pattern.[117]

No technique is foolproof until baptized by irony. Brazilian novelist Jorge Amado gives it that baptism in his picaresque story *The Two Deaths of Quincas Berro Dágua* (1961), amusingly questioning our habit, in life as well as in literature, of resorting to last words in our neverending search for meaning. The author of *Catch-22*, Joseph Heller, attempts the same, with a touch of the absurd, in the final part of his novel *Picture This*, entitled "Last Words": he has an Athenian court of law interpret Socrates' famous last words as a reference to a local leather merchant named Asclepius.[118] Again, if this bizarre variation on the well-known story is designed to question the institution of styles of dying and of corresponding last words, it succeeds only in confirming its vitality, at least in literature. Indeed, some scholars go even further, positing the existence of *regional* variations on this literary convention. At least one attempt was made to identify such a local style on the basis of what is said just before nothing can be said anymore: it is headlined, "How One Dies in North-German Literature," as if part of a "how-to" series.[119]

But let us not let it end like that. It may be instructive to turn to one of the finest and best-known examples of the literary use of the convention, the conclusion of Joseph Conrad's *Heart of Darkness*. The narrator, Marlow, gives an account of the last hours of Kurtz, the sinister agent of an ivory trading company in the interior of the Belgian Congo. As he dies of a fever on the boat taking him downstream through the jungle to the river's mouth, the truth of his mysterious life breaks out into the open, compressed into the last word: "It was as though a veil had been rent. . . . that supreme moment of complete knowledge. . . . he cried out twice, a cry that was no more than a breath: 'The horror! The horror!'" Marlow, profoundly shaken by this near-supernatural revelation, explains in his wordy way that we are face-to-face with "ultimate wisdom," self-judgment, with the truth and the sum of Kurtz's life. Rarely has a literary work presented last words

more poignantly in all their human and cultural meaningfulness. (Kurtz's cry has since become one of the most commonly known last words: *Newsweek* uses it without further explanation as a headline for a review of Martin Scorsese's
thriller *Cape Fear*.)[120] Yet, as Marlow describes Kurtz's last moments to the dead man's deeply mourning fiancée over a year
later, he bows to the expectation associated with the conven-
tionally sanctioned "sacredness of last words" (as Hardy put
it in the final chapter of *The Mayor of Casterbridge*). "The last
word he pronounced was—your name," Marlow lies, using a
cliché already parodied in Schiller's *Robbers* a century earlier.
He cannot bring himself to tell the truth in response to the
young woman's request, "in a heartbroken tone," for her
fiancé's final words: "I want—I want—something—to—to live
with."[121]

❖ ❖ ❖ ❖

There is no denying it: there
is something haphazard about this assembly of literary instances of last words. The multitude of techniques and types
of works offers no alternative. But to counteract the impression of infinite variety, it might now be interesting to focus on
the use of last words in a relatively coherent body of literary
works in hopes of finding a somewhat consistent, characteristic, and possibly meaningful or interesting use of last words.
How does Shakespeare use last words? What insight might
be gained from examining his practice? Insight into his plays
or even his intellectual stance at his particular moment in
history?

Why does Hamlet decide against killing Claudius when the
occasion presents itself? The opportunity, Hamlet realizes on
reflection, is no opportunity, as Claudius is praying: if he
were to be stabbed in the back at the moment of "the purging

of his soul" he would go straight "to heaven," no matter how
sinful his life (III.3.85, 78).[122] The real opportunity for revenge
would be

> when he is drunk asleep, or in his rage,
> Or in th'incestuous pleasure of his bed,
> At gaming, swearing, or about some act
> That has no relish of salvation in't—
> Then trip him that his heels may kick at heaven,
> And that his soul may be as damned and black
> As hell, whereto it goes.
>
> (III.3.89–95)

The condition of the soul at the moment of death appears
to be all-important in determining its destination in the here-
after. In comparison, the nature of the life preceding death
seems to fade into theological insignificance. Even sudden
death, death while asleep—that is, in a state of (conceivably
innocent) inability to commend one's soul to God or Christ—
would point the way to hell. Hence the Catholic litany's "A
subitanea et improvisa morte libera nos, Domine."

Hamlet's reflection about the right moment for dispatching
Claudius reveals that he is well versed in the teachings of the
ars moriendi. From the waning of the Middle Ages down to
Jeremy Taylor's *Holy Dying* (1651) and beyond, a veritable
flood of books using this title, either in the language of the
Church or in the vernacular, had admonished believers, be
they Catholics or Protestants, that their last moments on earth
were the most important in their lives: nothing short of confession of sins, repentance, affirmation of faith, prayer, forgiveness for all, and, ideally, the ritual "commendo spiritum
meum in manus tuas," addressed to Christ or the Lord (who
were thus the object of the last words) would guarantee the
passage of the soul into eternal bliss. Failure to live up to this
expectation or a sudden demise (to be feared most of all), both
implied God's disapproval, and there was no uncertainty

about the consequences. In this sense, the moment of dissolution was the moment of truth, indeed: an anticipated Last Judgment. Last words, like those of the thief on the cross, thus had the power to wipe the slate clean ("Nothing in this life / Became him like the leaving it," *Macbeth* I.4.7–8), or the power to end, by their nonconformity or by their absence, an exemplary life with a safe conduct to the flames eternal.[123]

This scenario, presented here in all its dogmatic severity (which was not significantly softened until late in the seventeenth century), was re-enacted in Shakespeare's time almost daily in public executions. For the "dying speeches," read by the "sufferers" at the scene of execution and printed soon thereafter as broadsides or small pamphlets, regularly followed the pattern set by the ars moriendi: the criminal confessed and commended his soul to his Maker, or, more rarely and specifically in the case of sectarian dissenters and Jesuits, he stood by his deeds and convictions. One way or the other, last words were "the most important part of an execution,"[124] and part and parcel of the ordinary living experience of Shakespeare's audience, nobles as well as groundlings. For them, last words were words of truth. Not only was there no longer any earthly motivation for lying, but a man about to die and to meet his Maker and judge would not forfeit the possible salvation of his soul by ending his days bearing false witness.[125]

Shakespeare was well aware of the convention. We might recall, for example, Emilia's dying words in *Othello*: "So come my soul to bliss as I speak true" (V.2.257). In fact, Shakespeare has become a sort of authority on the matter. For, oddly enough, a few lines from the dying speech of Count Melun in *King John* have been cited, from the late-eighteenth century to the present, in legal commentaries on the evidentiary status of so-called "dying declarations," which are recognized as exceptions to the exclusion of hearsay in English law and its derivatives in many parts of the world.[126] The passage runs:

What in the world should make me now deceive,
Since I must lose the use of all deceit?
Why should I then be false, since it is true
That I must die here, and live hence by truth?

(V.4.26–29)

The word *hence* is sufficiently clear in context to imply a reference to Divine Judgment (and, accordingly, legal authorities have, even quite recently, declined to honor the evidentiary quality of last words, as epitomized in the passage from *King John*, in cases involving "natives" who could *not* be presumed to believe in a supreme being empowered to punish them at the end of their days for untruthfulness committed at the moment of death).[127] Similarly, Shakespeare's audience would have recognized the Christian theological context (and, in particular, the doctrine of the ars moriendi) even when it was not explicitly stated. This is the case in the most famous of all of Shakespeare's many references to the aura of *hora mortis*, which occurs in *Richard II* when John of Gaunt, dying, is told that the king refuses to listen to him:

O, but they say the tongues of dying men
Enforce attention, like deep harmony.
Where words are scarce they are seldom spent in vain,
For they breathe truth that breathe their words in pain.
He that no more must say is listened more
Than they whom youth and ease have taught to glose.
More are men's ends marked than their lives before.

(II.1.5–11)

In the same scene, Gaunt also alludes to a related convention of thought: "Methinks I am a prophet new inspired" (line 31). Here, too, the affinity with the ars moriendi and biblical analogues would have been foremost in the mind of Shakespeare's audience—Jacob turning prophet on his deathbed, for instance, in Genesis 49—even though the notion that last words are prophetic is widespread in the folklore of cultures the world over.[128]

More interesting than Shakespeare's familiarity with such traditions of thought is the question of how, connoisseur of death scenes that he was, he confronted the traditions in his plays through creative manipulation or transformation.[129] The answer points to his attempt to offer a critical, or at least thoughtful, challenge to the generally accepted pattern of belief. Even in the passages just cited, which are commonly quoted at face value, there is more than meets the eye. While presenting conventional religious beliefs, Shakespeare seems to undercut them by their context. Hamlet's meditation on the state of the soul *in articulo mortis* also refers to the death of his father, who was killed in his sleep, unprepared, "with all his crimes broad blown" (III.3.81). Unquestionably a candidate for hell, one would assume, given Hamlet's own understanding of the matter, which in no way differs from the conventional view propounded by the ars moriendi[130]—and yet, Hamlet cannot help making a distinction between the murderer Claudius and his victim who, while not a saint, was not evil personified: "And how his audit stands, who knows save heaven?" (line 82). All-too-human wishful thinking, attempting to modify the clear-cut dichotomy of holy and unholy dying? And as far as Claudius's destiny is concerned, isn't there at least a hint of presumptuousness in Hamlet's assumption that it is he (and not the Lord) who is in a position to make the decision about his fellow man's eternal life, "sending" him to heaven or to hell. Isn't there a touch of irony in this arrogation of power, when in the same breath, thinking of his father, Hamlet is aware of the theological mystery of the potency of last words? Isn't Shakespeare in fact questioning the schematic dogmatism of the ars moriendi tradition when he has Hamlet meditate in this manner?

The light of irony cast over the theological convention of thought is even starker in the case of John of Gaunt. His words, powerfully summarizing the ancient mystique of last words, are disavowed by the situation. The king, for whose benefit the wisdom of a lifetime is designed, refuses to listen; he dismisses the dying sage as a "lean-witted fool" (line 116), and Gaunt is carried offstage. The near-supernatural, "prophetic" insight of the last moment remains unappreciated, powerless at the very moment when its power—again a widespread belief[131]—is extolled. And doesn't this suggestion of doubt about the conventional view turn our thoughts to the death of Percy Hotspur in *1 Henry IV*? Not only does Hotspur, fatally wounded in his duel with Prince Harry, turn his thoughts to worldly glory (or his lack of it) rather than to the life to come and its glories; even more ironic, he also articulates the topos of the prophecy of the dying, only to disavow it in the act:

> O, I could prophesy,
> But that the earthy and cold hand of death
> Lies on my tongue. No, Percy, thou art dust,
> And food for—
> > *He dies*

$$(V.4.82–85)$$

"For worms," Prince Harry finishes Percy's sentence: it is the living and not the dying who have the last word. And what a last word it is—the epitome of what, according to the ars moriendi tradition, man is *not* at the point of death, when the *anima christiana* leaves the body, *free* of "dust" at last, to join its Maker. "Prophesy" indeed.

Such casual remarks on Shakespeare's undercutting of traditional views may, at this point, require some suspension of disbelief. Matters become more self-evident, given the ideological background sketched thus far, as we turn to the death scenes of some of the major plays. Here Shakespeare reveals himself as a master of the last word by evoking a multiplicity of associations in the minds of an audience trained in the precepts of the ubiquitous ars moriendi.[132]

To start with the gentle bard's exercise in overkill, there is a wide variety of curtain lines in barely fifty lines in scene two of the final act of *Hamlet*. While Laertes comes close to dying a model death with his last-minute change of heart, confession of "treachery," and offer of "forgiveness" in *imitatio Christi* (lines 260, 281), Gertrude breathes her last without anything remotely like what might at the time properly have been called a last word: "The drink, the drink—I am poisoned" (line 264). There is a sort of poetic or even theological justice in this improvident demise—Hofmannsthal's Electra and her threat to take revenge for the murder of her father by preventing another criminal queen, Clythemnestra, from uttering her last word come to mind.[133] Equally hell bound is Claudius, of course, who dies not only unrepentant and with his mind on this world rather than the next ("O yet defend me friends! I am but hurt," line 276), but literally without a word; Hamlet forces him to drink the poisoned potion—"Follow my mother. *King Claudius dies*" (line 279). Hamlet himself, dying more slowly of the poison, and knowingly, is afforded the well-rounded dying scene so irresistible to Elizabethan dramatists. Yet it is surprising to see what he makes of it. Considering his more-than-adequate knowledge of the requirements of the ars moriendi demonstrated in act III, scene 3, his concerns are astoundingly this-worldly. First of all, he is preoccupied with his image on earth, a very Danish and dynastic earth at that:

> Horatio, I am dead,
> Thou liv'st. Report me and my cause aright
> To the unsatisfied. . . .
> If thou didst ever hold me in thy heart,

Absent thee from felicity a while,
And in this harsh world draw thy breath in pain
To tell my story.

(V.2.290–301)

If there is any religious overtone here at all, it comes close to parody and blasphemy—Christ's enjoinder to his disciples to "bear witness." Subsequently, the motif of prophecy comes up, but stripped of any religious mystique or connotation. The context is pointedly secular, almost parodistically so: it is not the Lord who has Hamlet's "dying voice," as he should according to the ars moriendi, but the new overlord from Norway:

I cannot live to hear the news from England,
But I do prophesy th'election lights
On Fortinbras. He has my dying voice.

(V.2.306–308)

As he lies dying, the protagonist, very much the Prince of Denmark, looks forward to the kingdom to come, but it isn't kingdom come. Viewed against the background of the ars moriendi, the dying speech of the play's expert in the theory of the art of dying is less interesting for what it says than for what it doesn't say. "The rest is silence"—Hamlet's very last words confirm it: *ultima verba* are conspicuous in their absence. Remembering Hamlet's soliloquy in act III, scene 3, the audience is left wondering about the destination of the prince's soul.

Similar questions might be raised about the death of King Lear. Kneeling by the side of Cordelia, he dies in a flush of ecstasy, apparently thinking that his daughter is showing signs of life:[134] "Do you see this? Look on her. Look, her lips. / Look there, look there. *He dies*" (V.3.286–287). The orthodox in Shakespeare's audience might at this point recall the didactic anecdote, told in some versions of the ars moriendi, about the *moriturus* who, having just commended his soul to his Maker, catches sight of his mistress who happens to enter his room: all preparation is to no avail, as "this world" (with its sins) forces itself on his mind at the last moment. However, recalling this horror story, the orthodox might be forgetting that they are also playgoers; and this play, unlike *Hamlet*, does not specifically thematize the matter of the last moment and its words.

We are on safer ground in *Othello*. For here the conceptual framework of holy and unholy dying is introduced *expressis verbis*, and it is "thrown in doubt" more challengingly than elsewhere in Shakespeare.[135] Questioning Desdemona about "that handkerchief / Which I so loved and gave thee" that Iago has played into Cassio's hands in order to arouse Othello's jealousy, Othello cautions her: "Sweet soul, take heed, take heed of perjury. / Thou art on thy deathbed" (V.2.54–55). They both know what is at stake: If indeed she is about to die, failure to tell the truth will commit her soul to hell. Othello, believing her to be lying when she truthfully proclaims her innocence, "smothers" Desdemona and leaves her for dead. And now, to make his point, Shakespeare defies the logic of nature and of the theater: suffocated, having died a death that is indeed "guiltless" at this point (line 132), Desdemona must nevertheless be permitted a last word to focus the problem Shakespeare all too obviously wants to thematize—a last word that changes everything. Or does it? In reply to Emilia's solicitous "O, who hath done this deed?" Desdemona says: "Nobody, I myself. Farewell! / Commend me to my kind lord. O, farewell! *She dies*" (lines 133–134).

The almost parodistic alteration of the canonical dying formula into a "commendation" to a "lord" who is not the Lord must have been obvious to all but the very young in the audience. Desdemona's *commendo*, unlike that of the Christian *moriturus*, articulates, for the last time, her love for her husband, whom her lie exonerates, as does her preceding self-

accusation in extremis, her false confession of the one unfor-
givable (because unrepentable) sin, suicide. This highlights
the other aspect of her dying: affirming her love of a man,
rather than of the Redeemer, as the highest value in her uni-
verse, she dies with a lie on her lips, irrevocably committing
what one might call suicide of the soul. The point is not lost
on Othello, who has just committed a mortal sin himself:
"She's like a liar gone to burning hell. / 'Twas I that killed her"
(lines 138–139). To which Emilia responds: "O, the more angel
she" (line 140). This dialogue poses the question unmistakably: if the ars moriendi would summarily consign Desdemona to the flames, as Othello reminds us, then why, at this
juncture, the pointed reference to the "angel" that Desdemona has been throughout the play—and more than ever in
her last moment, when she pronounces her loving lie, and
thereby practices the Christian virtue par excellence expected
of the dying believer, forgiveness? Will this angel, who condemned herself to hell by the very perjury against which she
had been warned, join the angels in the presence of the Lord?
Shakespeare's challenge to the theological *communis opinio*
could hardly be more provocative.

Iago and Othello condemn themselves to hell in less prob-
lematic terms. Iago, certain that he is about to be brought to
justice, abides by his vow, "From this time forth I never will
speak word" (line 310), thereby depriving himself of the last
word that might change the destination of the soul, even in
his case, which the ars moriendi would see as an analogue to
the thief on the cross. Othello stages his death in self-parody,
depriving it of whatever dignity, not to mention prospect of
redemption, it might otherwise have had. Concerned, like
Hamlet, with his image in this world, he dictates his own epitaph, adding:

And say besides that in Aleppo once,
Where a malignant and a turbaned Turk

Beat a Venetian and traduced the state,
I took by th' throat the circumcisèd dog
And smote him thus. *He stabs himself.*

(V.2.361–365)

Desdemona's "suicide of the soul," committed with a lie and culminating in her last words' reference to her beloved, amounts to a *Liebestod* of sorts. The lovers' suicides in *Romeo and Juliet* and *Anthony and Cleopatra* are more straightforward cases, yet they too are used by the dramatist to bring his challenge to the ars moriendi into focus, albeit a slightly different one: As the lovers die, each has the beloved foremost in mind; in the last words of each, the beloved's name takes the place of the Lord's. A kiss, verbal or real, seals their love at the moment of death, while the kiss of death in the book of the Lord is the kiss of Judas.

Even the last word of Paris, killed by his rival Romeo in a duel at Juliet's supposed grave, is, literally, "Juliet": "O, I am slain! If thou be merciful, / Open the tomb, lay me with Juliet" (V.3.72–73). Subsequently, Romeo, thinking that Juliet is dead, "drinks the poison." "Thus with a kiss I die. *He kisses Juliet, falls, and dies*" (line 120). Juliet, awakened from the sleep induced by the friar's potion, stabs herself on discovering Romeo's body, but not before completing her part of the duet: "I will kiss thy lips. . . . / Thy lips are warm" (lines 164–167).

The same substitution, of the love of man or woman for the love of the Redeemer, is pointedly thematized in Shakespeare's last tragedy of lover-suicides. Again, the beloved's name, rather than God's, looms large in each lover's last words. Not only that, it is Cleopatra's supposed last word, "Antony," communicated to her lover to test his love, that sets the whole denouement in motion. "Mardian, go tell him I have slain myself. / Say that the last I spoke was 'Antony'" (IV.14.7–8). And the messenger knows how to dramatize the weight traditionally attributed to last words:

>   The last she spake,
> Was 'Antony! most noble Antony!'
> Then in the midst a tearing groan did break
> The name of Antony; it was divided
> Between her heart and lips: she render'd life
> Thy name so buried in her.

>   (IV.15.29–34)

As he kills himself in despair on hearing this, Antony "will be / A bridegroom in my death, and run into't / As to a lover's bed" (IV.15.99–101). In the actual death scene that follows, he does pose as the noble "Roman by a Roman / Valiantly vanquished" (IV.16.59–60), but the dominant note of the long scene is the queen of Egypt, who is by his side.

> I am dying, Egypt, dying. Only
> I here importune death awhile until
> Of many thousand kisses the poor last
> I lay upon thy lips.

>   (IV.16.19–22)

Cleopatra follows suit, staging her own Liebestod. The expectations of the ars moriendi are again frustrated in a near-parodistic manner. When she says "I have / Immortal longings in me" (V.2.275–276), she does not have in mind what the Christian moriturus might put into the same words. "Husband, I come" (line 282) takes the place of "Jesus, I come," familiar from funeral sermons reporting on last words of the pious. Secularization continues with Cleopatra's anticipation of the afterlife, which is summed up in "that kiss / Which is my heaven to have" (lines 297–298). And then "O Antony" instead of "O Jesus":

> O Antony!
>   *She puts another aspic on her arm*
>   Nay, I will take thee too.
> What should I stay—   *She dies.*

>   (V.2.307–308)

One could go on citing examples, but it should be clear by now that the thrust of Shakespeare's challenge to the ars moriendi tradition implied in his death scenes is twofold. At issue is, first, *mors improvisa*: Death, sudden or otherwise, in the state of unpreparedness as the contemporaneous craft of dying understood it; death sealed not with the required last word but with a this-worldly exit line, or none at all; and second, as a pointedly secularized variation of this lack of proper preparedness, a life whose last word affirms the love of man or woman, rather than of the Lord.

Ariès, in his best-selling *L'Homme devant la mort* (1977), though not mentioning Shakespeare, tried to make the point that by the time of Shakespeare the ars moriendi-induced anguish was giving way to a more relaxed attitude; a change captured succinctly by Montaigne's remark in the *Essais* (1:20) that he would like to die "while planting cabbages." Others might silently have emended it to "while making love." And the stage of Shakespeare's time is, of course, one of the venues where the gospel of earthly love and delights begins to usurp the place of the Gospel, with Shakespeare himself acting as one of the protagonists. Still, Ariès's postulation of a historical divide has been criticized for failing to pay sufficient attention to what historians like to call the "simultaneity of the non-simultaneous," in particular to the persistence of the frame of mind expressed by, and reinforced by, the ars moriendi.[136] This would be the frame of mind of the rank and file of believers, whether Catholic or Protestant—including Shakespeare's audience. And it is to this mind-set that Shakespeare, no matter how subtly and covertly, would be addressing the questions that his death scenes suggest. Whatever the precise nature of the divide in intellectual history that Ariès and his many followers posit, the questions would have been topical. The ears they fell on were open, eagerly or reluctantly.

2

WHY THE INTEREST IN LAST WORDS?

Completion, Immortality, Mystique

Last words surround us everywhere—this is the obvious conclusion from the wide, and somewhat haphazardly assembled, variety of observations on the vitality of last words in our everyday culture. Nor is this a phenomenon only of the present; as indicated, the vigorous present-day life of the institution of last words is preceded by a tradition dating back to antiquity and biblical times. One might say (and Chapter 4, on anthologies of exit lines, will confirm this) that such serious attention over the millennia to what is said with the last breath, the passing on of such lore from generation to generation, is nothing less than the very idea of culture itself—of its self-awareness, its self-confirmation, and its insurance of its future. Culture is memory; what is remembered, lives; and we remember what we consider significant.

What is behind this willingness, even eagerness, of a civilization not only to preserve last words from oblivion but also to distinguish them with particular appreciation—an appreciation accorded to *"first* words" only in the most exceptional cases, for the good reason that the prophetic meaning attributed to them leaves too much room for arbitrariness? (A moderately well-known case is that of Michael Dukakis, whose reported first words, "All by myself" ["monos mou"], have inspired the jeu d'esprit that they amount to a foreshadowing of his adult personality.[1])

At first glance, it might be thought that what assures last words of attention always and everywhere is the banal fact that mortality is a sine qua non of the human condition. Accordingly, William Cowper, much like Joseph Addison and no doubt many others, thought that "few things are more interesting than death-bed memoirs. They interest every reader, because they speak of a period at which all must arrive."[2] That does not take us very far, quite apart from the fact that it does not explain what might motivate a dying person to leave a last word (assuming that it is not an utterance that just happens to turn out to be the last one). For one may take for granted that the *moriturus* shares the expectations associated in his culture with last words (see below, p. 96); and these do go beyond the mere confirmation of mortality. The fact is that, underlying the culturally sanctioned and indeed institutionalized attention to last words, there are more specific motivations, partly more plausible with a view to the predicament of the dying, partly more easily understood from the position of the survivors—although this is often not a matter of either/or.[3]

✣

There seems to be, first of all, some idea that the essence or the truth of a life, the "real" self, emerges in death and only in death. It is the idea—or is it a cliché?—that one dies as one lived (more so, perhaps), or as one "really" lived or was—whether one is, or is belatedly revealed to be, a saint or a sinner, a wit or a bore. It is the idea that a life should be rounded off, its pattern completed, per-

fect in its consistency, revealing its true identity as its unchangeable substance: "The ruling passion strong in death,"
as Pope put it in his "Epistle to Lord Cobham" (v. 263), which
concludes with a number of examples of such consistency
until the last word, some serious, some scurrilous. Without a
last word, life is not completed, not lived. Victorian accounts
of deathbeds will sometimes point out specifically, and with
undisguised regret, that the last word that was routinely expected, failed to materialize; Hofmannsthal's Electra alludes
to this sentiment when she threatens her mother, who helped
murder her father, that she will take revenge by preventing
her from pronouncing her "last word."[4]

This traditional mode of thought no doubt accounts for the
fact that, according to the best of our information, martyrs invariably depart from this life with the name of their Maker or
his son on their lips and that patriots of all nations predictably
turn their thoughts to the fatherland in their last moments on
earth (having left little room for imaginative variation ever
since Johann Zischka "passed on" in 1424 with the ultimate in
patriotic last words: "Make my skin into drumheads for the
Bohemian cause"). The idea of appropriately completing, indeed validating a life by dying as one lived accounts for the
fame of the most famous of last words: on the one hand,
Christ's words on the cross (dutifully repeated verbatim innu-
merable times by the dying, including Charlemagne, Christopher Columbus, Lady Jane Grey, Tasso, and Martin Luther,
who would probably have agreed on little else) and, on the
other, Socrates' proverbial remark to Crito moments after
drinking the hemlock: "We owe a rooster to Aesculapius," the
god of medicine and healing who had just cured him of what
Alexander Pope was to call "this long disease, my life."

A memorably consistent death, articulated in a characteristic last word, provides the motto for a life, or so it has been
believed only too willingly for centuries in the Western world.
"There is nothing more glorious," Addison writes about the

"good man" in the *Spectator*, "than to keep up an uniformity of his actions, and preserve the beauty of his character to the last" (no. 349); and more than two hundred and fifty years later, in 1971, the *Neue Zürcher Zeitung*, in a statement prominently reprinted in 1983, takes it for granted that "last words are likely to reveal something about people and how they lived. One expects of last words a sort of résumé of a life, and many a dying person has met this expectation of posterity."[5] Octavio Paz, a representative of a particularly death-obsessed nation, puts this line of thought, which has dominated occidental awareness for centuries in one form or another, rather more somberly, yet magisterially, in a ponderous passage of the essay "The Day of the Dead": "Death defines life. . . . If our deaths lack meaning, our lives also lacked it. . . . Each of us dies the death . . . he has made for himself."[6] Which is followed by the maxim which is not entirely logical but is nonetheless clear in its meaning: "Tell me how you die and I tell you who you are." Walt Whitman said it with less pathos and more realism: "Last words are not samples of the best, which involve vitality at its full, and balance, and perfect control and scope. But they are valuable beyond measure to confirm and endorse the varied train, facts, theories and faith of the whole preceding life."[7] Goethe, who remarked in his autobiography *Poetry and Truth* that it was the task of the biographer to show how an individual "had remained the same under all circumstances," cites a good example in a letter to his friend Knebel: "I don't know if you have heard that [Wieland's] last words were: 'To be or not to be, that is the question.' That's maintaining one's scepticism to the very end."[8] The tone suggests that Goethe was irritated by such consistency. One wonders how he would have felt about Thomas Mann's admiration for his own consistency in dying: No longer able to speak, Goethe raised his right hand to write letters into the air (as did Schiller and Heine, by the way). "He died writing," Mann commented in his 1932 commemorative address, "he did . . .

what he . . . had done all his life."[9] Eugene O'Neill, finally, gave a dramatic twist to the formula "as in life, so in death"; the standard biography reports that he expired shortly after cursing: "Born in a hotel room—and God damn it—died in a hotel room!"[10]

On the other hand, "confirmation" of life through the manner of death is not the only pertinent pattern. The opposite was not unthinkable—that in its last moments a life could take on or reveal shape and meaning quite different from the familiar or even the submerged or hidden "real" life. This was clearly the conviction underlying the artes moriendi, which endeavored to show the way to a manner of dying that would save the soul by achieving sinlessness through the last word, no matter how sinful a life might have been; the seventeenth- and eighteenth-century genre of deathbed recantation in the manner of Rochester continued in this vein. Somewhat secularized, the mode of thought occurs as early as *Don Quixote*, with the hero dying in the final chapter with the words: "I was foolish, and now I am wise." There is also an echo in Edward Young's *Night Thoughts*: "Men may live fools, but fools they cannot die" (IV.842), while a thoroughly de-theologized form may be encountered in the German highbrow weekly *Die Zeit*, which states that the last word encapsulates a "truth, which makes the entire rest of the life appear as a lie, as dissimulation."[11]

One way or another, then, it is the curtain line that matters in all these statements and sentiments, regardless of whether that line epitomized the play or gave it a surprise ending considered happy by the clerical audience that "collaborated" in some of the cases. (The theater metaphor is actually quite common in such writing as there is on this subject.)[12] And perhaps it is not an overstatement to add that the curtain line mattered more than the play itself—to the protagonist or the audience or both, at least in some cases that became well known. After all, for a long time, until the advent of the nondescript, depersonalized death made possible through modern medicine (whose ministrations normally deprive us of last words),[13] dying was a public or semipublic act—or even an art, as Ariès, to mention only the best-known thanatological authority, has amply shown in his monumental tome, *L'Homme devant la mort*. As such, the art of dying, in full consciousness and in the midst of family, friends, and followers, may indeed, more often than not perhaps, have outdone the art of living, or might even be said to have been designed to do so: "staged" to make up for opportunities missed or possibilities unrealized. As Malcolm says about the dying words of the Earl of Cawdor: "Nothing in his life became him like the leaving it" (*Macbeth*, I.4.7–8).

❖ ❖

A memorable last word, whether confirming a life or breaking with it, could grant a kind of secularized immortality. This is the second idea underlying the convention of taking last words seriously. For centuries, dying tended frequently to be an act of survival through last words, of survival through the signature of a life that could not be erased again, or in the intellectual or spiritual equivalent of the death mask. For a death mask is made precisely because it is not a mask in the conventional metaphoric sense of the word, but rather the opposite: it is the real or true face, widely thought to reveal itself only at the moment of death. This is how Tolstoy described the emergence of the real self, the epiphany of the ultimate that is within the individual's reach, in "The Death of Ivan Ilich." Similarly, Richard Curle reports in *Joseph Conrad's Last Day* that the marks of age had disappeared from the dead man's face, that it had regained its youth and thus revealed the signet of truth, for Conrad's work derived from the youthfulness of his personality: he "never ceased to be young."[14] The death mask will prove it forever. Gerhart Hauptmann's play *Michael Kramer* has a moving scene that is telling in this respect. Kramer contemplates the death mask of his son, who took his own life: "What is now on his face was all . . . in him. I sensed it, and yet I was unable to disclose it, the treasure . . . now death has disclosed it" (act 4). Just as the death mask *preserves* that real face, the last word is the enduring legacy—life transcending itself into artifact, time transcending itself into timelessness. In a manner unsurpassed to this day, English Renaissance drama has more than once recreated this apotheosis into immortality in its characteristic dying scenes (see above, p. 29).

This urge for self-transcendence, for leaving a monument that defies time and death, is a distinguishing, if often rather pathetic, human trait, which sets us apart from other mammals. It is the Faustian need to assure oneself "that the trace of my days on earth will not be effaced for eons to come" (lines 11,583–584).[15] This need was felt alike by Egyptian pharaohs and heroes of Icelandic sagas, as well as by modern mausoleum builders from Hadrian to Franco. Outside the Western world, it was felt by Yukio Mishima who, early in the morning of 25 November 1970, the day he committed his well-planned and well-orchestrated hara-kiri, just before leaving the house for his final and finest hour in the barracks on the outskirts of town, placed a note on his desk which said: "Human life is limited, but I would like to live forever."[16] Similarly, William Butler Yeats describes in *A Vision* how touched he was by the sight of a barefoot girl on the beach in Normandy who was looking out at the sea and singing a song about the civilizations that had flourished on this coast and disappeared without a trace. The refrain of each verse she sang was: "O Lord, let something remain!"[17] This desire is universal in time and in space. If one visits the Museo Nacional de Antropología in Mexico City's Chapultepec Park, for instance, one is struck by verses from the Songs of Hue-

xotzingo, originally composed in Nahuatl, sculpted monu-
mentally into the wall of the interior courtyard:

> This is how I have to go?
> Like the flowers that perished?
> Nothing remains in my name?
> Nothing of my fame here on earth?
> At least flowers, at least songs![18]

"At least songs" will remain as the only mementos of a life
troubling itself about one of the very few things worth troubling about, its temporality. Imbued with this thought are artists, writers, scientists, statesmen, and other men of action
who in one way or another make an effort to leave their stamp
on the world. Something is to bear witness "that I was there."
Powerful in antiquity[19] this concern about "what will remain"
enhanced itself during the Renaissance into the obsessive endeavor to ensure the survival of one's "fame" after death, as
in Petrarca's *Letter to Posterity* (*Posteritati*) and *Triumphs*, or in
Hamlet's pleading with Horatio "to tell my story." It is, characteristically, Hamlet's dying legacy: for the moriturus and
those by his side, the last words assume the significance that
the enduring, time-defying work has for the creative person
throughout his life. For, as the dying person endeavors to
summarize his life experience or "the lessons that life has
taught him"[20] in a last word, he does so with a view to passing
this knowledge and this self-image on, hoping to add something to the collective memory of his civilization and its future. Last words that have become familiar quotations would
seem to indicate that he is not entirely wrong.

At the same time, the very fact of the survival of so many
last words as the signet of their speakers' fame gives us a hint
as to their nature as seen against the backdrop of intellectual
history. Christians such as Dante and church fathers like Tertullian[21] rejected the cult of fame. Therefore, if a last word
(other than the Christian ones standardized by the artes mori-

endi) endures over the ages, this endurance reveals itself—
and the entire institution of last words—as a phenomenon of
secularization.

❖   ❖   ❖

But more underlies the age-
old fascination with last words than (first) the obsession with
life as the properly completed entity or pattern or the properly
completed work of art and (second) the obsession with self-
transcendence and a secular kind of immortality. There is a
third factor, quite apart from any individual case, which one
might call the mystique of the final moment (and its words).
This mystique becomes more interesting as life becomes less
constrained by a religious framework. Of course, even in an
age of belief, the final moment had its importance in that it
provided the experience of the threshold to a "life" of a different kind. "It was believed in at least the early Middle Ages,"
writes R. C. Finucane,

> that as [saints] neared death they could see over the boundary
> separating the worlds. Their deaths were transitions to an-
> other, higher and therefore more powerful state. This state
> could be anticipated: they could foresee their own deaths and
> other secrets of the future. Their statements were especially
> valued because in a sense they came from beyond the grave. It
> was a privilege to be present at their deaths and only "worthy"
> auditors should hear their last words. Conversely, it came to
> be expected that the dying holy man or woman would, even
> should, bequeath his special knowledge to intimates.[22]

But exciting and worthy of attention as such revelations may
have been well into the nineteenth century, they were revelations within the framework of Christian beliefs and were
therefore, strictly speaking, not entirely surprising. One had
an idea of what heaven and hell were like; and what saints, at

any rate, representing as they did the ideal form of life, had to say on their deathbeds was entirely predictable, as their numerous vitae confirm. More ordinary mortals confessed and regretted their sins and accepted absolution in equally routine fashion. As many anthologies recording Christian deaths amply and rather tediously demonstrate, these believers—whether long-term saints, or sinners reformed in the nick of time—always knew what to say at the last moment (see Ch. 4). This was not a time for originality. In fact, and to repeat, it was almost de rigueur to quote the very last words spoken on the cross ("Father, into Thy hands I commend my spirit"). Only later or outside the supportive framework of orthodox religion do the dying "not know what to say," and what they do say becomes rather more interesting and original and less predictable. Their words do not fit any dogmatically established pattern, and, as a result, the final moment, manifested verbally, gains an entirely different kind of importance: a nonstandardized one, so to speak. The search for a completed life, a meaningful life—the lifelong search perhaps, or the search initiated at the sound of the tolling bell—is brought to a different sort of conclusion in the last moment in which words are uttered. As such, this moment is often and rightly seen to have a mystique all its own.

Viewing the mystique, then, as a phenomenon of intellectual history, one may leave aside what physicians usually have to say about the moments preceding death. For them, the not-uncommon state of serenity or even euphoria at the dying moment and, more specifically, the "panoramic vision" of the dying (which fascinated Henri Bergson, among others) is primarily a correlative of the physiology of incipient organic decomposition.[23] The tradition of folklore is less inhibited. It provides us with the notion (or is it an old wives' tale?) that a dying person, or at any rate a drowning or a hanged one, sees his entire life recapitulated before his mind's eye in his last moments. But this does not take us very far either, even though it may inspire arresting literary works such as Ambrose Bierce's story "An Occurrence at Owl Creek Bridge," or William Golding's novel *Pincher Martin*. This bit of folk wisdom led German writer Theodor Däubler to realize in a flash of inspiration that the life review of a man being hanged "can only be Expressionism!"[24] Surely there are more comfortable ways to excel in Expressionist style. And the only clinical account of the state of mind of a person drowning and about to die that I have found records nothing but trivialities.[25] In any case, one finds it difficult, on the basis of such empirical evidence (essentially a string of impressions of teenage dating, a recent Rose Bowl game, etc.), to see that the folk belief in the life review of the drowning or the hanged person is essentially a metamorphosis of the concept of the Last Judgment and the afterlife, as A. Alvarez claims in his famous study of suicide, *The Savage God*.[26]

Whatever the significance of the moment, it is less specific and less dogmatically circumscribed than that, and it does not take hanging or drowning to see it. There is in fact quite a respectable, if informal, tradition of attributing special meaning and quality to the last moment and the words said in it—meaning and quality best described with this admittedly vague term, mystique. This tradition exists primarily outside the specific sphere of influence of the Christian churches, which used to teach that one's behavior at the last moment may decide the ultimate destination of the soul that is at that point preparing to embark on its journey to parts unknown to most. For Samuel Johnson notwithstanding—"the act of dying is not of importance" and "it matters not how a man dies," Boswell quoted him as saying[27]—there has been a fair amount of speculation, albeit frequently aphoristic, on the importance of the last moment and the utterance it yields on the part of those who are not specifically committed to religious orthodoxy, and even on the part of those who are *not* eager for those glimpses of the life of the soul after death which have become the *dernier cri* in our postrationalist time under the label of "near-death experiences."[28] Goethe, for example, in his *Maxims and Reflections*, commented on a victim of the French Revolution, whose last words are reported to have been "O Liberty! How are you mocked!":

> On the scaffold, Madame Roland asked for pen and paper in order to write down the very special thoughts which occurred to her while she was taking her last steps. It is unfortunate that her request was denied; for at the end of life, ideas dawn on the composed mind, previously unthinkable ideas; they are like blessed spirits gloriously descending upon the peak of the past.[29]

"Previously unthinkable ideas"! Or, as Thomas Mann said in his aforementioned comment on the death of Goethe himself: "Definitive knowledge, and eminently worth communicating."

In *Moby Dick* one comes across a similar sentiment: "For whatever is truly wondrous and fearful in man, never yet was put into words or books. And the drawing near of Death, which alike levels all, alike impresses all with a last revelation, which only an author from the dead could adequately tell."[30] In the South Seas as well as in Weimar: the mystique of the last moment, of the last word.

The "moment" (articulated in language) so greatly interests the religiously "uncommitted" because it represents a threshold experience—or a bona fide *Grenzerfahrung*, as existentialists, especially those of the Jaspersian persuasion, would say. It is a moment wherein being and nonbeing merge, a moment of experiencing what is indeed beyond experience and yet may leave a verbal record which forces or teases the ineffable into the effable, producing the last word. What passes understanding, the ultimate knowledge (or is it knowledge of the

ultimate?), is seen "through a glass darkly." Or is it? Whatever the answer, the mystique of the unique moment begins
with this question.[31]

Even present-day psychiatrists will wax mystical and mysterious when discussing this moment, revealing their affinity
with a more ancient breed of initiates. Gone are the days of
physiological "realism" when an authority of the stature of
Herbert Spencer could blithely assure his readers that near
and at the point of dying both the "thinking faculty" and the
"feeling faculty" are "almost gone," so that on the deathbed
"the sentient state is the farthest possible from that which ac-
companies vigorous life";[32] a person's last utterance could
therefore hardly be telling or significant (as other and less
qualified observers have noted as well). Modern psychiatrists
do not necessarily agree. This is not to say that they revert to
the position of Sir Thomas Browne, for example, who in *Re-
ligio Medici* was confident that at the moment of its separation
from the body the "soul" began "to discourse in a strain above
mortality."[33] But present-day soul specialists may, in principle, concur with Goethe's speculations about last moments
and last words expressed in his observation on Madame
Roland.

True, some will not venture beyond the observational
donnée "that the dying patient, . . . in the face of death, remains more or less true to his basic personality," which is
then defined as "an individual's total responsive attitude to
his environment and his habitual behavior patterns regarding
his physical and mental activities irrespective of the picture he
presents to the outside world." This last qualification allows
for surprises in the deathbed scene. If the patient's behavior
in his last moments differs from "his earlier behavior," Dr. Arnold A. Hutschnecker continues in his essay, "Personality
Factors in Dying Patients," it is the final behavior that counts.
For "an individual in his basic unrestrained structure" is "revealed" precisely at the moment of "a breakdown of conscious

controls."[34] And the most incisive breakdown revealing the true face comes at the last moment—from which the last word issues. This is little more than a clinical restatement of Edward Young's line, "A death-bed's a detector of the heart,"[35] although the Rev. Edward Young was surely closer to disquisitions on "holy dying" than was the New York M.D. Another psychiatrist, Gerald J. Aronson, however, does indeed see a remote connection between the late-medieval ars moriendi and latter-day psychiatric bedside experience: "No man is different from the martyrs who died according to a code of ethics, with an inbuilt script still rolling out."[36] (He may be alluding to the word-filled bubble that one occasionally sees projecting from a dying saint's mouth in late-medieval pictorial art.) Aronson's documentation—the case of A. E. Housman frivolously commenting with his last gasp on a lewd story told to the dying classics don and connoisseur of pornography by his thoroughly understanding physician—may be less than well chosen, though it was confirmed by the physician himself in a letter to the editor of the *Daily Telegraph*.[37] The point is clear, however: in his final moment, a dying man retains "his sense of individuality and identity," and this, to some, has become the secular analogue of the anima Christiana. Such psychiatric evaluations of the significance of the dying moment and the last word do, however, all but explain away the mystique.

Other psychiatrists, though no less secular in their basic outlook, give greater credit to the mystique of the last moment and its verbalization. K. R. Eissler, known to many as the author of a psychoanalytical biography of Goethe, claims in his pioneering study *The Psychiatrist and the Dying Patient* that "the moment of death is still the most important and the most decisive in man's life." But he has more in mind than "the idea—often expressed by philosophers and well supported by the psychoanalytic conception of the personality— that the whole preceding lifetime is reflected in the terminal phase of a human being"; more in mind than the idea (which he, of course, finds psychoanalytically "correct" as far as it goes) that "in dying, man consummates his whole previous life."[38] Like Aronson, Eissler takes his cue from the Christian conception of death as the one moment when the believer, through repentance, absolution, and Holy Communion, may achieve the state of sinlessness. But, unlike Aronson, Eissler retains the sense of *tremendum* and *fascinosum* that gives this moment its unique aura in dogmatic contexts. For, as he translates the dogmatic concept of sinlessness into its secular equivalent, namely "the state of maximum individualization," he preserves a sense of the transforming power, the mystique, of the final moment. What may be achieved at that point is not only a *summation* of a life or a given individuality (which may also "immortalize" it in a secular sense). On the contrary, *beyond* the stage of individualization attained in life some "last few steps of individualization . . . may be possible along the terminal pathway." These steps beyond the status quo, the very last stages of psychic growth, may or may not "facilitate the last farewell to life," may or may not lead to true happiness. For there is at least the possibility that "the futility" of the entire past life may be realized in the process of terminal, maximum, individualization. On the other hand, even this perceived futility may be turned into what Eissler calls "a triumph of individualization," adding that "the final processes of structurization during the terminal pathway may provide the past life with a meaning which it would never have acquired without them" (p. 55).

Eissler's formulation of the mystique of the last moment and, by implication, of the last word may perhaps also be seen as a translation into psychiatric language of what Rilke in *Malte Laurids Brigge* and the *Stundenbuch* had adumbrated poetically as the mystique of a "death of one's own," as opposed to the anonymous or, as Rilke says, "factory-like" death of the modern Everyman who dies in a Paris hospital designed for the masses, in effect cheated out of the experience of his dying. Eissler, like Rilke in his way or Heidegger in his,[39] seems to articulate a secular form of salvation when he extols the individual and individuality-enhancing death:

> The full awareness of each step that leads closer to death, the unconscious [or does he mean conscious?] experience of one's own death up to the last second which permits awareness and consciousness, would be the crowning triumph of an individually lived life. It would be taken as the only way man ought to die if individuality were really accepted as the only adequate form of living. (P. 57)

The all-importance of the dying moment and the dying word, which the Catholic Church has held axiomatic for centuries, reappears here in new language. But one cannot help noticing that in a sense secular psychiatry makes the final moment even more mystical and mysterious, indeed more ineffable than it had been, and still is, in orthodox theology. Theology will speak of the certainties of heaven and hell, of the "fact" of the survival of the soul and the meeting with its maker (as does, for example, the Rev. Herbert Lockyer in his collection, *Last Words of Saints and Sinners*: "When the soul is face to face with eternal realities, true character is almost invariably manifest" and the believer may "bear witness . . . to the reality of Christ and the glorious assurance of heaven"[40]).

The modern psychiatrist, Eissler, on the other hand, speaks of "possible stimulation of new structural processes through the terminal phase," which in his view raises the final moment and the final word far above the significance of a mere summing up or a consummation of previous life (p. 263). But what do "evolvement of new structures," or even "growth" mean to someone to whom "forgiveness of sins" no longer holds the meaning that was once self-evident? There is a curious emptiness of specific meaning about those "psychic processes of the terminal phase," and this void is not really filled by the negative definition; that is, by the rejection of the common medical idea that "disturbed physiological functions" or the "disturbed biological apparatus" accounts for whatever changes might be observable in the personality of the dying and which might prompt last words (p. 263). Paradoxically, then, the last moment may become even more ineffable if viewed within a secular horizon. Much the same is true of views expressed by Karl Jaspers, a philosopher well versed in medicine and psychology, whose existentialist stance has been summarized as follows: "Faced with death, existence emerges from its true depth to its essential potential."[41] Again, what does this mean?

In comparison, the deathbed scene in literature which habitually makes the ineffable effable—an exemplary literary rendering of existential growth may be found in the final chapter of "The Death of Ivan Ilich"—becomes all the more striking in its imaginative and evocative concreteness.

Not unexpectedly, poets will also come up with statements on the commonly felt mystique of the last moment and the last word, statements which are rather more memorable than those of mental health professionals, and not only because poets do not normally have phrases like "the possible stimulation of new structural processes" in their active vocabulary. One could indeed have a field day going on a safari through the world's classics, gunning down appropriate lines with minimal concern for the textual environment. Even if one resists that temptation, one could bag some birds of very different feathers not usually found in the same habitat. At the risk of assembling a zoo, then—Shakespeare, if I may repeat myself, is hard to overlook:

> O, but they say the tongues of dying men
> Enforce attention, like deep harmony.
> Where words are scarce, they are seldom spent in vain,
> For they breathe truth that breathe their words in pain.
>
> (*Richard II*, II.1.5–8)

Typically, there is no suggestion here that the truth emanating from the lips of a dying man might be illuminated by a ray of light from beyond. At the other end of the scale one finds Willa Cather's description of Father Lucero's deathbed in *Death Comes for the Archbishop*:

> Among the watchers there was always the hope that the dying man might reveal something of what he alone could see; that his countenance, if not his lips, would speak, and on his features would fall some light or shadow from beyond.[42]

Brazilian novelist Moacyr Scliar's much-noted story of "magic realism," *Max and the Cats*, takes this fascination to the point of absurdity. In a lengthy parenthesis it tells how, during the Nazi period, the German professor Kunz switches from animal experiments to experiments with humans (the passage is also singled out for quotation in extenso in the review in the *New York Times* of 11 July 1990):

> In one such experiment, young Gypsies, with microphones hanging from their necks, were thrown out of airplanes; the Professor hoped that during the plunge to their deaths, the subjects would supply him with a statement, or if not, with at least a clue—like a scream, primordial or not—that would throw light upon the meaning of existence, which was the Professor's major concern in those days, for with the Allies already at the gates of Berlin, he wanted to learn something about the transition to eternal life. His hopes were frustrated.[43]

Taken together, these quotations capture well the wide scope of the arresting power that last words have over the imagination and the secular "piety" of the survivors in our culture. And again, this is by no means entirely a matter of the past. Botho Strauß's much acclaimed *Paare, Passanten*, contains a casual reference to the "omnipotent force of what a man said at the last"; and the duration of the power of such a last word is described here, with equal casualness, as nothing short of "eternal."[44] But regardless of whether the truth of the dying pronouncement is understood as the reflex of a thresh-old experience—a Grenzerfahrung that involves the "totally other" in metaphysical terms (as in the passage from Willa Cather)—or in what appear to be purely human terms (as in the lines from *Richard II*), there is, in either case, a hint of an awareness that the moment and its words are *sui generis*, dis-tinct from any others by virtue of their mystique. This para-dox of life articulating its own transcendence or, conversely, its own cessation (more than one scientist is said to have ex-pired saying his own heartbeat stopped) is expressed aptly in Alice James's remark in a letter to her brother William, dated 30 July 1891: "[Death is] the most supremely interesting mo-ment in life, the only one in fact, when living seems life."[45] An echo seems to reach us from turn-of-the-century Vienna, from Hofmannsthal's Claudio in *Death and the Fool*: "Only now as I am dying do I feel that I exist."[46] At the same time, both of these formulations take us at least close to the absurd. For un-like Eissler's comments, they in effect declare worthless all stages of growth experienced before this crucial moment—what makes life worthwhile is experienced only as it is being lost. Yet, as is so often the case, it is the absurd extreme that points back to the essential truth.

3

PORK-PIE OR
FATHERLAND:
AUTHENTIC OR
BEN TROVATO?
The Last Word as
Artifact and
"Inherited
Mythology"

✛

Some commonsensical res-
ervations and objections are overdue. If the moment of dying
is significant for our understanding of human nature in general or in particular, does it necessarily follow that last words,
too, are significant, be it as indicators of true character or of
the quality of the Grenzerfahrung from which they supposedly derive? More specifically, does it follow that the utterance reported or generally "known" as the last word is of significance? If one pays attention to last words and ascribes
significance and meaning to them, as is customary in our culture, then one would first of all like to be certain that they are
authentic. One would like to know whether the last words
reported in biographies or in anthologies, or passed on by
word of mouth or preserved in the collective memory of the
educated—and only those are the subject of this study—were

in fact (and in their reported form) the final words spoken. Such doubts about authenticity are familiar even from cocktail-party conversation; they tend to be the first objection raised against any and all interest in this subject. And, needless to add, it is especially those "appropriate" curtain lines that have become familiar quotations that raise these doubts in the first place.

Napoleon by some accounts died with the name of his beloved Josephine on his lips, and Josephine reportedly sank into a coma after she pronounced the word *Napoleon*. But one of the greatest love stories did not end with "Héloise" (Abélard's last word was a disappointing "I don't know"). But, then, does a banal *mot de la fin* of this sort not inspire more confidence in its genuineness than does the all-too-neat duet of Napoleon and Josephine, which is so obviously suspect? Tallulah Bankhead died with bourbon on her lips, or the word, rather. Chekhov passed on after saying "champagne"—entirely insignificant it seems, even though Chekhov's coffin was shipped to its final resting place in a freight car of the imperial railroad labeled "fresh oysters," as gourmets rarely fail to note. Wordsworth said in extremis: "Is that Dora?"; Emily Dickinson's concluding remark was: "I must go in, the fog is rising"; Lord Chesterfield's last words, as everyone in the English-speaking world knows, were addressed to his valet, referring to a visitor: "Give Dayrolles a chair"; George Eliot complained of pain "in the left side"; Samuel Butler (the younger) asked his servant whether he had brought the checkbook. Entirely banal, all of these curtain lines, yet one is conditioned to feel that writers and artists should be able to do better, should be able to die more memorably. Or take another disconcerting fact (as facts go in this line of inquiry; but more of that soon): George Washington, Immanuel Kant, and André Gide not only died saying insignificant words, they died saying exactly the *same* insignificant words, though their lives, personalities, and claims to fame are arguably different (all three said, "'tis well"). Rabelais, Beethoven, and Emperor Augustus mumbled a roughly identical statement about the farce of life being over; Harriet Beecher Stowe and the Maréchal de Saxe both remarked with their last breath that they had had a "beautiful dream." Do the same last words imply the same summation of the "same" life? Or was "the last word" not the last? Or again, isn't the last word (and hence the question about authenticity) meaningless in all these cases, perhaps in *all* cases; meaningless, indeed, by definition? This is what Stephen Macdonald is driving at in his much-praised play *Not About Heroes*. He lampoons the hero's death on the battlefield with its obligatory "memorable last words" by having nothing more memorable occur to Siegfried Sassoon, dying, he himself thinks, of a shot in the head, than the observation that his head hurts[1] (not borne out, incidentally but significantly, by Sassoon's diary). By implication, isn't Macdonald debunking the whole institution?

The last words of others are controversial in the sense that very different sets of exit lines have been reported as the very last ones. In the case of Chekhov, for example, was it the traditional "It's been a long time since I've had champagne" or, as V. S. Pritchett has it in his *Chekhov*, "I'm dying," first in Russian, twice and to no avail, then, successfully, in German?[2] Everyone seems to have heard of Nelson's dubious exit line addressed to staff captain Hardy as the admiral was rasping out his last during the Battle of Trafalgar, a French bullet in his chest: Was it "Kiss me, Hardy" or "Kismet, Hardy"? Or was it, as other anthologies of last words report, "Thank God, I have done my duty"? (Nelson's physician, William Beatty, in his *Authentic Narrative of the Death of Lord Nelson*, records that Nelson did say "Kiss me, Hardy," whereupon Hardy kissed Nelson on the cheek, but that his *very* last words were indeed about duty fulfilled.)[3] The strange and similar case of George V might best be relegated to the coy discretion of a note for fear of becoming either obscene or blasphemous (and guilty of lèse majesté in either case) in the pursuit of scholarship, for it appears, in the light of recent documentation, that the official "How is the Empire?", so considerate of national expectations, were not the only recorded last words of the colonial overlord.[4] British Prime Minister William Pitt, generally supposed to have been as patriotic in his final hour as King George, is controversial in a less off-color manner. There are two main versions of his last words, both of which are suspected of textual corruption: "Oh, my country. How I leave [or was it love?] my country," and "I think I could eat one of Bellamy's pork pies" or was it "veal pies"?[5] *Many* of the famous apparently left more than one set of last words, "dying up" to what appears to be the status requirement of their class and leaving us wondering, even in the absence of controversy and scholarly assessment of the "evidence," which words were really last—and whether they, too, were not followed by yet more, deemed too insignificant or too revealing to be recorded, or simply not heard by anyone of importance. Goethe, in spite of everybody's favorite "More light!" is in this class; so is Schiller (did he mumble about the "judge" of us all or about lighting fuel?). Oscar Wilde is another (he, at least, was dependably entertaining in the alternate, but again not literally "last," version as well: dying in that dingy hotel room in Paris, he commented to Claire de Pratz on the bad taste of the wallpaper: "One or the other of us has to go"). Did Diderot have philosophy on his mind as he died (see above, p. 5)—or an apricot that his wife tried to prevent him from having for dessert?[6] Heinrich Heine can claim several last words, though not all witty, as can Daniel Webster, while the world record is believed to be held by Rabelais, with a grand total of five sets of last words, with Voltaire and Queen Victoria as the runners-up[7] (rather an odd couple when one cares to visualize it). But one must hasten to add that there may be doubts even when there is only *one* recorded version of the last word, as in "I have lived as a philosopher and die as a

Christian," supposedly the parting shot of Casanova, of all people.[8] There is controversy even about the all-but-sacrosanct wording, though not the sentiment, of Nathan Hale's universally known words pronounced under the gallows, "I only regret that I have but one life to lose for my country." Did Hale echo a printed source? Was the patriot a plagiarizer?[9] And if the wording itself is beyond doubt, its interpretation may still be acutely controversial, as in the (to some) esoteric but most-learnedly debated case of Pope Gregory VII: into his—undisputed—deathbed legacy posterity reads what it wants to hear, and that can be highly contradictory.[10]

The reasons for all these problems are obvious: How well are "last words" authenticated? A reputable handbook of historical errors—the genre does exist—states matter-of-factly that the telling last words of "great men" that are the historians' stock-in-trade were "almost without exception invented post mortem."[11] Whoever reports last words *as last words* (hence laden with significance) may have a bad memory or a motive—he may want to prove, for example, that Haller died either a Christian death or the death of an empirical scientist without "faith"; with the name of his Savior on his lips *or* with his hand on his pulse.

Given this state of affairs, it is not surprising that some scholarly anthologists of last words consider concern about authenticity the badge of their connoisseurship. Edward Le Comte, for example, is at pains to point out that only last words that are authentic and in fact last have been admitted to his *Dictionary of Last Words*, [12] and many agree that this should be the way to proceed in this difficult terrain. In fairness it might be added, however, that authenticity or legitimation is, in principle, of limited interest to the cultural historian. For he is interested in last words because they have been handed down from generation to generation as last words, as precious heirlooms or sacred relics, and have thus become part of the vocabulary of the educated—in an unchanging form, as a *fable convenue,* myth, or legend. To the cultural historian, last words are artifacts that have developed a life of their own, independent of the "truth" of the deathbed situation. Hence their legitimacy and flawless pedigree are less important than their agreed-upon status as words of the last gasp (see below, pp. 95–96).

But the special taste of cultural historians aside, the difficulty of any claim of authenticity of last words remains that it can only be proved with "evidence" whose weight inevitably differs from case to case. There is no general standard for the evidence, and the nature of the source material differs so widely that there can be no litmus test. Each case requires its own procedure of analysis and depends on such variables as the character of the dying person, the circumstances of his death, the profile of the witness or witnesses, and the manner of transmission; and it is not even to be taken for granted that in a given case such an analysis would yield a clear and incontrovertible result.[13] If one reads a number of biographies of leading figures of public life, one is in for strange surprises. It may therefore be interesting to look at a few examples in the humorless spirit of strictly factual examination of the evidence. Perhaps one might gain, above and beyond the entertainment value of pedantry, a sense of the natural laws of legend formation, a glimpse of the natural history of last words.

❖   ❖

Let us start with Edgar Allan Poe. Two versions of his last words are common currency, Rodger Kamenetz stated recently in an essay, "Last Words." One is "sentimental," belonging to the realm of "poetry": "Lord help my poor soul!" The second is "sensational" or "prosaic," a reply to Poe's physician's inquiry whether he had any friends he would like to see before the end: "'Friends!' exclaimed the dying son of genius—'friends!' repeating the word for a moment as if it had no longer a definite meaning;

'my best friend would be he who would take a pistol and blow out these damned wretched brains!'"[14] How to decide which version is more credible or better authenticated? Kamenetz bases his decision in favor of the latter on intuition; no reasons are stated. If, however, one looks into the matter, there are surprises.

The first volume of *The Works of Edgar Allan Poe* (New York, 1880) reprints a report by Poe's physician, Dr. John J. Moran, about the last days of Poe's life—a report first published on 28 October 1875 in the *New York Herald* (Poe had died on 7 October 1849). Dr. Moran gives neither of the two versions mentioned above as the last word, but instead cites a third version which has never become general knowledge. It is an outpouring of a lyrical monologue, unmistakably literary, about suicide, gulf and stream, buoy and lifeboat, "ship of fire, sea of brass," culminating in "Rest, shore no more!" (p. cxxii). This is the last word as of a quarter century after Poe's death, and hardly credible, even less so when one hears that Dr. Moran traveled up and down the country lecturing about Poe's last days and that his memory of the facts became ever more precise and detailed as time went on.[15] Still, Dr. Moran's 1875 report does include Poe's statement that his best friend would be he who would blow his brains out, though not in precisely the same wording. But, according to Moran, this was said days before the end and before several other remarks which he reports—"Lord help my poor soul!" not among them (p. cxviii).

A very different impression of Poe's last days, hours, and words emerges, however, from the "Official Account of his Death," which none other than Moran published ten years later as *A Defense of Edgar Allan Poe: Life, Character and Dying Declarations of the Poet* (Washington, 1885). There is no mention here at all of the bitter remark about the best friend who would kill him; instead, the dying man answers the question whether he would care to see friends with the most famous of all quotations from Poe: "Nevermore." The lyrical effusion on the stream, lifeboat, etc., is unaccountably missing as well; its place is taken by an equally incredible poetic homage to the Creator—finishing without anything like "Lord help my poor soul!" (p. 72). But, oddly enough, *this* final word can also be traced back to that ever-resourceful physician by the dying poet's bedside. In a letter written to Maria Clemm about six weeks after Poe's death, on 15 November 1849, Moran does refer to Poe's wish to be murdered by his best friend if he had one, not as the utterance of the last moment, but as a remark dated two days before the curtain fell; the real last words, spoken two days later, are unambiguously stated to have been the God-fearing version that, as one of two, has become reasonably well known: "Then gently moving his head he said, 'Lord help my poor soul!' and expired!" (This letter was generally accessible as early as 1902 in the Virginia edition of Poe's works.)[16]

So no case can be made for the "finality" of the cynical postulate about murder and friendship which, as a last word, would contort the poet's image to a grimace? So it would just have been a matter of some survivors thinking it fitting that the writer notorious for his dark moods would have sent his "poor soul" on its way in this manner? One may grant this, but does it necessarily follow that the God-fearing version of Poe's last words can be accepted as authentic, especially as we have it on the authority of the Dr. Moran of 1849, who had yet to develop his creative penchant for imaginative embellishment of the circumstances of Poe's death? Would the God-fearing last words that Kamenetz considered not only suspect but also categorically fictitious then be authentic? Le Comte's *Dictionary* does in fact list "Lord help my poor soul" as the sole and hence legitimate exit line. The most recent biography, Kenneth Silverman's *Edgar A. Poe*, considers it the only reliable last word.[17] But it is not necessarily authentic, and more likely not. For one should consider the addressee of Dr. Moran's letter of November 1849 following Poe's death. It was a woman to whom Poe was very close, his aunt Maria Clemm, who was also his mother-in-law. Did not pious consideration rather than the love of truth dictate this document? Are we not witnessing a legend in the making? And does it not follow that *no* word can in good conscience be claimed as Poe's last testament and legacy, no matter how desirable to posterity, as Moran's reports of 1875 and 1885 bear the clear stamp of fiction?

The case of Walter Scott leaves us even more empty-handed. The biography produced with all due dispatch by his son-in-law J. G. Lockhart, *Memoirs of Sir Walter Scott*, is considered one of the great biographical feats in the English language, along with Boswell's *Life of Johnson*. From it one gathers that, his consciousness and linguistic competence ebbing away, the bard of the borders kept lingering for months after several strokes, until on 21 September 1832 his heart stood still at last in Abbotsford, the neo-Gothic manor he had built for himself in the Lowlands at prodigious expense. Lockhart, called to the deathbed, reports that Scott's last words, spoken on September 17 in expectation of his imminent demise, were a pious admonition: "I may have but a minute to speak to you. My dear, be a good man—be virtuous—be religious—be a good man. Nothing else will give you any comfort when you lie here." This was followed immediately by the remark that his daughters Anne and Sophia should not be called, they should not be disturbed after they had been up all night, and then: "God bless you all."[18] After that, Scott succumbed to unconsciousness from which he did not awaken.

Scott's edifying oration of the final moment is listed in Le Comte's *Dictionary* of 1955, the self-proclaimed last word on authenticity, though the compiler has it followed by the statement "I feel myself again"—an addition that comes out of insight which must remain unfathomable, as Lockhart is given as the source, cited by chapter and verse. The admonition to be virtuous and religious is quoted with the air of authority as late as 1973 in Carola Oman's both scholarly and popular biography of Scott, *The Wizard of the North*.[19] Yet in 1938 Sir Herbert J. C. Grierson had debunked this edifying exit as a "pious myth" in his *Sir Walter Scott, Bart.* (a book known to Oman, by the way). He had been lucky enough to find in the National Library of Scotland a letter to Lockhart from a relative of Scott's, preserved by an unknown pack rat, that unabashedly all but dictated such a pious last word to the biographer-to-be, along with a plausible motive for this deathbed scenario:

> When you write anything of the last very melancholy weeks at Abbotsford I think it will be most valuable to mention any of the few remarks he uttered when his mind was clear of a religious tendency such as I heard he said occasionally, Oh be virtuous! It is one's only comfort in a dying state! and anything of that kind, for there *are* wicked people who will take a *pleasure* in saying that he was not a religious man; and *proving the contrary will do much good*.[20]

Here, then, we encounter an undeniably invented last word (testifying, of course, to the need for one, and to the persuasive power of the institution)—a last word whose fictional quality, solemnly confirmed by Edgar Johnson in his monumental biography of Scott,[21] has by no means hampered its long career in the popular imagination. *Or*, to play devil's, or rather God's, advocate, was it fictitious? After all, there is a literal overlap between the solicitous letter and the authoritative biographical account of no more than two words. Could Lockhart have been trustworthy in spite of the suggestion of the contrary? Should one not give Scott the benefit of the doubt?

Oscar Wilde was lucky in a different way. His last quips, in both familiar versions already mentioned, sound far too witty, too irreverent in extremis, too much "like him," to be taken seriously as the truth about his last moment. And yet

they are commonly quoted in biographies,[22] even though reports on his last days appearing shortly after Wilde's death
might have produced enlightenment—had anyone been sufficiently interested in being enlightened. There is no doubt:
both commonly known sets of exit lines are documented *not*
as last words but as pronouncements from the last weeks of
Wilde's life, more than a month before his death. Richard Ellmann's justly praised recent biography now gives us the evidence with unprecedented narrative charm and sympathy[23]—
but also documentation of other utterances that *followed* the
"exit lines" and which would definitely have been less appropriate in one of Wilde's comedies. Or, to go back to the ultimate sources of information on the last days and hours, what
did Reginald Turner and Robert Ross, Wilde's intimates until
the end, report on the final moments? Ross's notes, "Oscar
Wilde's Last Days," which incorporated numerous letters
from Turner on the final phase, appeared in German on 15
November 1909, while still unpublished in English, in the
magazine *Nord und Süd* (pp. 313–328) and soon after caught
the eye of the *Mercure de France* (1 January 1910, pp. 182–186).
Here neither a witty nor even an insignificant last word is reported; instead, Wilde "talks nonsense all the time, sometimes in English, sometimes in French" (p. 321). His friends
cannot even confirm that he accepted, willingly and consciously, the rites of the one and only church, though they do
tell of the "satyr play" following his death that even Wilde
could not have improved on (though Joe Orton might have):
only after the authorized French government official had determined the number of shirt-collars the deceased had owned
and the resale value of his umbrella, were plans for the funeral—sixth class—allowed to proceed.

This kind of detail may offer connoisseurs of *Morts bizarres*—the title of Jean Richepin's book of riveting stories[24]—
a limited compensation for last words fit for cocktail-party
conversation lost through an all-too-scholarly craving for authenticity. They should count their blessings; for in another

justly famous case, that of Thomas More, one ends up with even less.

Richard Marius's biography *Thomas More*, like that of More's son-in-law William Roper (another son-in-law as biographer!), provides us with an impressive series of last words of Henry VIII's Lord Chancellor.[25] He was tried for high treason on account of his steadfastness in the Catholic faith in 1535 and is said to have uttered all of these exit lines on his way to Tower Hill and indeed on the scaffold, facing the executioner's block. His words confirm not only that it was customary and expected to leave this world with such memorable utterances (which is why the king had expressly enjoined his victim that he should "not use many words" at the execution, p. 512), but also that such words were considered public property, to be bequeathed to one's issue. However, more than one eminently quotable version appears in one lexicon or another, not to mention biographies. Marius wisely leaves open the question about their sequence and authenticity, thus in no way cutting back the thicket of anecdotes. Different witnesses and biographers simply claim to have heard or know different things. The most moving and at the same time wittiest story—More drapes his long grey beard over the block so that the executioner's sword will not cut it, for "this hath not offended the king"—does not make its appearance until the hagiographies of the nineteenth century, while a similar version (that his beard "had never committed treason"), which the *Dictionary of National Biography* preserves, did not gain currency until a century after More's death.[26] Sixteenth-century biographies know nothing about the beard's fate. The mindset of the later accounts is easy to understand: The holy man might as well have been witty; not only was he more spiritual than his worldly superior but also more spirited—certainly true, but no doubt false as far as evidence for his last word goes. Yet conforming to the natural law of literary legend formation?

The critical examination of the wording and the moment of utterances canonized as last words has in these cases thrown a certain light on the circumstances of reporting and transmission that at least allow us conclusions about which word was *not* or could not have been the final one, and therefore conclusions about which general interpretation of the life and death in question cannot be confirmed or sealed with a fitting last word. The case of Samuel Johnson is different. Here the sceptical analysis of the traditional sets of last words and their circumstances leaves the case even more puzzling than it had seemed at the outset. It becomes increasingly clear, however, why it is that one or another version was preferred; clear which overall image of Dr. Johnson was to be confirmed or unmasked through a particular last word.

Johnson is well known for his view that it did not matter how one died; what counted was how one lived. His friends and biographers did not honor this sentiment, resulting in no fewer than three crassly contradictory versions of his last words. And these versions have been in circulation "almost from the moment of his demise on December 13, 1784"—not, as in the case of Thomas More, since some considerable time after his death—so one reads in the most recent critical contribution to the old controversy about the three versions' claims to authenticity which flared up again in the 1980s.[27] On the basis of a careful examination of the textual sources and their authors, as well as the comings and goings in Johnson's house during his last hours, this study, by Mary Jane Hurst, arrives at the conclusion that each of the three versions labors under a grave credibility gap. The question of what was said by the famous master of cultivated conversation before he passed into unconsciousness must remain open. Future biographers, Hurst feels, cannot simply decide in favor of this or that version; the challenge would be, rather, to give its due to each of the three and thereby also to the difficulties they involve, separately and in relation to each other—and she cannot see how this could be brought off "elegantly." It is all the more interesting to see the effect of having the curtain fall on the life of the unsurpassed practitioner of the mot juste at each of the three versions.

What is there to choose from? "God bless you" (perhaps followed by "my dear," addressed to a Miss Morris, to whom Johnson was not exactly close)—this was the last word according to Boswell, who was at pains to stylize the end with a view to that Christian equanimity prominent in his image of Johnson. Johnson's friend John Hoole, on the other hand, reported in his account of the last days of the grand old man that at the very last he had mumbled something (not recorded verbatim, alas) about a cup of warm milk not being handed to him properly. Boswell knew of this account, but the communication of this all-too-human detail would have besmirched the image of the admired father figure. The third version is definitely more sublime. It surfaces as early as 1787 in the biography of Johnson by Sir John Hawkins—another regular in the Johnson circle—as secondhand information; but then, the rival "God bless you" may have been thirdhand: It is not to Hawkins, but to Italian teacher Francesco Sastres, that the dying man said: "Iam moriturus."

Walter Jackson Bate, in his *Samuel Johnson*, finds this curtain line eminently fitting. True, in his description of the deathbed scene, Bate is careful to specify that this was only one "among his last words"; but the biographer tellingly adds that the remark seems to echo the gladiators' ritual final salutation to the emperor, and he suggestively entitles the last chapter "Iam moriturus" (though he does at least mention, without comment, one of the two competing versions, "God bless you," in his narrative context).[28] Let us assume that the echo of "Morituri te salutant" was not misheard by Bate, the artistically inclined and classically educated biographer. Let us further assume that "Iam moriturus" was indeed the last utterance (diligent detectives have determined to their own satisfaction, Hurst reports, that at the moment in question Sastres was not in Johnson's bedroom but in the dining room; also, Boswell did not use his testimony). There is no denying that *this* death of Johnson would seal a very different life: that of the intrepid fighter, raising an angry fist against his fate. At one point in his biography Boswell had likened Johnson's mind to that of a gladiator, which Bate hailed "a fitting comparison" in his 1955 *Achievement of Samuel Johnson*.[29] The choice of last words reveals the biographers' true colors.

Finally, and inevitably, we come to Goethe. "Educated men and women," even those who have never read a line of Goethe's, know with which exclamation he closed his eyes. Le Comte's *Dictionary of Last Words* lists the timeworn "More light!" as the last pronouncement on the authority of G. H. Lewes's *Life of Goethe* of 1855 (which, incidentally, added the heavy-handed commentary: "He whose eternal longings had been for more Light, gave a parting cry for it").[30] The problem could not be stated more clearly, or unwittingly. To be sure, the "More light!" story has been repeated hundreds of times in biographies and commemorative addresses; it is a treasured part of the national mythology of a country whose unity was usually more cultural than political. Thus in the year of the centenary of Goethe's death, one reads in an essay authored by Max Hecker:

> From early on, Goethe's last word (that it was really the last is attested by Coudray in his notes written immediately after Goethe's death and by Chancellor von Müller) was interpreted as a rich symbol of the poet's entire life: "More light!" Such spiritualization was natural; it was not unjustified. For the dim light of that early spring day too flowed from the sacred sun which Goethe's eye, being sun-like itself, strove to meet even when it broke—it, too, an expression of everlasting divine nature into whose womb his divine essence was preparing to return.[31]

But this does not adequately reflect the "state of research" even of 1932. (The leading Goethe bibliography, by Hans Py-

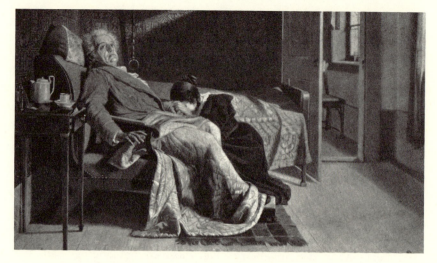

Postcard of "Mehr Licht," an engraving after the painting by
Fritz Fleischer.

ritz, contains an entire section, brought up to date from time
to time, assembling scholarship on Goethe's last words.)
There have been various and contentious schools of thought
on this subject. The most recent, substantial scholarly biography, on the other hand, Karl Otto Conrady's, strains to
reserve judgment about the words that were spoken or not
spoken at the last, on the morning of 22 March 1832 in the
stately mansion on Weimar's Frauenplan square: "Some claim
to know that he said something memorable."[32] The memora-
bilia were painstakingly collected and critically reviewed by
Carl Schüddekopf in his book on the event, *Goethes Tod*.

Schüddekopf presented himself as a biographical dragon-
slayer of the first rank. He destroyed the "More light!" version, already "frequently" and regretfully deemed untenable
by that time, with a reminder that it goes back to a report by
the grand-ducal director-general of construction, Clemens
Wenzeslaus Coudray, who was present at Goethe's deathbed,

or rather chair. Goethe had asked his valet Friedrich Krause: "'Open the shutter in the bedroom so that more light can come in.' These were his last intelligible words."[33] This is what Coudray reports in his "Notes concerning Goethe's last days and death" of 24 March 1832, not published until 1889, by which time the "More light!" story, passed from mouth to mouth ever since 1832, had already made its appearance in print many times over, as Schüddekopf duly noted (pp. 27–28, 104). But Schüddekopf in his turn called attention to an earlier note of Coudray's, of 22 March 1832, the very day of Goethe's death; interestingly, this document says nothing about more light. Instead it offers a last word faintly reminiscent of Samuel Johnson's (possibly) banal demise. The grand-seigneur said to his valet in this version: "You didn't put sugar in the wine, did you?" (p. 22)—which presents a real challenge for anyone trying to find symbolic significance in last words. So much, gloats Schüddekopf, for the favorite notion that great men offer the "sum of their existence" with their final breath (p. 24); Houston Stewart Chamberlain echoed this triumphant conclusion in his *Goethe* in 1912.[34] Schüddekopf is generous, though: he is not carried away to the point of denying outright that the famous words about more light might have been spoken, although he does note that other sources do not report them and that in any case they could not have been as succinct as they are usually quoted. The grand master of pedantry is more interested in pointing out that in the actual semidarkness of the small back room, the last words could not possibly have had the symbolic meaning that had for generations been attributed to them with so much piety and consideration (pp. 24–27). After all, the desire for light, he tells us, is "quite common" with the dying. Shortly before the end, darkness dims their sight, a phenomenon called amaurosis, we learn (pp. 26–27).

But what does this intrepid destroyer of the legend offer in compensation? Letters written at the time by such Weimar residents as the bookdealer Friedrich Johannes Frommann, the painter Luise Seidler, the scholar Wilhelm Weißenborn, and one Pauline Hase, the wife of a professor in nearby Jena, all report, Schüddekopf discovered, that Goethe's last word had been directed to his daughter-in-law Ottilie: " 'Come, my little daughter, and give me your little paw' or something like that."[35] This surely satisfied those biographers and others who delighted in the debunking of the "More light!" story. One of them, the widely read English Goethe enthusiast Chamberlain, hastened to quote "the core of eternal love" from *Faust* (line 11,853) for clarification (p. 78). Another must have been Ottilie herself who, along with her children, was the only signer of the official death notice, in which she describes her father-in-law as "in the full possession of his intellectual powers and loving to his last breath" (Schüddekopf, pp. 28–29). Unfortunately, it is the scholar who is called upon to be the spoilsport here. With all due professional timidity he needs to remind us that neither the one nor the other symbolical interpretation would in principle have had the blessing of the grand old man himself. True, Goethe's remark about Madame Roland's last moments (see above, p. 59) would suggest some fascination with the mystique of the transition; but in a letter to Chancellor Friedrich von Müller of 12 October 1828, concerning a "relation" about the death of Grand Duke Karl August of Weimar, he generalized peremptorily: "Such last hours are always like plaster-cast death masks, pathologically passive caricatures of even the most active life."[36]

But apart from the symbolic interpretation, the touching story about Ottilie's "little paw" and eroticism to the last, which Schüddekopf triumphantly paraded as the true last word, has problems of its own. First of all, Goethe's valet Friedrich Krause's notes about the last conscious moments of his master do not mention the "little paw" at all,[37] yet Krause was present throughout; that should have given Schüddekopf and his followers pause. A more incisive and significant criticism, however, can be found in the essay "Goethe's Last Words" by Dolf Sternberger, the political scientist:

> Not one of those who report the charming remark [about Ottilie's little paw] was in a position to hear it himself or herself, and none of those present at the final hour recorded it. So it is not hard to guess the source: the story can only go back to Ottilie herself, the little daughter or little woman who was so kindly asked to offer her little paw. It may even have been whispered or murmured in such a low voice that nobody else could actually have heard it. Ottilie, the daughter and granddaughter of ladies-in-waiting, no doubt politely told her friends who came to offer their condolences about it, one after the other, and so the story rushed and skipped through the entire town in no time and still delights us today. Old-fashioned courtesy will prevent doubts as severe as those about the other last word from gnawing at the authenticity of this one as well.[38]

Are both familiar versions of Goethe's last words suspect? In his turn, Sternberger—who at least hints that Ottilie's self-interest came into play—hopes to shore up the "More light!" story. He wonders aloud why Coudray remembered "More light!" only in his second note on the grand old man's death. His explanation seems plausible at first blush: Coudray must have heard it from Chancellor von Müller who was also in attendance at the deathbed, and Coudray himself indicated that he talked to Müller on the evening of Goethe's death (Schüddekopf, p. 102). And Sternberger found that Müller had written up his own account of the dying scene, which Sternberger says Schüddekopf overlooked (pp. 40–42). But Schüddekopf, for his part, merely tucked it away in a footnote (p. 166). Müller's version runs as follows (the wording reveals an early penchant for seeing symbolism where none was intended or plausible): "He died the most blessed death, lucid, serene without any intimation of death. . . . His last demand

was for light, half an hour before the end he ordered: 'Open
the shutters so that more light can come in.'" As Müller and
Coudray knew each other, the "More light!" version may indeed have been taken by one from the other (both were present during the last hour). But, at the risk of getting into the
spirit of the quibbling—or is it detective work?—endemic in
these investigations, who echoes whom?

Coudray's second account bears the date 24 March 1832;
Müller's statement is dated March 22 in the Artemis edition of
Goethe's conversations (1950) as well as in Biedermann's collection of the conversations on which it is based.[39] However,
the ultimate source—Bettina von Arnim's *Tagebuch*,[40] which
quotes from an alleged letter of Chancellor von Müller to Bettina—gives no date at all for the text. It follows that it cannot
be determined that the date of Müller's statement preceded
that of Coudray's, and Sternberger's thesis (that Coudray got
the "More light!" story from Müller) thus collapses: it cannot
be determined whether Müller refreshed Coudray's memory
or the other way round. One must conclude that the March 22
date given in the Artemis *Gespräche* just mentioned is no more
than a reference to the day when the remark was made,
Goethe's last day, not to the day when Müller recorded it in
writing. Equally undated is an English translation of Müller's
passage on "More light!" quoted by Sarah Austin in 1833, two
years before Bettina von Arnim, in the third volume of her
"documentary" *Characteristics of Goethe*—presented, however,
not as an excerpt from a Müller letter to Bettina but as part of
an apparently lost letter of his to Prince Pückler-Muskau.[41]
The different addressees make the text even more suspect
than it would have been in its German printing (Bettina is a
notoriously unreliable source of information). Hence it is perhaps not surprising that Bettina's text is omitted entirely in
Wolfgang Herwig's recent revised edition of the Artemis *Conversations*; it is "replaced," as the editorial account puts it in
1987, by a letter from Müller to Goethe's close friend Karl
Friedrich Zelter which says: "'Open the shutter in the [other]

room ["Stube"—not the bedroom, where we are at that point]
so that more light can come in!' These were the last words *I*
heard."[42] This letter from Müller, however, in print since
1928, is dated 29 March 1832. Are we to assume then that
Coudray, who for his part had recorded the "More light!" version as early as 24 March, told Müller about it or refreshed
his memory—and not the other way around, as Sternberger
took for granted on the basis of a misinterpretation of a date?
Yet Coudray had said nothing about more light in his note
written on the very day of Goethe's death and is therefore
suspect himself as a source for "More light!"; it looks rather
like an afterthought when it makes its appearance two days
later in his second account. So one wonders: Is the credibility
of both Müller and Coudray increased or diminished by their
agreement?

"Goethe's death was an event which even at that time of
feverish political unrest commanded awed attention; the public did not tire of listening to the reports on Goethe's dying
hours," wrote Max Hecker, a prominent Goethe scholar, in
1928 in the *Jahrbuch der Goethe-Gesellschaft.*[43] The passing of the
sage of Weimar, the living legend of German *Kultur*, was generally seen to signal the end of an era, as Heine stated so
memorably at the outset of his *Romantic School*: "The gods are
leaving." But what is the final word in the more than 150-year-
old argument about the universally known expression that
seemed to encapsulate everything Goethe stood for?[44] His demand for more light (whose analysis happily turned out to be
a parody of positivist *Quellenkritik*) had supposedly been directed to his valet Friedrich Krause. Krause confirmed in his
own awkward notes on the event that he was called by
Goethe to the green biedermeier chair in which the old man
was about to die, but not, as he pointedly notes, to have the
shutter opened so that more light could come in, "but at the
last he asked for the pot de chambre, and he took it himself
and held it firmly to his body until he died."[45] Is there a biography that mentions this? Better known to many Germans is

Friedrich Rückert's poem "Goethe's Last Word" which cele-brates "More light!" with high pathos as the exit line summing up the singularly sublime life.[46]

American schoolchildren are more familiar with Anthony Hecht's poem, which is anthologized in Lawrence Perrine's reader, *Sound and Sense: An Introduction to Poetry*.[47] The poem recounts an act of extraordinary physical and mental cruelty in the Buchenwald concentration camp and points out that no light from nearby Weimar appeared in this darkness of mind and soul. The poem is entitled " 'More light! More light!' "—a title that is not in the least explained in the poem itself. It is apparently taken for granted that the American reader is fa-miliar with the quotation. Le Comte's remark, cited earlier, does not seem so farfetched: "Those who never read Goethe in prose or verse can still tell you that he said on his death-bed, More light!" We might also recall some other testimo-nies, referred to earlier, to the currency of Goethe's final re-mark in the non-German world: Antler's poem featuring "More light!" among other curtain lines, without seeing a need for attribution; the English moth yearning for "mehr Licht" during the blitz; Umberto Eco's *Foucault's Pendulum* in which a Mr. Dee dies with a request for "more light." Goethe is almost never passed over in the numerous, mostly non-German anthologies of last words, which will be discussed in the next chapter. In them, he is featured not only among the most august of philosophers (as in G. W. Foote's *Infidel Death-Beds* of 1866) but also among the unfortunates distinguished by trivial last words (as in Brian O'Kill's *Exit Lines* of 1988). Knowing this, one is not surprised to discover that a recent bilingual art-book on holograms and light objects is entitled *Mehr Licht/More Light*, without further explanation.[48]

We cite one final exhibit demonstrating the familiarity of Goethe's alleged farewell to life in the English-speaking world—one quite innocent of those doubts that have troubled scholars for many decades. In the *New York Review of Books* of 27 October 1988, Gore Vidal reviewed an anthology of articles

published in the earliest issues of that magazine; Vidal's article took the form of a dialogue between Eckermann, Goethe's
ever-present recorder of conversations, and a visitor. In it,
Eckermann luxuriates in reminiscences of the sage with quips
such as "Echt lousy, as Goethe would say." "Our Japanese
masters currently prefer comic books," Eckermann comments
at one point in the conversation; the outlook for the future of
literature is correspondingly somber. Accordingly Eckermann
sends his visitor, who has already heard that Goethe was
"chatty to the last" (p. 82), on his way with the request: "On
your way out, open the second shutter so that more light can
come in" (p. 83). No explanation deemed necessary.

But perhaps the ultimate canonization of "More light!" occurs not in the literary weekly *Mehr Licht!* (1878–80), but in the
Austrian writer Thomas Bernhard's *Der Stimmenimitator*,
where a passage focuses on the matter of authenticity in a
pseudoanecdotal manner:

> A man from Augsburg was committed to the Augsburg insane
> asylum for the sole reason that all his life he had claimed at
> every opportunity that Goethe's last word had been *mehr nicht!*
> (no more!) rather than *mehr Licht!* Over the years this had got-
> ten so much on the nerves of the people who had to deal with
> him, that they had plotted to have this Augsburg citizen, who
> remained so unfortunately obsessed by his claim, committed
> to an insane asylum. Six physicians reportedly refused to com-
> mit the unfortunate man; the seventh ordered him to be com-
> mitted without delay. This physician, I read in the *Frankfurter
> Allgemeine Zeitung*, has been awarded the Goethe Medal of the
> City of Frankfurt for his action.[49]

❖ ❖ ❖

Let us pick up the thread
again. Authentic or apocryphal? That is the question that any
master of the raised eyebrow will ask the moment the matter

of last words comes up. Underlying this question is that of the significance or insignificance of the last word (indeed of *any* last word) as a sort of testament or motto of a life, the question of the legitimacy of the institution. Of course one could, with a little effort, see some "meaningful," "telling" significance even in the prima facie most insignificant last words, clearly not meant to be a "message" or a "summation"; for example, Lord Chesterfield's offering a visitor a chair. The man who was so concerned about manners all his life was "polite to the last," as one anthologist explains, following Chesterfield's first biographer, Matthew Maty, who found these words "characteristic" as early as 1777 and quoted the commentary of the physician attending the dying aristocrat: "His good breeding only quits him with his life."[50] Much could similarly be made of other last words that were not last by design, but by chance: Marie Antoinette's "Pardonnez-moi" to the executioner, or Samuel Butler's "Have you the check-book, Alfred?" And one might chuckle over the understatement of the year 1914: Archduke Francis Ferdinand of Austria muttering feebly "It is nothing" as he expired from the wound from that other gunshot that was to be "heard around the world," signaling what then appeared to be the end of the world. This last word "could hardly have been less appropriate," Theo Aronson has commented;[51] yet, does it not put the "nothingness" of the whole era into a nutshell?

But even the trivial or commonplace last word that *resists* any efforts at interpretation (which somehow is to show its telling appropriateness and symbolical meaning) will find connoisseurs delighted by precisely its triviality, pleading "human interest": Richard Wagner, obsessed with time throughout his life, wondering in his last minute about his watch, which fell from his pocket as he was seized by a heart attack; Alfred Jarry's properly absurdist request for a toothpick (a "cure-dent"—or was it, as academic spoilsports surmise, a more properly spiritual "cureton" that he wanted?);

Thomas Mann, the notoriously habitual close observer, asking for his glasses, etc.[52] But even in these cases, as my strained formulations show, the recorded last words are not *totally* inappropriate or meaningless. In many others they no doubt are; and one can understand equally well the frame of mind of those who try hard to see meaningfulness and of those who are delighted by the opposite. A memorable life must have a memorable concluding line; a trivial last word, on the other hand, such as William Pitt's in version 2, highlights the sorry fact of life that the sublime and the ludicrous are usually entangled with each other. We all know this, but while some would have it another way, some emphatically would not. Tragedy ends in sublime death, or does it end with the satyr play that follows? Writers of saints' lives liked to report last words of exemplary piety; modern biographers may be exhilarated by the find of a last word that lends itself to the debunking of a myth surrounding the great. While some make much of the Aufklärer's "Mehr Licht!" others hear the Frankfurt dialect in it, and a complaint about physical discomfort ("mer liecht . . . "—"so schlecht," perhaps). Both types of commentators, to be sure, do attach significance to the last word, one way or another. Whether profound or trivial, such last words are telling in that they affirm, and seal as it were, what this life was "really" all about or "really" amounted to—in the observer's view.

This field of inquiry apparently allows anyone to play, to exercise his ingenuity, with only minimal demands made on his sense of responsibility. For the significance of last words— if any—is even more questionable than their authenticity. To limit the damage, one should consider the manner and circumstances of death and their impact on the last word and its alleged significance. To begin with, "last words" as defined here (the alleged last verbal utterance passed on as common knowledge) should properly exclude what is frequently termed last words in a loose or metaphorical way:[53] suicide notes, last diary entries such as those of a sister of Saint Teresa's which were published in German as *The Last Words of a Saint*; documents such as the Antarctic explorer Captain Robert Scott's farewell message to his countrymen from the frozen continent; as well as last letters such as, among many others, *Last Words: Letters and Statements of the Leaders Executed after the Rising at Easter 1916, Der letzte Brief,* and *La Dernière Lettre: Prisons et condamnés de la Révolution 1793–1794* by Olivier Blanc.[54] Nor would one include reflections on life and death that are not the fruit of the extreme moment described earlier, even though this seems to be what Kierkegaard, for one, means by "the last word" in *Fear and Trembling* where he says that many tragic heroes would all along have such a last word in themselves which would embody the meaning of their life like an epitaph.[55]

Still, even if one excludes these varieties of "last words" entirely, there remains a whole range of circumstances of death that will throw a very questionable light on last words. Last words, even if clearly last, would arguably have to be considered and assessed differently if, on the one hand, they precede an unexpected or accidental death and therefore just happen to be the last, without the slightest foreknowledge of death (Abraham Lincoln being shot in his Washington theater box, for example); or if, on the other hand, they are the final deathbed utterance at the conclusion of a drawn-out, consciously experienced process of dying which (to use Dr. Johnson's famous remark on the prospect of hanging) "concentrates [the] mind wonderfully."[56] One must then consider the circumstances of the deathbed itself: Is the dying person delirious or fully conscious? Is he or she under the influence of consciousness-altering drugs or guided by an intention? What interests do the witnesses harbor, especially in the case of a sole witness, as when Elisabeth Nietzsche at 2 a.m. on 25 August 1900 brought her brother refreshments and heard his last word: "Elisabeth"—which, if true, would have flattered her possessive and power-obsessed love.[57] Common sense will have to be the guide here. Nonetheless, or perhaps precisely because of this, the question of authenticity of last words will keep dogging anyone in search of their possible significance.

Authentic or not? Apocryphal or not? This question has all too often dominated the discussion of last words.[58] One collection, Burton E. Stevenson's, is prefaced by the well-meant warning that "the reputed last words of famous men are always open to suspicion." But if this is "always" the case, Stevenson seems to draw the wrong conclusion when he continues by assuring his readers that the ones he has collected "are among the best known and best authenticated."[59] For, quite apart from the suspicion that the best known may not be the best authenticated, is "best authenticated" really good enough? To the purist turned cynic by experience, the answer is most certainly "No." To him it is in the nature of things that last words are not likely to be genuine, and the less genuine the more proverbial they have become or the more quotable or telling they are, like many of those quoted at the beginning of Chapter 1, or, for good measure, Alexander Pope's: "I am dying of a hundred good symptoms"—history, the inexact science once again.

Nigel Dennis takes this position in his spirited "Study of Last Words," with all the wit and charm appropriate to the subject. He casts doubt on what D. J. Enright in the *The Oxford Book of Death* has called "the entire institution of Last Words" precisely because so many of the reported last words of the great are so appropriate, or, as Dennis puts it, because they are "examples of great men being expected to say what little men feel they should say and thus being denied the right to speak for themselves."[60] That is to say, the recorded last words, which have been passed on from generation to generation, are inauthentic or even deliberately falsified (as—Dennis claims to know—in Elisabeth Nietzsche's report on

her brother's last word being "Elisabeth"). Dennis also glee-
fully points out that for some great men more than one last
word has been transmitted to a puzzled posterity. And,
where there is only *one*, it is its metaphoric interpretation, so
welcome in some quarters, rather than its meaning in context,
that has made it common knowledge, regardless of whether
such interpretation was called for or not. Goethe's "Mehr
Licht!" for example, had nothing to do with the Enlightenment, but everything to do with the shutters at Goethe's window. And even this remark, decoded as harmless, was, Dennis claims, a last word deliberately induced by bystanders
who would have found it unbearable to think that the grand
old man died asking for something as banal as the "little paw"
of his wife. (His wife in fact had died many years earlier, so
here Dennis himself is being creative about the words of the
dying man which, in point of fact, if spoken, were addressed
to his daughter-in-law Ottilie). For such reasons, Dennis sees
all last words as "post-mortem counterfeits," pure inven-
tion by interested parties (p. 30). He further suggests that,
because modern death in the hospital bed under the influence
of the hypodermic needle does not lend itself to last words
anyway, it might be helpful to "postpone all last words until
after death"—which, in his opinion, is what in fact has happened all along. Such a generally agreed upon postponement
"would have beneficial results. Genuine last words, often
spoken in haste, could be replaced by falsifications more in
keeping with the character and dignity of the deceased"; such
a practice would also "supply biographers with a conclusion
to their books"; and, finally, "it would give each of us a
chance to choose his official Last Wordster and so prevent the
bickerings and differences that now attend upon the verbally
intestate" (p. 30). There is charity, in addition to wit, in this
view, as Dennis warns that the effort involved in pronouncing last words should be avoided in any case, at least by "the
common man." It tends to raise the blood pressure, which

hastens the end and might in turn cut last words short so as to make the whole exercise self-defeating . . .

Such charm is difficult to argue with. Nor does D. J. Enright, who does argue with it in *The Oxford Book of Death*, come up with the correct objection when he says that the last words *he* has collected at least are, "if not literally authentic, . . . authentically in character" (p. 314). Similar, if rather more hesitant in a scholarly manner, is the view of Alan Shelston, who fears that the last word so dear to the biographer's heart is all too often "an inherited mythology rather than a provable fact. . . . Whatever reliability we may feel able to place in it, however, we would not want to give it up, for it seems such an ideal story with which to conclude the life of such a man."[61] This is a doubled-edged argument, for the last word that fits the known character so well is suspect for that very reason. Still, Shelston and Enright may lead us in the right direction, if *contre coeur*. Authentic or not? The correct answer is that it does not matter; the institution of last words does not stand or fall with their authenticity.

Authenticity does not matter because what aficionados and connoisseurs of last words are *really* interested in, or should be, is not necessarily and exclusively the empirical deathbed truth, but what we might call the legend, the (sometimes anecdotal) fable convenue or the myth that may have a truth of a different kind. Last words, which our culture cherishes, more often than not are not historical facts of documentary status but artifacts; and even when they are documented beyond the usual doubt, it is as artifacts that they survive: as the artifacts they have become through the collective imagination of those who have recorded them *as last words* and passed them on *as such* over the decades and centuries, thereby surrounding the possible empirical truth with a far more appealing aura. The question of authenticity vs. inauthenticity consequently becomes somewhat academic. Is a myth authentic or inauthentic? Myths are not transcriptions of historical, factual truth, but truths in their own right, truths we live by, for better or for worse, and sometimes very much for worse. Last words as understood in this study are closely related to this large and somewhat vague category of artifacts that the human race leaves behind, as a legacy to itself. Such myth-making begins at the deathbed. As a result, dying speeches and last words are, loosely speaking, a *literary* genre, *artifacts*, not historical documents like last wills or death certificates.

As such, last words are a somewhat neglected genre, com-monplace though they are in our everyday culture. And yet the cult of last words, as evidenced in best-selling biogra-phies, in literary works of all kinds, as well as in the media that shape our popular mythologies, might prompt inquiry. What could one expect from such an inquiry? It might, in a minor and modest way, shed some light on an emerging lay anthropology or body of "truths," words of wisdom people lived by or pondered or hoped to live by or wished they had lived by. And one might suspect that these truths, preserved in last words, have changed over the centuries and that, as such changing lodestars, they might suggest something about the changing self-image of those who came before us. It is safe to say, for example, that in the Middle Ages (and wherever the Christian system of beliefs was and remains unchallenged and unquestioned) one died in accordance with certain spiri-tual expectations and with corresponding last words, ideally a standard formula. One knew what one had to say (see below, pp. 159–160). However, with increasing seculariza-tion, by the time of the Renaissance or the Enlightenment (at the very latest) one not infrequently died not knowing what to say, or at any rate not repeating the obligatory Christian formula in the manner of imitatio Christi. One died, instead, with words that were unpredictable, original, or conforming to a new, emerging convention and sociocultural expecta-tion[62] (always assuming that the last words were not last by "chance").

Viewed from this perspective, last words may reveal (beyond the image or self-image of the deceased) something akin to the needs or the intellectual profile of the time and the milieu: Why was *this* myth rather than *that* one made at the deathbed and then passed on at a given point in the history of a civilization? It has been argued that there are styles, even fashions, of dying; are there corresponding styles and fashions of last words? What are these styles? And what is their history? Again: such questions become more interesting whenever and wherever dogmatic religious frameworks of intellectual life break down or lose their grip on the believers. Beginning in the Enlightenment, then, or even in the Renaissance (both periods are ill defined and have some affinity with each other), one might expect different emphases and trends to emerge in the kinds of last words reported and in the importance accorded to them. These would then also be trends in the manner in which last words were made into literary artifacts, not only by biography but also by word of mouth as it were. There is indeed evidence, ever since the end of the Middle Ages, as some of our examples may already have indicated, of a significantly increased general or even popular attention to what the great and the not-so-great had to say as they were about to die, and it is an interest that is by no means limited any longer to the standard "good" and "bad" death and last words. One indication of this is that people started collecting last words. After uncertain beginnings in the sixteenth century, a steady and ever-broadening stream of such anthologies of last words has continued unabated from the seventeenth century to our own day, preserving the oral mythology of the ages. One wonders what can be learned from the various types and thematic emphases of such anthologies of last words. Might they not throw some light on historical *changes* of interest in what is said at that unique moment when nothing can be taken back?

4

GUIDANCE, ENTERTAINMENT, AND FRISSON

Anthologies of Last Words

✤

Montaigne confessed in the *Essais* that he found nothing so intriguing as the manner in which people died: "What words, what look, what bearing they maintained at that time." If he were a writer of books, he continued in the same essay (1:20; 1580), he would compile a "register" of "various deaths" with a view to teaching not only how to die but also how to live. The project, essentially an anthology of last words—that is, of a *variety* of dying words—confirms what was anticipated at the conclusion of Chapter 3: such a collection would have been timely. A hundred years earlier there could not have been any real interest in such last words—that is, in a *multiplicity* of last words—for the simple reason that utterances of the final moment followed only one pattern in the Christian world. A century before Montaigne, the artes moriendi were one of the most popular "consumer" genres all over Europe, and they were unequivocal in their instructions concerning the "good" death: the believer was to

---

Due to the partially bibliographical nature of this chapter, publication information will be given in the text rather than in the Notes where appropriate.

die commending his soul to his Maker (see below, pp. 159–160). Hence a sudden death, which took the sinner unprepared and did not allow for the standard last words, was to be feared above all else. Montaigne, for his part, admitted to hoping for precisely this unforeseen death (*Essais*, 1:20; 1580). Clearly, something had changed in the Zeitgeist; the artes moriendi were beginning to lose their compelling power. Under such circumstances, last words of the dying become more unpredictable or even "original"—nonstandardized and hence more interesting. But interesting in what respects?

Collections of last words of the sort Montaigne had in mind might answer this question. Curiously, however, such compilations remained an all-but-unknown genre in Montaigne's own century when he himself thought that there would have been a demand for it, and they remained sporadic well into the seventeenth century. Even in the mid-nineteenth century, when Chateaubriand expressed a similar desire for a *recueil* of last words in his *Vie de Rancé* (1844),[1] there were only rather specialized, though by that time numerous, anthologies of dying words, limited to martyrs and other exemplary Christians, criminals, or infidels (never, however, in the same volume). As a more inclusive general collection, the genre did not establish itself until the 1860s, but it has flourished ever since.

Even though last words are rarely heard in this age of "medicalized" death (Rilke called it "the physicians' death"),[2] they are still somehow expected to reveal the true face, to sum up a life and provide a motto for it, which survives, conquering mortality, transcending time, contributing something (a digest of the experience of a life, most notably) to the collective memory of the civilization. The hospice movement may have contributed to this attention to last words in recent years, and may even ensure the future of the convention. Dame Cicely Saunders's conviction that the end of a life might prove to be its "most important part" may come to mind, or

Elisabeth Kübler-Ross's interviews with the dying collected in
On Death and Dying, or Daniel Berrigan's *We Die Before We Live:
Talking with the Very Ill.*[3] Another factor contributing to the increasing interest in last words, as evidenced by the current
flourishing of anthologies of last words, may be the taboo: the
traditional or at any rate widespread public or semipublic *staging* of the act of dying ceased some time in the early twentieth
century—all the stronger, perhaps, the desire for the voyeur-
ist thrill that at least some such anthologies have provided all
along.

Collections of last words, whether all-encompassing as they
have generally been since the second half of the nineteenth
century, or more specialized as to the types of dying persons
as they were as early as the seventeenth or even the sixteenth
century, usually have prefaces or introductions that suggest
why such a project was undertaken and what it hopes to
accomplish. One might think it worthwhile to study these
suggestions—especially with a view to the significance attributed to last words whenever and wherever the Christian
frame of reference is either nonexistent or no longer unchallenged. What might emerge is a peculiar facet of the need of
humans to reassure themselves of their significance and their
permanence.

The historical origins of the anthologizing instinct in this
particular field of inquiry are obscure. Last words were an institution, recorded and passed on from parents to children,
teachers to pupils, as far back as antiquity, playing a considerable role in literature and historiography even then. This
phase of interest in the subject has been summarized in a
Latin dissertation, *De ultimis morientium verbis,* accepted by the
University of Marburg in 1914 and written by a man whose
name would have delighted Theodor Fontane because he had
invented it, and for a classics professor at that, in one of his
novels: Willibald Schmidt. Still, interest in *collections* of last
words does not really appear to have arisen in antiquity; Mon-

taigne's mention in the *Essais* (1:20) of such an anthology assembled by Dikaiarchos could at best refer to a lost work of
this obscure Aristotelean. In a real sense the collecting instinct
seems to have stirred, and not very productively, during the
late Renaissance at the very earliest. And that makes sense, as
it was then that the generally accepted Christian tradition of
what to say on the deathbed was beginning to break down; as
the artes moriendi, which had standardized the proper exit
line, were beginning to lose their grip.

One of the first to offer his readers a—very short—catalog
of last words was Francis Bacon in his 1612 essay "Of Death."
He lists less than half a page of deathbed utterances to prove
that the approach of death makes "little alteration in good
spirits": the dying "appear to be the same men till the last instant."[4] His examples are without exception the last words of
Roman emperors, revealing that this arcane knowledge of the
pagan world was handed down across the Christian main-
stream. But Bacon himself, who reportedly died with words
of Christian piety on his lips, disavowing his endeavor to find
God in "fields and gardens," does not seem to have pursued
the matter further.

The man with a much more sustained interest was Michel
de Montaigne, who was indeed inclined to find his God in
fields and gardens, and who went on record in 1580 (*Essais*,
1:20) as wanting to die while planting cabbage (of all vegeta-
bles)—to die that sudden death which the Catholic litany
even today exhorts us to fear ("A subitanea et improvisa
morte libera nos, Domine"). For Montaigne, such a death
(which today is probably the universal favorite in civilized societies, as it had been in antiquity) has the proto-Nietzschean
appeal of "living dangerously," as Jacques Choron somewhat
intrepidly observed.[5] Montaigne is, thus, understandably interested in finding out just how people, the famous and the
not-so-famous, said farewell to life. In judging others, it is important to observe how they bore themselves in the end, he

notes. For in the moment of death a man will show his true face; confronting death, a man will tell the truth, Montaigne continues, not unlike his contemporary Shakespeare, and what such a dying person says is an indication of the real essence and worth of his life (1:19; 1580, 1588). It is easy to see that this is a secularization of the Christian view, propagated by the artes moriendi, concerning the value of the deathbed confession and reaffirmation of faith in extremis. And it is equally clear that such a secularization of Christian expectations allows for many more variations of the kinds or types of dying words than were possible in the Christian range— where, at least in theory, the only variation could have been the failure to live up to the required exit line. Indeed, the change signaled by Montaigne allows for individual "style" on the deathbed. And the range of possibilities becomes even greater if one includes that accidental, sudden death that Montaigne himself was so fascinated by, if only in the form of a wish with respect to his own demise. Not surprisingly, then, his remark about his interest in a collection of last words runs as follows:

> And there is nothing that I investigate so eagerly as the death of men: what words, what look, what bearing they maintained at that time; nor is there a place in the histories that I note so attentively. This shows in the abundance of my illustrative examples; I have indeed a particular fondness for this subject. If I were a maker of books, I would make a register, with comments, of various deaths. He who would teach men to die would teach them to live. (*Essais*, 1:20)[6]

The project does not seem to have progressed very far. Nor did Pierre Charron's similar and similarly worded interest result in a collection of last words. In his discussion on the need for constant readiness for death as a "fruit of wisdom" in *De la Sagesse* (1601), he too expresses his conviction that the day of death is the "master and judge of all other days," the day of accounting for one's life: "To judge life, one must look at how it was borne at the conclusion; for the ending crowns the work, a good death honors the entire life, a bad one defames it."[7] Again, the idea is that the dying person shows his real face; and here, too, this real face no longer needs to correspond to the pattern of Christian tradition that allowed no valid variations. Although Charron knows of at least five very different *manières* of the farewell to life,[8] he, too, failed to produce an anthology of last words.

❖ ❖

The earliest anthologies that did appear are by no means as all-encompassing as Montaigne or Charron envisioned nor as the genre was to become in the nineteenth century. There is one exception, valid only if one allows for a somewhat generous definition of anthologies of last words: Jacobus de Richebourcq's compilation in two hefty quarto volumes, published in Amsterdam and Antwerp in 1721: *Ultima verba factaque et ultimae voluntates morientium philosophorum virorumque et foeminarum illustrium &c. &c. plurimis e scriptoribus descripta [,] compilata [,], collecta & variis e linguis in Latinam linguam translata.* And an outlandish work it is: an alphabetical listing of many hundreds of names under which a few lines or several double-columned pages record the circumstances of the death of that person, with exact source references, including not always the last words but, rather, everything about the death that might possibly be memorable with a view to the life of each person, ranging from antiquity to the early eighteenth century. (Women have their last word in a 113-page, separately paginated appendix, while men fill the 720 pages of the main part of the two volumes.) Why Richebourcq compiled this "vast work," as he calls it in the preface without false modesty, is not apparent in his heavy-handed account of his labors; he fails to raise his index finger in Christian exhortation, nor does he admit to a fascination with the curiosity value of what he has assembled. *Ultima verba* is an exception that confirms the rule, for what is typical up to and beyond this time is not Richebourcq's global interest in deaths, including last words, but rather a closer thematic focus on certain groups of persons, with a corresponding pursuit of a particular purpose.

As a rule, the very titles of the typical collections of this time tell of their somewhat narrow specialization. And not unexpectedly, the genre starts out as a branch of Christian edification literature. Indeed, the earliest collections, dating back to the late-sixteenth century, specifically identify themselves as parts of orthodox artes moriendi, providing examples of "dying well," preceded or followed, as a rule, by sections containing pertinent prayers, meditations, or pastoral directives. These earliest compilations form a well-defined, coherent group which will be treated in the context of the artes moriendi in the final chapter (see below, pp. 162–168), though they also belong to the present one.

When, by the middle of the seventeenth century, the ties of such collections to the "art of dying" become looser and less explicit, its proximity can nonetheless still be felt. Some of these memorably curious collections are enveloped in the aura of the esoteric and macabre. This is true of pastor David Lloyd's crassly didactic *Dying and Dead Men's Living Words* (London, 1668). It is an anthology of words of wisdom designed to convince the readers of the vanity of this world and to motivate them to turn to God, while there is still time, to save their souls. Lloyd is not squeamish in the use of his sources; emperors and kings, Christians and non-Christians, biblical figures, and personalities of political life are pressed into service rather indiscriminately. Their golden words, as a rule, though not always a summation formulated on the deathbed, unfailingly drive home the message that there is just barely time for turning back to God. If it were not for the pagan authorities and the great variety of individual expressions of piety, one might think of Lloyd's compilation as a late descendant of the artes moriendi and their listing of worthy "exempla." But the overwhelming impression is that of a memento mori which leaves nothing untried, not even pre-Christian sayings, and as a result also allows the specific category of "last words" to be submerged in a welter of multifarious words of wisdom. While *Dying and Dead Men's Living Words* never quite made it into the limelight, the no less didactic and exquisitely macabre anthology *A Token for Children* by James Janeway (London, 1671) was exceedingly pop- ular (that is, frequently reprinted) as a book for young readers in those years of high infant mortality.[9] It promises *An Exact Account of the Conversion, Holy and Exemplary Lives and Joyful Deaths of Several Young Children*. Less macabre, but not without esoteric colonial charm, are the twelve pages of *The Dying Speeches of Several Indians* (Cambridge, Mass., ca. 1683), collected and translated by the Massachusetts preacher John Eliot. He puts his cards on the table in the preface: it is not the North American "noble savage," whose popular mythology was emerging at the time, that is to be celebrated here (as it was at exactly that time in *The Dying Words of Ockanickon*). On the contrary, Eliot memorializes eight Indians who "dyed in the Lord," and what they have to say in their brief farewell addresses—in only a very few cases do they still bear their native names, such as Waban or Piambohou, rather than newfangled Old Testament or nondescript English names— confirms that they learned the lesson Eliot taught them. Without fail, all eight have the Lord or Jesus Christ on their lips as they prepare to move on to the eternal hunting grounds, Christian style.

The less esoteric line of didactic Christian anthologies starts out with the almost one hundred page "Account of the Death and Last Sayings of the Most Eminent Persons from the Crucifixion of Our Blessed Saviour, Down to this Present Time" in

John Dunton's collection of devotional pieces, enticingly entitled *The House of Weeping* (London, 1682; 2d ed. 1692; pt. 2,
pp. 161–256). Saints and church fathers, reformers and martyrs, English monarchs and leading figures of European
church history, and John Eliot too, pass review here, without
exception as inspiring examples of godly living and holy
dying. This pioneering work is followed by two documents of
the religious (and political) persecution of dissenters in England: *The Dying Speeches, Letters and Prayers, &c. of Those Eminent Protestants who Suffered in the West of England, (and Elsewhere,) under the Cruel Sentence of the Late Lord Chancellour, then
Lord Chief Justice Jefferys* (London, 1689), and the several volumes—published over more than a century—of *Piety Pro-
moted*, an anthology of "brief memorials and dying expressions" of Quakers (vol. 1, London, 1701). The first significant
collection of this sort was *A Cloud of Witnesses, for the Royal
Prerogatives of Jesus Christ; or; The Last Speeches and Testimonies
of Those Who Have Suffered for the Truth, in Scotland, Since the
Year 1680* (n.p., 1714).[10] It is a memorial to Scottish Presbyterians, the Covenanters, who, during the last years of the Stuarts before the Glorious Revolution brought William and Mary
of Orange to the throne in 1688, were severely persecuted and
often executed for their unwavering faith. These and all other
collections of last words discussed so far (with the exception
of Richebourcq's) still adhere to the traditional Christian
frame of reference which Bacon and Montaigne had already
ignored.

A different kind of narrow focus is represented by *A Collec-
tion of Dying Speeches of All Those People Call'd Traitors, Executed
in This Reign, from Colonel Henry Oxburgh to the Late Mr. James
Shepheard. To Which Is Added, Some of the Speeches Left by the Like
Sort of People Executed in Former Times. By Comparing Which, It
Will Appear That It Has Been the Practice of Most Times, for Men
to Justify Their Own Conduct on All Occasions, Even to the Last*
(London, 1718). Whereas in the 1689 anthology of last words

the followers of the Catholic Stuarts were the persecutors, they are the victims in this compendium. (In the meantime, after the death of Queen Anne, the last ruler of the House of Stuart, George I had inaugurated the rule of the Hannoverians who had quelled the Stuart rebellion of Bonnie Prince Charles in 1715). What is interesting about *A Collection of Dying Speeches* is—as already signaled in the title—that the editor in his lengthy introduction takes issue with the entire institution of last words which by this time was well established in British public life in the form of the "Last Words" statement made by the condemned—political prisoners in particular—shortly before their execution. As a critical observer of this custom, Daniel Defoe, to whom this anthology has been attributed,[11] adopts a pointedly nonpartisan political stance. He does not choose to go into the question of whether a man executed for treason was right or wrong in defending his cause in his last speech (p. 16). Instead, he reminds his readers of the political turmoil of the preceding decades and recalls that rebels against the state would habitually make claims for the justice of their cause in their final words, Protestant opponents of the Stuarts as well as Stuart loyalist adversaries of Protestant George I. Those taking offense at such self-justification and protestation of innocence expressed immediately before execution were reminded that they too at some point were rebels and traitors and would have acted the same way (p. 9).

> Rebels of all sorts, Whig-Rebels as well as other Rebels, have always satisfied themselves so, by the Perswasions of their own Minds, as to go out of the World justifying the worst Actions of their Lives, whether Treason, Rebellion, Assassination, or of what kind soever it was; and therefore it can be no more wondred at now, than heretofore. (P. 13)

As a result, the anthologist arrives at the conclusion he had stated at the outset:

We are come to an Age in which the Dying Words of Men are
little more to be credited than their Living Words; and tho' one
would in Charity suppose that at the Gallows, and on a Death-
Bed, Men were past disguises, and that it was not worth their
while to speak doubtfully, or deal deceitfully; and therefore we
ought to lay an uncommon Weight upon Words spoken at
those Times, let the Persons who speak them be of what De-
nomination soever: Yet there are some Circumstances attending the Quarrel of the Age, and upon which most of our State
Criminals are brought to Execution, which render it less possible to judge of the Men, or of their Cause, by their Last Words,
than has been the Case perhaps in any other Age of the World;
and this has been so for some Years past, as well as now.
(Pp. 3–4)

This is not political cynicism but realistic psychology. For
Defoe, if it is Defoe, takes for granted that the stubborn persistence on all sides has "natural causes." Whoever risks his life
for a cause is certain that he is doing the right thing: only firm
conviction would motivate a person to engage in a risky political enterprise and then stand by it when faced with the
executioner.

A comparable, if more sophisticated, conclusion is reached
by the anonymous editor of a similar collection, published in
London in 1720: *The Dying Speeches and Behaviour of the Several
State Prisoners That Have Been Executed the Last 300 Years*. It specializes in "Gentlemen, who have been charg'd with High
Treason" against the various de facto or de jure governments:
Thomas More, Babington, Essex, and the rest, including Mary
Stuart. The public is supposed to know about these causes
célèbres, but the anonymous anthologist feels that "it would
have added much to the Satisfaction of the Reader . . . if he
had been inform'd . . . how they behav'd in their last Moments." And this is the information he proposes to oblige
with. The convention of taking last words seriously, he too

suggests between the lines, is already well established. For he finds it necessary to attach a lawyerly codicil that warns, as did Defoe's very title page, against drawing the wrong conclusions from the supposed truthfulness of words spoken on the way to execution. He pointedly leaves it open

> whether this Regard to the Words of dying men proceeds from an Imagination that one who stands on the Confines of each State, has juster Notions of both, than he, whose Views seem more remote; or from an Opinion, that the Character of the Man is best understood from his Behaviour in this last Scene of Action. . . . Many indeed take upon them to judge of the Cause, as well as the Man, purely from what he says at that important Hour, and great Stress they lay upon every the minutest Action; they take his Words as the Result of a sincere disinterested Mind, not sway'd by any secular Motives, and therefore then best qualify'd to make a Judgment of the State of Things.

The anthologist cites this tradition of thinking only to add his loyalist caveat: that the constancy, serenity, and even exultation of the "sufferer" at the execution are by no means "any Signs [that] he is in the right; or that the Justification of the Enterprize at the last Gasp, adds any weight to the Justice of his case, tho' the Suffering Side are always ready to ascribe much to the Resolution of their Martyr'd Hero."[12] With this encouragement of scepticism, comparable to that which was aroused by the Jetzer case in 1679 against the Jesuits' ultima verba, this collection makes a nice counterpoint to the several collections of last speeches of martyrs in the manner of *A Cloud of Witnesses*, which gave last words an exemplary and indeed revelatory status.

A third kind of focus is represented in the early history of anthologies of last words by André François Boureau Deslandes's *Reflexions sur les grands hommes qui sont morts en plaisantant*, which was published anonymously in Paris in 1712 and in many subsequent editions until the 1770s; it was also translated into English by Abel Boyer as *A Philological Essay: or, Reflexions on the Death of Free-Thinkers* (London, 1713). Here the anthological genre seems to flirt with triviality. Why entertain the public with such bagatelles? Why waste their precious time with a collection that is "useless," if one is after "a profound discussion or moral treatise" (Amsterdam, 1732; preface)? Deslandes is quite willing to face this charge. But when he playfully retorts, Is it not permitted to laugh occasionally and to make fun, does one always have to immerse oneself in serious writing? he is in fact hinting that, as an alternative to the theology of death, one might consider the merits of an anthropology of death—a deathbed without fear and terror or beatific transfiguration, a final moment reaffirming that mastery of life, that triumphant superiority of mind over matter, defined in nonreligious terms, in which the Enlightenment believed or tried to believe. The *Reflexions* are not strictly speaking an anthology of such last words but rather a series of meditations on the theme of secular death and its "truth." Still, a considerable number of last words are cited and discussed with a view to the possibility of that kind of calm, serene, and even cheerful death that remained unprovided for in the artes moriendi and for which Montaigne, extensively quoted by Deslandes, had already pleaded. In the *Reflexions* the speakers of last words are no longer only Roman emperors as they had been in the collection by Bacon (whose essay on death is quoted in the 1713 English version), but also such modern figures as Madame de Mazarin, Rabelais, King Henry VIII of England, Gassendi, and Hobbes.

These three kinds of early, major anthologies of last words (represented by *A Cloud of Witnesses*, Defoe's *Collection*, and Deslandes's *Reflexions*) each had a limited focus, and though they may not exactly have established a pattern, each has had what might be loosely termed "descendants" well into the nineteenth century (the Christian variety even into the twentieth).

The lineage is a bit open to doubt in the second category, the anthologies of last words of prisoners. For they had been preceded, ever since the late sixteenth century, by countless pamphlets and broadsides containing the last speeches of individual traitors and criminals or of small groups of political and nonpolitical criminals. Of these, *England's Black Tribunall* is among the better-known specimens. It is a collection of the speeches made from the scaffold by Charles I (executed in 1649) and his followers, from the Earl of Strafford to Dr. John Hewet, published in London in 1660. A New England counterpart, if that is the word, is the appendix to Cotton Mather's *Pillars of Salt* (Boston, 1699), which brings together the invariably contrite and verbosely pious "dying speeches" of twelve criminals executed in the colony as a chilling warning of the infallibility of the Lord's revenge for any and all acts of ungodliness.[13] But in spite of such quasi-predecessors, one may say that *A Collection of Dying Speeches* of 1718 and the anonymous *Dying Speeches* of 1720 were the prototypes, and that it was their lead that was followed by the several popular eighteenth-century collections of more or less picaresque "rogues' biographies," though their history, too, does go further back.[14]

Their emphasis is not specifically on last words, but last words are rarely omitted if the story ended at the gallows—as was usually the case, even with pickpockets. A major French example is Pitaval's frequently imitated and continued multi-volume *Causes célèbres et interessantes* (1734–1742), preceded by François de Calvi's *Histoire générale des larrons* (1623–1625). But it was in England that the genre flourished most profusely. Early on, there is Captain Alexander Smith's *A Compleat History of the Lives and Robberies of the Most Notorious Highway-Men* (1713–1714, frequently reprinted well into the twentieth century in various versions). Others are *A History of Executions* brought out by Defoe's publisher, Applebee, in 1731, and *The Lives of the Most Remarkable Criminals* in 1735. Both endeavor to break away from the merely entertaining character of the romantic-picaresque collection of Captain Smith, as does *The Ordinary of Newgate, His Account of the Behaviour, Confessions, and Dying Words of the Malefactors* (1731–1770). Following in this vein are the most famous compilations of this kind: *The Tyburn Chronicle . . . Containing an Authentic Account of the . . . Executions, and Last Dying Speeches of the Most Notorious Malefactors* (1768) and *The Newgate Calendar* (1773)—each named after a venue infamous in the eighteenth century: the place of execution and the prison in London. Here too, and in the many later editions, revisions, and imitations, grim realism instead of Smith's fictional embellishments reigns supreme, last but not least through the inclusion of the "dying speeches of the most notorious criminals of both sexes." With these and other gripping details, *The Newgate Calendar* promised to be "extremely useful for families." "Parents and guardians will find it one of the most useful books to be put into the hands of the rising generation, before their tender minds have been led astray from the practise of virtue." This appeal remained undiminished far into the nineteenth century, as the publishing history of related works indicates.

A later example from France, covering more than four centuries, are the two volumes of *Derniers sentiments des plus illustres personnages condamnées à mort; ou, Recueil des lettres qu'ils ont écrites dans leur prisons, des discours qu'ils ont prononcés sur l'échafaud* (Paris, 1775; attributed to Antoine Sabatier. It is worth noting that a translation in three volumes appeared in 1777–1778 in Germany, where—with the one exception of Johann Jacob Moser's several installments and versions of an anthology entitled *Seelige lezte Stunden einiger dem zeitlichen Tode übergebener Missethäter* [the title varies slightly] appearing from 1740 to 1767 and again in 1861—collections of last words of criminals, political or otherwise, are unheard of, no doubt because the intertwining and indeed identification of politics and religion was less acute there than in England and France). The preface of *Derniers sentiments* reveals that the somewhat legalistic interest in the truthfulness of last words that had been characteristic of the early English anthologies (1718, 1720) is now giving way to a more broadly human, even "philosophical," concern. For this anthology presents itself as a "collection of documents of the history of the human heart" (p. i). But what exactly does it teach the reader about the human heart? The qualities that are claimed to manifest themselves when one is face-to-face with death oscillate strangely between Christian and stoic virtues.

> [We witness] that heroic strength and valor that Heaven [!] awarded to great souls. . . . And so we do not hesitate to say that the picture we are offering in this work is the history—a great credit to mankind—of the battles of the human heart against the terrors of the most cruel death. . . . Serenity and dignity [raise the victims, at the hands of the executioner,] beyond the measure of man. . . . But what gives us the most sublime idea of man is hearing him give vent to clever remarks and even word play on the scaffold. (Pp. i–vi)

This may turn our thoughts to Deslandes's anthology of last words of free—and strong—spirits, only to surprise us with the information that it is "religion" that is the source "from which all these noble unfortunates derived the strength and sublimity which we admire" (p. vii). These last words are overwhelmingly those of English men and women such as Cardinal Wolsey, Thomas More, Anne Boleyn, Jane Grey, Mary Stuart, Essex, Walter Raleigh, etc. The preface explains this (a decade and a half before the French Revolution) by referring to the political tensions and upheavals in the British Isles since Henry VIII's break with Rome (p. x). But what distinguishes Sabatier's from the two prominent English anthologies of the last words of the same "traitors" is his fundamen-

tal sympathy with the victims. Their persecutors, the loyalists
of the "state," can count on it that the verdict of history will
spell their shame and curse (p. xii), even if it does not exoner-
ate their opponents completely. The "traitors" may indeed
have done wrong in one instance ("une fois"), but their conduct over many years, demonstrating exemplary qualities of
heart and mind—confirmed by their last words—ensures that
their "honor" is by no means extinguished by their death on
the scaffold; their fatherland can be proud of them (pp. xiii–
xiv). Only as an afterthought does the preface mention that
some of the victims actually did receive their just deserts and
forfeit all claims to posthumous honor, namely those oppres-
sors who committed "the most horrible and most unpardon-
able crime against humanity": they abused their power,
"which is entrusted to them only so that they will work for the
glory of their prince, endear him to his subjects and make
them happy" (pp. xiv–xv). An afterthought or—along with
the glorification of those who violated formal sanctions in
pursuit of their good cause—a tentative articulation of a hidden leitmotif? The last words of famous traitors as writing on
the wall, a foreboding of the Revolution?[15]

Even after the Revolution, such works remain the exception
rather than the rule in France. One should therefore pay some
attention to Léon Thiessé's anonymously published anthology *Derniers Momens des plus illustres personnages français condamnés à mort pour délits politiques, depuis le commencement de la
monarchie jusqu'à nos jours, avec les lettres qu'ils ont écrites dans
leur prisons, recueillis et rédigés d'après les chroniques et journaux
du temps par M**** (Paris, 1818). Like Sabatier's, this account of
the last moments of twenty-nine French men and women
(from the fourteenth to the early nineteenth century, including Joan of Arc and concentrating primarily on figures of the
French Revolution) is designed not so much to throw light on
political life as to contribute to the knowledge of the *coeur hu-
maine* and its history, in support of which La Rochefoucault

is quoted on the *terres inconnues* of the human heart. But this promise is not really kept, for to hear "M***" tell it, everyone executed went to his or her death with words of French patriotism on their lips (or in their letters)—from which, oddly enough, only one lesson is to be learned: moderation. Whereas in the last-words anthology of 1775, with all its nonpolitical interest in the history of the human heart, the Revolution appeared to announce itself with faint tremors, interest in the human heart in Thiessé's collection has already transformed itself into a post-Revolutionary form of wisdom.

Religiously oriented compilations are also numerous, and here the line of descent from one or the other of the key texts mentioned earlier is sometimes quite clear, especially in *A Collection of Memorials Concerning Divers Deceased Ministers and Others of the People Called Quakers, in Pennsylvania, New-Jersey, and Parts Adjacent, from Nearly the First Settlement Thereof to the Year 1787. With Some of the Last Expressions and Exhortations of Many of Them* (Philadelphia, 1787; London, 1788) and in *The Dying Testimonies of the Scots Worthies* (Glasgow, 1841; preface, dated 1828, by William McGavin; a companion piece to John Howie's *Biographia Scotiana*, frequently reprinted since 1775), which expressly identifies itself as collated from *A Cloud of Witnesses*, among other sources. This is another memorial to the steadfastness of Protestant Scots, Presbyterians, and others, who paid with their lives for their opposition to the Church of England, chiefly during the twenty-eight years preceding the Glorious Revolution.

Throughout the eighteenth century, the German-speaking territories contributed a fair amount of such anthologies. More often than not, their last words were gleaned from protestant funeral sermons which, flourishing particularly in Lutheran lands from the mid-sixteenth to the mid-eighteenth century, would normally include the circumstances of the demise, often complete with last words of "the gently and blessedly deceased." Gottfried Feinler apparently attempted exhaustiveness in his compendium *Theatrum morientium*, featuring the "last words" of five hundred "Christians [who] died in the state of salvation," to be followed, according to the title page, by the swan songs of two hundred (in fact only one hundred, but entirely sufficient) "protestant pure theologians" (Leipzig, 1702). Everyone dies in the state of grace in this theater, even those who die suddenly, as their pious life is now seen to make up for pious last words (p. 234). Nonetheless, some categories of cases (Feinler is very methodical about ordering his quarry) give one pause—there are those who died immediately before, during, and soon after their wedding; on Good Friday; on their birthday, etc. This resourceful tome is followed in 1710 by Conrad Mel's *Die letzte Reden der Sterbenden* (3d ed., Berlin, 1723; preface, 1713). In fact a collection of sermons, this volume is, however, distinguished by its preface of fifty quarto pages. This offers not only an anthology of—even then—famous last words, "good" ones and less-good ones, pronounced by pagans and Christians; it also captures the aura or mystique that surrounded last words even in the view of Protestants at the time, much as they were concerned about Christian edification in the narrower sense. The soul, says Mel, "begins to communicate the quintessence of its best thoughts" during the last breaths, encouraging bystanders to "a holy following-suit" (*Nachfolge*); indeed, even heathens, such as they are, can be pressed into this service.

Unlike Mel's *Letzte Reden*, Pastor Johann Christoph Ludwig's *Letzte Stunden und Reden großer Herren und vornehmer Standespersonen aus vorigen Zeiten, zur Erweckung zusammen getragen von L.P.* (Dresden and Leipzig, 1758) specializes in the dying words of Christians of elevated social standing— emperors and kings and especially Electors and their wives; nonetheless it hopes to appeal to *all* "lovers of God" and their need for "awakening" and "edification" (preface). An interesting variation, in spite of its very similar title and intent, is

Count Erdmann Heinrich Henckel's three-part *Die letzten Stunden einiger der Evangelischen Lehre zugethanen . . . verstorbenen Persohnen . . . zu allgemeiner Erweckung, Erbauung. . .* (Halle, 1720). Polemically anti-Catholic, the aristocratic Lutheran has not saints or monarchs, but more ordinary people pass review, with their last words carefully checked for authenticity—funeral sermons, he says, were already commonly known as lying sermons. The people thus chosen to encourage the pietistic "awakening" and "edification" promised on the title page range from a count to a theology student, from a three-year-old to a church superintendent. A comparable service was provided for Calvinists by Pierre de la Roque in his *Recueil de diverses dernières heures édifiantes, choisies pour la consolation des âmes fidelles* (Amsterdam, 1706) and, stressing the connection with the ars moriendi, in his *La Science de Bien Mourir mise en pratique ou Recueil tout nouveau de dernières heures édifiantes* (Utrecht, 1722). "There is nothing more powerful," he quotes a theological source in the preface of the latter book, "to induce to a Christian life than seeing a true believer die."

In the nineteenth century, England again held the lead. Less sectarian in outlook than *A Cloud of Witnesses*, but no less sure of the one and only right (i.e., Christian) way to die, is the anonymous *Death-Bed Scenes and Pastoral Conversations* authored, it was later discovered, by John Warton, pseudonym of William Wood (London, 1826–1828), a highly successful work, judging by its printing history. Its three volumes are intended to be "a manual for the information and direction of the Minister in his daily intercourse with sick persons and other members of his flock" (4th ed., London, 1830, I:ix) and, as last-word anthologist Herbert Lockyer assures us, "interesting reading for all those who have the care of souls."[16] Each chapter of *Death-Bed Scenes* is about the death of one parishioner, invariably not without a last word of some weight, and headlined unmistakably: "Infidelity," "Atheism," "Parental Anger," "Penitence," "Impatience," "Religious Melancholy," and the like. Each chapter, the author feels (alluding, no doubt unwittingly, to Horace) "may possibly both amuse and instruct every description of readers" (I:xii). Possibly; the raised index finger is hard to miss, though. The entertaining element is in any case more obvious, if perhaps unintentional, in a similar work by one Timothy East, "author of the Evangelical Rambler": *Death-Bed Scenes: or, The Christian's Companion on Entering the Dark Valley* (London, 1825). Here the mood is a bit less somber, as befits a book that promises "consolation to the timid Christian." It is "placidity," "hope," "joy," and "fortitude" in death that demonstrate Christianity's "exclusive ability of turning the shadow of death into the brightness of the morning; and of giving to the deathbed scene all its interest and glory" (p. xlix). The cases—without exception descriptions of deathbed scenes and last words of inconspicuous people, many of them clergy and all of them pious—are arranged in five classes "according to the relative degrees of interest which they possess": "first class," "second class," and so forth, although it is hard to make out whether they are in ascending or descending order; that is, whether first class is better or more interesting than fifth, or the other way round. "First class" are those who "departed in triumph"; "fifth class" assembles "the sayings of the eminently wise and good, when in immediate prospect of their dissolution" (pp. l–li). In any event, whichever class may be best, here is an example from fifth class, the death of the Reverend Robert Bruce, which is not half bad:

> When he was very old, and through infirmity confined to his chamber, he was asked by one of his friends, how matters stood between God and his soul? To which he made this return: "When I was a young man I was diligent, and lived by faith in the Son of God; but being now old, he condescends to feed me with sensible tokens of his favour."
>
> And in the morning before the Lord removed him, being at breakfast, and having as usual eaten an egg, he said to his

daughter, "I think I am yet hungry; you may bring me another egg." But having mused awhile, he said, "Hold; daughter, hold; my Master calls me." With these words his sight failed him: whereupon he called for the Bible and said, "Turn to the 8th chapter to the Romans, and set my finger on the words,—I am persuaded that neither death nor life, etc. shall be able to separate me from the love of God, which is in Christ Jesus my Lord." When this was done he said "Now is my finger upon them?" Being told it was, he said, "Now God be with you, my children: I have breakfasted with you, and shall sup with my Lord Jesus Christ this night." And immediately expired.
(P. 342)

This particular subgenre of last-word anthologies continues with somber collections like Ingram Cobbin's unrelentingly educational *Dying Sayings of Eminent Christians, Especially Ministers of Various Denominations, Periods, and Countries* (London, 1828), ordered alphabetically for handier use and ominously printed in large type for the benefit of the old and the sick, and the unabashedly proselytizing *The Last Hours of Eminent Christians* by the Rev. Henry Clissold, who harps on the "advantages" of religion in the hour of death (London, 1829, p. v). Both compilers allude verbatim to their seventeenth-century prototype, *A Cloud of Witnesses* (p. x and p. xiv, respectively), and neither of them seems ever to have heard of a single case of human frailty in the face of death. Continuing in this vein, there are Joseph Miller Chapman's *Brief Memorials of Departed Saints* (London, 1842), which as a rule incorporates last words and shows its flag as early as the subtitle: "designed to exhibit the animating and supporting influence of Christianity in Labours, Suffering, and Death"; E. C. Sharpin's *Death Scenes*, (privately printed in Yarmouth, 1842), also amounting to a soul-saving devotional tract with its nearly two-hundred positive and negative cases from all periods, countries, and professions; and finally the anonymous *Dying Testimonies in Favour of an Atonement for Each and for All of Sinners*, part one of which specializes in clergymen from Luther and Calvin via Bengel and Bishop Butler to early nineteenth-century divines (2d ed., Dunfermline, 1843; apparently no sequel was published, which may indicate that the particular mission was accomplished). *Dying Testimonies* was followed by Jabez Burns's *Death Bed Triumphs of Eminent Christians, Exemplifying the Power of Religion in a Dying Hour*, (Halifax, 1848), featuring mostly modern B-team theologians; by Andrew Redman Bonar's *The Last Days of Eminent Christians* (Edinburgh, 1847; mostly clergymen but also one colonel and a chief justice of Bengal) and by Bonar's *Last Days of the Martyrs* (London, 1865), which is "interesting and instructive," as the introduction assures us.

The United States contributed *How They Died; or, The Last Words of American Presbyterian Ministers* by Alfred Nevin (Philadelphia, 1883). These men of God, though overwhelmingly obscure, generally pass on with respectable Christian quotations or similarly devout pronouncements. But, unlike his just-mentioned British colleagues in Christ, Nevin does not shirk the admission that some of his exhibits are less than edifying: a smattering of his pastoral witnesses left this world in despair rather than transfiguration. His explanation—at the height of physiological materialism—is interesting: it is "something morbid" in the lifelong bodily condition that accounts for the anxiety or "depression" of the final hour, "physical depression with which religious encouragements contended in vain" (p. 10)—which, however, does not deprive these dying men of the grace of God by any means. The rigorism of the *artes moriendi* is now a matter of the past.

On the fringes of this edifying variety of anthologies, one chances upon one specimen of a truly bizarre species: the pedagogical novel built around all-too-resourceful conversations about the last words of Christian martyrs, entitled *Last Words; or The Truth of Jesus Sealed in the Death of His Martyrs*, "by the author of 'Little Mary,' 'Ellen's Visit to the Shepherd,' etc."

(London, 1834). While this oddity may be a symptom of an intensively religious age, religious anthologies of last words do continue well into the twentieth century, catering to increasingly specialized tastes. One of the rare German contributions takes the prize here, Christian Wilhelm Stromberger's collection *Letzte Reden der Sterbenden: Zeugnisse des weltüberwindenden Glaubens* (Giessen, 1879; 2d ed., Gütersloh, 1898). Like his American colleague, Stromberger is aware of what is going on in the world. What is needed "in these times of unbelief and doubt" is an antidote to the "naturalist and materialist world views" that deny the afterlife (2d ed., pp. vii, xii); and the truly Christian, indeed Christ-like, overcoming of the world in death is just the thing to remind us of the promise of "God's blessing" (pp. iii–iv). A wide variety of heroes and heroines of piety rendezvous under these, if no other, auspices: not only New Testament but (as is occasionally the case in such adamantly Christian anthologies) also Old Testament figures, church fathers and hermits, religious reformers and missionaries, artists, scholars and humble folk, including a child in the state of grace and a wounded Silesian, but also a New Zealand chieftain, an eskimo as well as an otherwise unknown contemporary of the compiler, Otto von Zitzewitz, whose last words were: "Oh, the Emperor's birthday. May God bless him." This calls for editorial comment, though Stromberger had been considerate enough to promise that he would let the last utterances of his "blessed people" speak for themselves and generally lived up to this pledge: "So deep and strong is the love of the earthly king and lord in the heart of a Christian conservative" (p. 234). This was reported in 1898. But as recently as 1964 one finds a collection of last-word testimonies of nineteenth-century religious visionaries, mostly from a place called Pulverbatch, in Shropshire, entitled *More than Notion* (3d ed., London, 1967), by J. H. Alexander, i.e., Jean Hester Buggs. But this subgenre does not necessarily become more interesting with age.

Of greater intellectual attraction is what in Pulverbatch circles might have been called enemy propaganda: reports on
non-Christian, though in the enlightened view noble, deaths
in the wake of Deslandes's *Reflexions*. The fourteenth of the
Marquis d'Argens's *Lettres morales et critiques* (Amsterdam,
1737) is dedicated to such deaths. Though strictly speaking no
more a formal anthology than Deslandes's work, this "letter"
does assemble a large number of cases that are to prove that
at the moment of death, when all masks fall or lifelong character is reaffirmed under the seal of finality, "greatness" of a
pointedly secular nature may manifest itself in all its glory,
"and I endeavor to prepare myself to follow their example one
day" (p. 118). The proud lineage of such "grands hommes"
and "esprits-forts" who have become guiding figures through
their last words extends from Hobbes and Spinoza to St. Evremond and Locke.

The first real anthology of such last words kept free spirits waiting until 1886; it is George William Foote's *Infidel
Death-Beds* (London: Progressive Publishing Company, 1886),
which appears to also be in some line of descent from works
such as Deslandes's *Reflexions*. Here, however, the anti-Christian polemics have become rather more pronounced, for the
purpose of this collection of descriptions of dying scenes, usually complete with last words, is to show the groundlessness
of the frequent Christian claim that freethinkers tend to con-
vert on their deathbeds or else die distraught by terror. Such
a claim had indeed been routine; one might think, for example, of the pamphlet by John Collett Ryland whose title tells
all: *The Death-Bed Terrors of an Infidel; or, A Modern Freethinker,
Exemplified in the Last Awful Hours of a Young Gentleman, Who
Departed from the Principles of Christianity, and Turned Deist*
(London, 1770; Dublin, 1812); or one might recall Gros de
Besplas's *Le Rituel des esprit-forts, ou le tableau des incrédules
modernes au lit de la mort* (Paris, 1762). In reaction to such

works, Foote gives us more than fifty pages of case histories (alphabetically arranged for reasons not altogether clear) of famous freethinkers who did *not* recant with their last breath, among them (in reverse alphabetical order, to try out a different sort of arbitrariness) Voltaire, David Friedrich Strauß, Spinoza, Percy Bysshe Shelley, Thomas Paine, John Stuart Mill, David Hume, Victor Hugo, Thomas Hobbes, Goethe, Frederick the Great, Diderot, Danton, Lord Byron, and Giordano Bruno. To Foote in 1886, this was an honor roll of free spirits who remained so until the end and defied the lies and distortions of pious zealots.

By this time, however, these two strands of last-word anthologies—the last words of the pious, of saints, or martyrs *and* of figures of worldly fame or infamy—had already come together, and pointedly at that, in volumes that, while not actually entitled Last Words, constitute large depositories of last words. (They were preceded, incidentally, by the pathologically comprehensive genre of tomes, mostly German, providing preachers with edifying and deterring "examples" of holy and unholy dying, invariably incorporating more than a fair share of bizarre, grotesque, and curious cases, painstakingly indexed, along the lines of death from toothpicks, library dust, grave monuments, tame pigs, splinters in the behind, etc.[17]) The first volume combining and polarizing last words of saints and sinners was apparently *The Book of Death*, a collection of "sketches" of the deaths of famous believers and unbelievers culled primarily from Chalmers's *Biographical Dictionary* and compiled, according to the British Library catalog, by Samuel Dobree (London, 1819). It was followed by Daniel P. Kidder's *The Dying Hours of Good and Bad Men Contrasted* (New York, 1848; 1853). The first is basically evenhanded; the second continues the Christian apologetics and polemics: Last hours are of universal interest, primarily to the young, because they teach the value of the Christian religion.

"By beholding, too, the deathbed scenes of infidels and
wicked men, we shall see the value of that religion which they
have neglected and despised; and for doing which they met a
dreadful end," the preface reminds us. Thus John Wesley
confronts Voltaire, Addison puts Thomas Paine to shame,
and so forth. Similar in focus are Erskine Neale's two volumes
of *The Closing Scene: or, Christianity and Infidelity Contrasted in
the Last Hours of Remarkable Persons* (London, 1848–1849; Philadelphia, 1850), an unflinchingly pastoral collection assembled
by a retired village rector who tells, with a raised index finger,
of the last words of wretched infidels of the caliber of Paine,
Bolingbroke, Hume, and Frederick the Great, and of others
with his eyes turned upward; as well as Osmon C. Baker's
handily pocket-size *The Last Witness; or, The Dying Sayings of
Eminent Christians and of Noted Infidels* (Boston, 1851), which,
true to his country's constitution, uses last words to "ascer-
tain what real progress has been made in the pursuit of happiness" in the hope of thereby encouraging "experimen-
tal and practical godliness" (preface); and finally Davis W.
Clark's *Death-Bed Scenes; Dying with and without Religion: Designed to Illustrate the Truth and Power of Christianity* (New York,
1851). Christians in Clark's anthology "triumph" in anticipation of "the felicities of the redeemed" while sinners "despair"
in view of "the appalling retributions of the future state"—
making this compendium, which starts with "Our Lord Jesus
Christ" and ends with Hume, Rousseau, Byron, Burns, and
Mirabeau, "a part of 'the portable evidence of Christianity'"
(pp. 21–22).

The ultimate in systematized completeness is achieved
along these lines by the grand master of fussiness, the Rev.
(C.) Seelbach of Züsch (wherever that may be), in his anthology *Tod der Frommen und Gottlosen in geschichtlichen Beispielen
aus allen Jahrhunderten der christlichen Zeitrechnung* (Eisleben
and Leipzig, 1865). Through the characteristically different

deaths of the godless and the believers, the examples are to reveal the "just judgment of God," namely the wages of sin and the rewards of virtue (pp. V–VI). The deathbed of the pious (children, martyrs, pastors) is accordingly neatly separated from the demise of the unbelievers who depart in blasphemy and doubt, raving and despair. Nobody is left out: we hear of kings and lords, reformers and novel readers, a "negro" and a tanner, an East Indian heathen and Klopstock, author of the epic *The Messiah*, of Roman emperors, Englishmen and a fringe maker, among many others.

In all such collections, the last words of the moribund usually remove any possible doubt about the destination of the soul. An anthologist straggling behind such missionary efforts makes this clear with all unrequired rhetoric: it is either the realm of God with its angels or the abodes of eternal doom with their hideous demons—so we are assured in the preface and the introduction to *Pebbles from the Brink, or Last Expressions of the Dying* by M. C. Pritchard (Ottawa: Holiness Movement Print, 1913). With such sectarian zeal, the genre enters into the twilight zone where the sublime and the ridiculous uneasily meet. Great names such as Jesus Christ, Byron, Tasso, Cato, Napoleon, Rochester, and Voltaire, without a perceptible sense of order, join ranks with less well-known ones such as "William. (A Negro)," "Mrs. Cicely Ormes. (Martyr)," "Rose" (a young man who, lacerated by an agricultural machine, sang a chorale for three hours before he expired), the chieftain of the not easily located island of Aimeo, who died with the word "Jesus" on his lips, and finally a mere "Mr. ——," who had nothing much to say either. Such curiosities are no doubt the side effects of a genre that had seen better days. Herbert Lockyer's later—and more successful—collection is a similar curio.[18] It can be no coincidence that, in the meantime, a new type of anthology of last words had established itself, at once less susceptible to religious abstruseness and more assured of a future: the *general* collection of last words, without the village vicar's penetrating examination of the heart.

❖ ❖ ❖

The first anthology to use "Last Words" in its title without limiting itself to a specific socioreligious group (again with the exception of the hodgepodge assembled by Richebourcq in 1721) is Joseph Kaines's *Last Words of Eminent Persons* (London and New York, 1866). The subtitle indicates how the "Last Days" or "Dying Hours" type of anthology now merges into the genre of the "Last Words" anthology proper: *Comprising, in the Majority of Instances, a Brief Account of their Last Hours*. This anthology is the first that can be said to have made Chateaubriand's wish come true: "One would like to have a collection of last words of famous people" (see above, note 1). From then on there is a stream of such books (most of them featuring "Last Words" on the title page) right through to the present. Most are in English, but French, Spanish, German, Swedish, Danish, Russian, Hebrew, Arabic, and Japanese collections exist as well, though they are apparently far fewer, with the possible exception of the Japanese genre. They are universal in scope, listing the famous of all kinds and nations (thus uniting all three selective categories of anthologies current earlier and, of course, expanding their repertoire). The one exception to this universality of scope is John Robert Colombo's *Colombo's Last Words: The Dying Words of Eminent Canadians* (Cobalt, Ont.: Highway Book Shop, 1982), which does, however, include such unfamiliar distinguished Canadians as Queen Victoria, Tecumseh, Frankenstein's monster, and King George VI, who is reported here to have used his last breath to pronounce "Oh." In spite of the only slightly moderated exclusivity of this collection, its preface pays lip service to the human condition in general when it reminds the reader that all the last words brought together in the volume throw light on human nature and hence also on the nature of Canadians (p. xi), not the other way round.

In fact, it looks as if the genre of last-word anthologies is becoming increasingly popular at the present time; certainly there are significantly more of them than ever before. And perhaps this makes sense in light of the widespread conviction that death has replaced sex as the ultimate taboo in our society: death *"as a natural process"* as Geoffrey Gorer qualifies it correctly in his seminal 1955 essay "The Pornography of Death," which is still the last word on the subject.[19] For what is taboo is not only "too horrible to contemplate or to discuss" and therefore the object of prudery, it also becomes the object of interest, not necessarily "prurient."

As interest increases, it also changes; or does it? What do the introductory statements of anthologists reveal about the reasons for their interest in last words? These reasons are certainly not always the same, but do their varieties fall into a historical or typological pattern? What have compilers and readers—those whose interest went beyond the search for "entertainment"[20]—hoped to learn, over the years, from anthologies of last words?

Most agree that what is behind such collections is not the endeavor to gain some statistical information on how certain categories of people have left this world—that is, whether famous poets die with a larger average number of words than do famous statesmen, or whether a higher percentage of distinguished physicians and scientists die with words of contentment than with words of indifference, and how they differ in this respect statistically from well-known philosophers or members of the military profession.[21] This is "all very interesting," as Lady Mary Wortly Montagu said in a different context, namely on her deathbed. But there are other reasons for developing an interest in last words.

A manageable approach might be to look first at each of the earlier of the all-inclusive anthologies of last words—the pioneers straggling into print like lone explorers—up to the turn of the century or slightly beyond, before the stream of anthologies gains real momentum. Quite a welter of motivations will be found in this transitional phase between the primarily religiously or otherwise ideologically motivated collections with their narrow focus and the less "committed" ones of the more recent period. This mix can then be seen as crystallizing the ingredients of an emerging typology of interest, which it might subsequently be possible to trace in the twentieth century when the genre bursts into full bloom.

Whereas Kidder's *Dying Hours of Good and Bad Men Contrasted* (a "deathbed" rather than a "Last Word" book, strictly speaking) of 1848 still relied heavily, indeed heavy-handedly, on the Christian frame of reference, the first specimen of the pure breed, Kaines's *Last Words of Eminent Persons* of 1866, draws a sharp line between those works that have a "religious object" in contrasting the dying hours of infidels and Christian believers and his own enterprise, which professes to be "psychological" in orientation and to have "no theory to prove" ("Advertisement"). In other words, the interest has become secular and the focus all-inclusive. The principle of selection is eminence alone. "Illustrious characters of all nations, ranks, and occupations" are included, and, from the contemplation of their last words, not only the religiously committed but "all might derive advantage." What sort of advantage? Clearly, a new beginning is signaled here; Kaines is aware that he is striking out into uncharted territory. But what does the pioneer find? Why are dying words "always interesting," and why can one not read them "without profitable meditation"?

What fascinates Kaines most is what could be called the "mystique of the moment": the meeting ground of the this-worldly and the other-worldly in the instant of death. In other words, although Kaines is no longer interested in the Christian alternatives of salvation or damnation, he is still intrigued, as some later anthologists are not, by the edge of the transcendental or metaphysical. "Dying is an act we cannot report of," he states matter-of-factly and then continues with the understatement: "It has an awful newness for every living being. It is for each of us the one untried thing." (Oscar Wilde was to specify: "The one thing no one can survive.") Therefore—and here the stiff upper lip begins to quiver—watching the process of death, we are "eager for the merest indication of what [the dying] are beginning to know, peering anxiously to see if we can trace their footsteps over the boundary of existence, or catch the slightest glimpse of 'the land of darkness and the shadow of death.'" Undoubtedly, a quasi-religious frisson is a component of such curiosity about last words, even if the intimations of the beyond remain nondenominational. "Dying men are nearest to the gods, and are being initiated into grand mysteries by the highest intelligences. Their words are often rich in the wisdom which is not of earth" (pp. vii–viii).

This fascination with the supernatural mystery of the last moment only barely conceals a kind of nostalgia for the world of belief, which Kaines seems to locate somewhere in the recent past. But he clearly feels the need to counteract this nostalgia when he takes issue with the common notion that the manner of a person's death, his last word, is an indicator of the worth of his life. In his rejection of this view as both "unsafe" and "unfair," we feel the unmistakable materialist scientism of the nineteenth century breathing down our necks. The reason the last phase of life is not necessarily representative is physiological: "Bodily weakness" may cloud the intellect, dim the faculties, produce last words that are in no way telling. And this applies pointedly to Christians as well as to others. To make his point, Kaines appends a repulsively detailed physiological description, cited from a medical authority, of the process of natural death. Biological science meets super-naturalism, and indeed Christian dogma, head-on in this re-flection about the true significance of last words, which the traditional believer, as the artes moriendi keep reminding us well into the eighteenth century, considered to be the key to the destiny of the soul. Kaines is diplomatic but nonetheless clear in his intent: "That for death as for life the hope of the Christian is the safest and the best, there can be no question. Whether He who knows all will be satisfied with less than this it is not for man to determine" (p. x).

So what remains to be said for an interest in last words if they cannot be guaranteed to epitomize a life, let alone indi-cate the destination of a departing soul? Kaines's answer, self-contradictory in part, is a kind of hero worship that, like his materialist skepticism and "profitable meditation," fits into his century, which was also Carlyle's and Victoria's. As only the great, those who "powerfully affected the destinies of mankind," of all ages and all nations and all varieties are fea-tured, we may perceive in their last words "how the world's beacon-lights expired—in what glorious light, or impenetra-ble gloom, they went out." Last words are not forgotten; they keep "thrilling" us, "we cannot rid ourselves of them." What they bring about in our culture is a secular immortality of the great figures of the past. "The dead are ever with us"—if we preserve their last words in our collective conscious (p. xi). Much like figures of Greek mythology, great personages of our past thus become transformed into constellations in the firmament and, as such, points of orientation for the genera-tions that follow them.

This is a remarkable indication of the state of the disinher-ited mind in the second half of the nineteenth century. As old certainties are—politely—discarded in the name of contem-porary knowledge, the aura of transcendence that traditional religion had to offer is not destroyed categorically. Instead, there is a bold effort to create a new, secular mythology, a pantheon of heroes classified according to area of activity; i.e., kings, warriors, poets, philosophers, philanthropists, and the like. These heroes give us guidance, last but not least through their dying words, imperiled though they may be by "bodily weakness."

But Kaines's anthology cannot, in fairness, be said to have set the tone, even though it was marketed by a leading commercial publisher (Routledge in London and New York) and cited on the Continent as much as twenty years later. The next anthology published, J.M.H.'s *Last Words of Remarkable Persons* (London, 1876), is a throwback to Christian certainties. Not only does it repeat uncritically the cliché that "deathbed words afford an index to the lives of the utterers" (p. 5), the author refers on the very first page of the preface to "eternal realities" and "the glory beyond," which are believed to be reasons for the great attention paid to the voices from the "border land." This collection, then, its neutral title notwithstanding, is a kind of Christian edification book providing applicable wisdom in capsule form. The same is even more true of S. B. Shaw's *The Dying Testimonies of Saved and Unsaved* (Elkhart, Ind.: Mennonite Publishing Company, 1898; selections appeared in 1964 in Kansas City as *How Men Face Death*). This anthology, which, like several others before Kaines, limits itself to the Christian era, is structured around the "awful contrast" (p. ii) between the dying words of infidels, including atheists and skeptics, and those of believers, including saints. (Charity is observed, however, by omitting the names of the unsaved out of consideration for friends and families, except when they were of such stature as to be "noted," though there are precious few of these, while believers like one Hulda A. Rees are featured by name.) The book is indeed, as it claims to be, nonsectarian; its proselytizing stance, however, is unmistakable, and it spares no one. The historian might hear in this collection the last distant tremor of the rhetorical thunder of the late-medieval artes moriendi, so unabashed is the missionary impetus of this volume. As late as 1910, a faint echo of this hectic persuasion can be heard in Colonel Thomas H. Lewin's compilation *Life and Death, Being an Authentic Account of the Deaths of One Hundred Celebrated Men and Women* (London). Not much proselytizing zeal is evident in the title, to be sure; but although this anthology, chronologically arranged, starts with figures of antiquity, the words spoken in the "hour of sincerity" clearly do gain a greater claim to attention with the advent of Christianity and its promise of a future life for the soul (pp. vii–viii). No matter how indirect, the guiding inspiration again must be a latter-day Christian *Sterbehilfe*, an attempt to reconcile to death all those who are not confirmed infidels; hence also the emphasis on the "fearlessness and ease with which human beings in general leave their mortal habitation" (p. v).

Compared with this, the sophistication of the pioneer Joseph Kaines, although not overwhelming, is not unremarkable. His intention to be helpful to his readers is rather more subtle. And such understated didacticism or aid to the dying and the living is also behind those nonreligious collections that may be said to follow in Kaines's footsteps. One of these, to be sure, Frederick Rowland Marvin's *The Last Words (Real and Traditional) of Distinguished Men and Women* (New York, 1900; 2d ed., New York, 1901; rpt. Detroit, 1970), is no more than an alphabetical listing, without a preface or introduction offering an apologia for the undertaking, a reference work that simply takes for granted the need for such a checklist. *Last Words of Famous Men and Women* by Walter R. Egbert (Norristown, Pa., 1898), on the other hand, avows that its purpose is to "contribute something to mitigate the terrors of dissolution" (p. 6). But what the *something* is remains obscure when Egbert defines the "precious legacy to the world of thought" that he has collected as "food for the theologian, shelter for the psychologist, and clothing for the moralist" (p. 5). This does not make anyone feel left out, or addressed for that mat-

ter. The classification here ("admittedly weak," even according to Egbert) is roughly thematic, as was Kaines's: Last
words are organized according to the classes or professions of
the dying. Rulers get one chapter; naval heroes get another,
as do spies (though the total is only two) and men of letters
(who are rather more plentiful); patriots are lumped together
regardless of country; philosophers (of ancient Greece) are by
themselves, and so on. But Egbert is so reticent about his specific motivation that it is not even clear whether each section
is meant for the corresponding section of readers.

Samuel Smiles, in the chapter on last words in his *Life and
Labour* (London, 1887), is a bit more forthcoming. The preface
to the book promises "many instances of what can be accomplished by honest force of will and steady perseverance." This
Victorian, hero-worshipping ethos has indeed informed
Smiles's selection from the world's treasure trove of last
words. He is particularly gratified by those last words of the
great that demonstrate (instructively, of course) that one can
persist in one's chosen, and usually profitable, line of work
until the very last moment, thereby setting a good example:
Doctors and scientists continuing to be diagnosticians and
empirical observers with their last breath, like Albrecht von
Haller feeling his own pulse, Archimedes doing geometrical
problems, and Cuvier analyzing his paralytic symptoms. The
exhibit also includes a distinguished judge mistaking his family for the gentlemen of the jury, Plato writing, and Napoleon
having war on his mind rather than Josephine. Obviously, the
old ideal of an appropriate death crowning a life has been
taken out of its Christian frame of reference and reinterpreted
within the horizon of the Victorian ethos, and the didactic
bent has been redirected correspondingly. In a way, this is a
development or practical specification of Kaines's suggestion
that last words are a key to a worldly pantheon or mythology
of heroes who provide guidance at a time when Christian values are no longer widely held as binding.

The first German anthology of dying words of this nature, Feodor Wehl's *Der Ruhm im Sterben* (Hamburg, 1886), also takes its cue from Kaines (who is mentioned in the preface), but in a different and perhaps more interesting manner. Much like Kaines, Wehl arranges his account of the death and last words of the famous according to the professional classes of the dying (careful, however, that the "entertaining" aspect of this sort of undertaking will not overshadow the "more significant and important side" of the matter). Emperors and kings do not die in the same way as philosophers and artists or even warriors or poets (these have been closer to the transcendental all along, we are told [p. 11]). What Wehl is after, then, is a typology according to station in life (*Stand*), and the purpose is again a sort of secular *Seelsorge* or Sterbehilfe: worldly edification designed to reconcile us, or rather "the thinking head," somewhat ("einigermaßen") with death—our own mortality—and to make us aware of its "mysterious connection with divine justice and the spirit of the time" (p. x).

This last note alerts us to a second and more significant motivation of the collection—another organizing principle that may lead to valid insights. Modes of dying are classified not only according to the role one plays in public life (ruler, poet, warrior, etc.) but also according to the age in which one lives. For within each section Wehl orders his cases chronologically to show that although individuals die as is appropriate to their respective profession, they also die "as it were in the spirit of their age" (p. vi). The argument may be circular, but it follows that we study last words to gain both an insight into human nature (or is it class?) and, to a certain degree, into the time and its "spirit" (pp. vi, viii). This idea certainly deserves some attention. Whereas under Christian auspices there had been really only one way of dying (not counting the incorrect one), and whereas Montaigne and Charron considered different ways of dying a given *at their own time*, Wehl now, at the turn of the century, claims that one died differently (and by implication, lived differently) *in different ages*. The questions that are suggested are, clearly: Has human nature always been the same, or has it a history? And are last words, the manners of dying, indicators of such alleged change?

The formulation may be a trifle old-fashioned in its simplicity, but to us today this is surely a more intriguing notion than the claim (not entirely compatible with the idea of historically variant death) that one dies—and lives—in the manner imposed by one's profession, using this term in its widest possible meaning. To belabor the obvious for the fun of its absurd potential: Not all poets, for example, not even contemporaries, are comparable in their life-styles and death-styles: take Dylan Thomas and T. S. Eliot; nor are military men, for that matter: take field marshals Rommel and Montgomery, to go no further afield. In fact, as early as 1901, a certain Firmin Maillard piled up, with serious mien, impressive evidence in his privately printed anthology of last words *Le Requiem des gens de lettres* (Paris: Henri Daragon) to the effect that writers leave the scene of their activity with as many different types of words as do members of less word-obsessed professions. Obviously, arrangement of last words according to the profession of the speakers is only marginally superior, for purposes of humanistic understanding, to the alphabetical arrangement (which creates strange bedfellows in its turn: Stalin and Gertrude Stein, Oscar Wilde and William the Conqueror, the Buddha and Robert Burns, Robert E. Lee and Leo X, Kafka and Boris Karloff, Saint Bernadette and Sarah Bernhardt). On the other hand, that styles of dying have a history we have all heard in the hundred years or so since Wehl's book (from W. Rehm, J. Choron, R. Favre, and others).

As the debate about Ariès's *L'Homme devant la mort* (1977)[22] shows, this is a controversial subject, and catalogs of college-course offerings indicate that it has widespread appeal. But the idea of studying last words with a view to throwing light on such a history of death and dying styles is still a novel one, especially if one attempts somehow to get around the circularity of Wehl's proposition. Wehl, in his intrepidly brief sketch of the history of dying styles based on last words, discovered only what he had known beforehand (pp. vii–viii). The real question is: Can the study of last words add something to our understanding of this history—or help us determine whether there was such a history? The prima facie value of last words for such an objective is not insignificant when compared to other types of evidence that have been used, such as last wills and testaments, philosophical meditations, funeral fashions, and epitaphs. It is tempting to think that one could go beyond the sort of demonstration Wehl has to offer: In heroic times one dies heroically (the Crusades, the German Wars of Liberation); in the Age of Enlightenment one dies uttering freethinkerly sarcasms; in ages of religious unrest one dies a martyr; in a period of frivolity one dies like Queen Caroline, wife of George II, who, "infected by the spirit of the time," used her last breath to urge her husband to remarry. George replied that he would take mistresses instead, to which Caroline responded, "Mon Dieu, that's no obstacle," and passed away (pp. vii–viii).

The challenge is to see if a study of last words can contribute to our understanding of the changing human condition over the centuries. This challenge, also implied in all anthologies that arrange their material chronologically, is indeed taken up by some of the twentieth-century anthologists. To be sure, they do not get us very far either; but they do suggest that an attempt to write a history, not of collections of last words but of last words themselves, might be worth some effort.

Let us turn now to these more recent anthologies and inquire into the motivations behind their interest in last words.

Is it the same plethora of divergent motivations that we have encountered up to the Edwardian period, or do some dominant concerns emerge?

❖ ❖ ❖ ❖

It is perhaps not a coincidence that the next anthology to appear after Colonel Lewin's *Life and Death* of 1910, entitled *Last Words of Famous Men*, by "Bega," pseudonym of A. P. Codd (London, 1930; rpt. Folcroft, Pa., 1973, and Philadelphia, 1977), expresses dissatisfaction with its own system of classification, which is "according to the nature of men's position and work": religious leaders, monarchs and statesmen, military figures, philosophers, lawyers, educators, and so on, in somewhat arbitrary order of precedence, except that Bega expressly defends the position of clerical dignitaries at the head of the procession (pp. 7, 11). And that betrays his dominant motivation. For the light that last words "throw on human nature" does not so much illuminate professional or historical attitudes and sentiments (p. 140) as it reveals the latter-day vitality of the ars moriendi tradition. At first sight these *Last Words* seem to be a thoroughly *secularized* "art of dying," as the "legacies of parting words" that distinguished men of all walks of life have left us are to help us, in all walks of life, to find our own "peace at last"— vaguely enough (p. 127). We, the undistinguished, are to look to the great for "guidance." The motif of Carlylean hero worship, which loomed large in earlier anthologies, crops up again verbatim and is now identified as "an essential factor in human nature." "We would learn what we can from them, and particularly we like to know how our heroes meet the common lot of mortals, because therein lies the appropriate fulfilment of the life" (p. 128). Given such strong a priori convictions and expectations, Kaines's caveat (and not only his)—that one may not always be answerable for what one says in extremis—can be mentioned but not taken seriously. For "under normal conditions" the ruling passion of a life will declare itself "on the verge of the tomb" in language that is loud and clear—especially in the case of the great who, after all, dislike leaving work and life "unfinished" (pp. 130–131). While this sounds all-encompassing and secular, Bega's real sympathies lie with those who become the objects of hero worship because they died a Christian death. In other words, he turns out to be closer to the ars moriendi tradition and less secular in his orientation than his broad spectrum of heroes might suggest. "The world's greatest hero" is Jesus Christ; intellectuals and statesmen cannot really compete with him when it comes to giving guidance (p. 136). Specifically and significantly for this moment in intellectual history, the "guidance" that matters cannot come from science. Christianity, on the other hand, "transcends" all other religions, although we are assured that there is "good" in each of them, too (pp. 137–139).

A modern observer might note that the arrangement of last words by profession of the speakers is not the only unsatisfactory feature of Bega's anthology. Another such collection, which came out the same year and which is a truly major one, *The Art of Dying: An Anthology* by Francis Birrell and F. L. Lucas, "published by Leonard and Virginia Woolf at the Hogarth Press" (London, 1930), is pointedly different in focus. Commenting on Bega's just-published volume, the prefatory note elegantly rejects any edifying intent (which Wehl, despite his historical inclinations, was not able to shake off): "*Too much* gravity is unbecoming to such a subject; human interest, not edification, has been our aim; we sought for the piquant or the poignant, for the comic, the tragic, or the ironic. We trust that the result will interest many and depress none." The human interest here is not, as this formulation might suggest and as is sometimes the case in more recent collections of this kind, the mere curiosity value of the hodgepodge of ways of dying; rather, it is historical interest (and in this respect this collection strikes a dominant motif of twentieth century anthologies of last words). For the arrangement of *The Art of Dying* is chronological in the expectation that "a certain light might thus be thrown on the changes in human life through the centuries, even from under the shadow of death. . . . Dying too has its fashions, and at rare periods may even become an art" (p. 9). Of course, one has to be careful here not to rush in where professors fear to tread. Deathbed utterances, we are told, can be "surprisingly characteristic" not just of the particular speaker but of the time as well, if only "often." This qualification alludes to the dilemma of quantification: How many instances are enough to prove anything along these lines? The sketch of a history of last words as indexes of their times that Birrell and Lucas give is just that, a sketch, and again the question of circularity comes up: Does a study of last words add to our knowledge of past ages or does it just illustrate the well known in a novel manner?

In *The Art of Dying* the historical sketch looks like this: The irony and grace of classical Greece is found in the dying words of Pericles and Socrates; the incisive brevity of Roman culture in the last words of Nero or Vitellius; the humanism of the Renaissance in "the quiet jesting" of some famous dying utterances and in the "fervid patriotism" of others; the temper of the Reformation and Counter-Reformation is reflected in the final farewells of Cranmer and Saint Teresa, Jacob Böhme and Cromwell, and so on through the Age of Reason. That age's last words echo its urge for knowledge and truth, its cultured passion for elegance and amiability, making the Enlightenment the age that in "style" of dying words leads all others, especially the nineteenth century, which "in this department of life, as in others, . . . lacks style" (pp. 8–13). When the case is put this baldly, and with the assumption that last words issue from a state of at least semiconsciousness, we are tempted to add a big question mark to the proposition of a *history* of last words. It is the same question mark that has been added to Ariès's periodization, which rests on a much broader foundation of evidential material.

The question mark was replaced by an exclamation point a decade and a half after *The Art of Dying* in Virginia Moore's book about last words, boldly entitled *Ho for Heaven! Man's Changing Attitude Toward Dying* (New York, 1946). Last words are used here as the building blocks of a history of the human mind from earliest times to the present; Moore posits them as "a mirror of man's evolution in consciousness . . . not unique, of course, for there are the arts, but a true reflector of world changes, wherein one can see not only the character of the dying, but the character of his period." For "men have not always died the same way," as the typological arrangement of last words preferred by Bega and others somehow assumes. And if people did not die the same way over the ages, it follows that they did not live the same way either. "Fashions" and "trends" in dying ultimately point to fashions and trends in living. "Really, a period's whole attitude toward life and death was summed up in [a] last remark," Moore concludes, giving as an example Diderot's supposed last words, which in her version are not the well-known philosophical ones ("The first step towards philosophy is incredulity") but the irritated remark to his wife who tried to stop him from eating an apricot: "What a devil of a way to treat me"—typical of the Zeitgeist, says Moore, because it shows that the spiritual realm lay beyond the ken of French rationalism (pp. 17–18). It is doubtful, of course, whether Moore succeeds with this admittedly original argument, based as it is on a faith in apricots that is beyond all rationality. We may also wonder what is "a typical nineteenth-century death." Or, in the absence of quantitative statistics, are not the "exceptions" more "typical"? (pp. 214, 225). On balance, Moore does not inspire us to share her robust confidence in the telling quality of—purposefully selected!—last words as indicators of the spirit of the time. As a result, the book, despite its sweeping period generalizations, degenerates into a hodgepodge of anecdotal "cases" and becomes a depository of last words rather than a history of them.

Whereas Moore offers hundreds of last words, Manuel Iribarren, the author of the next book on the subject, chooses only one "representative" for each period or civilization—and thereby gives the *illusion* of a history. This results in chapters like "Socrates or Greece," "Julius Caesar or Rome," "Michelangelo or the Renaissance," and so on, in his weighty volume *Los grandes hombres ante la muerte: capítulos decisivos* (Barcelona, 1951). Iribarren blithely proceeds from what remains to be proven: that each civilization has its own distinct style of dying, which reveals "the essence of life," that last words produce the "emotional synthesis of each epoch," and that it is, of all people, the "exceptional" ones who prove to be "representative" in their last words (pp. 15, 17). This sort of approach seems to be dear to the Latin heart. A similar tour d'horizon of civilizations is promised, though hardly offered, by Luis Angel Rodríguez in his *Las grandes muertes de la historia* (Mexico City, 1938), as well as in Enrique Chao Espina's anthology entitled *Cien frases ante la muerte* in 1945, which blossomed into *Doscientos frases ante la muerte* in its third edition (La Coruña, 1979).

Intriguing as the historical line of inquiry is, as yet no explorer who has ventured into this difficult terrain has brought back a convincing report. True, the next anthology to appear, Edward Le Comte's magisterial *Dictionary of Last Words*, published in the prestigious *Philosophical Library* series (New York, 1955), does make reference to the historical idea when it states, almost in passing, that this collection contributes to "a survey of human history from a uniform vantage point" (p. xx). But Le Comte warns Virginia Moore (and others) that "the seeker of Zeitgeist must beware of finding only what he is looking for" (p. xiii). Le Comte's dominant interest is elsewhere, as his alphabetical arrangement (by speaker) suggests. Undeterred by James Gordon Bennett's advice to a cub reporter, "Remember, son, many a good story has been ruined by oververification," Le Comte in his valuable introduction is mainly interested in weeding out inauthentic last words and keeping only those that (he thinks) can be considered both last and genuine (which is irrelevant, of course, to those who value last words as cultural artifacts, i.e., as a literary genre). And there are others who in the introductions to their anthologies give a nod to historical interest without pursuing it further. Thus, a German collection, Erich Worbs's *In die Ewigkeit gesprochen: Letzte Gedanken. Eine tröstliche Anthologie* (Munich, 1970), professes to avoid the "purely conventional" in preference for what is "telling from the point of view of psychology or cultural history" (p. 10); Worbs accordingly arranges last words (the term is defined somewhat broadly here) in chronological order, he cites Jean Paul: "There is an important immense world history, that of the dying" ("Erinnerungen aus den schönsten Stunden für die letzten"); and the introduction suggests that last words might give at least a glimpse of that immense, lost history (p. 6). Nonetheless, in spite of such suggestions of historical interest, the emphasis is on something else: the by-now familiar, secularized Sterbehilfe that last words promise. They are, after all, those utterances that allow us a glimpse into "the final mystery" (p. 6), utterances that show the face without the mask—from which we can learn valuable lessons (p. 7). Similarly, Åke Ohlmarks's collection of last words, *Sista Sucken: Vad stora och små människor sagt eller säga vid sin död* (Stockholm, 1970), arranged chronologically from 600 B.C. to the present, postulates in its brief postscript that the ages reveal their own distinctive style in last words. But not only do we not hear exactly what these styles are, the main fascination seems to be with the infinite and un-classifiable richness and variety of last words, with their word games and puns, expressions of faith and sarcasm, of duty and fear, fatigue, magnanimity, baseness, and the rest.

It is easy to see that this sort of "human interest" can degen-erate into a mere love of the odd and curious, which might put collections of last words into the company of the *Guinness Book of World Records*. This does indeed seem to be the case with a number of more recent anthologies.[23] Such craving for entertainment is notably satisfied also by one of the most recent and perhaps most "popular" collections, Malcolm Forbes's *They Went That-a-Way* (New York, 1988) which pre-sents, chronologically, "the extraordinary exits," not *just* the last words, of 175 personalities of public life and of show busi-ness in particular. The ultimate in last words anthologies as-sembled for entertainment, however, is Barnaby Conrad's *Fa-mous Last Words*, with a foreword by Clifton Fadiman (New York, 1961). Conrad, too, treats the subject lightly, as befits most serious matters in countries that have a taste for *Arsenic and Old Lace* or *The Wrong Box*. For instance, Conrad's restate-ment of the well-worn observation "how comparatively pleas-ant dying is reported to be" is followed by "especially when compared with other ordeals. Such as living, for example" (p. 15). His own collection of last words (or at any rate what he quotes from it in his introduction) is geared toward the curi-ous and the macabre, the bizarre and the funny, such as the murderer who, asked by the rifle squad about to execute him whether he has a last request, replies: "Why, yes—a bullet-proof vest"; Thoreau's puzzled notation, in *Walden*, about one Tom Hyde whose last message under the gallows was: "Tell the tailors to remember to make a knot in their thread before they take the first stitch"; Dylan Thomas: "I've had eighteen straight whiskies. I think that is the record." Conrad's sug-gested titles for anthologies of last words are equally funny, with first prize going to *Learn to Speak Effectively While Dying,* with *Words to Die By* and *Before I was So Rudely Interrupted* running close seconds.

But some attempt to arrive at an *aesthetics* (as distinguished from a history) of exit lines, comparable to the aesthetics of other literary genres, does emerge from this and similar collections assembled primarily for their entertainment value. For instance, Fadiman in his foreword makes a playful yet critically serious search for the appropriate last word, for the artistically appealing consistency of life and death, for the stylistic continuum uninterrupted by the prospect of the end: he is delighted to find "true Yankee farewells" (no fuss); a writer dying with precision of language; Gertrude Stein sibylline till the last moment; and "the most wonderfully British farewell utterance"—the beau geste generally. Conrad adds "dying in character," truth to one's profession (Corot dying confident that he would paint in heaven), as well as the vainest, the coolest, the most intemperate, the most poignant exit lines and other stylistic prize winners. A typological stylistics of verbal taps beckons here as an alluring possibility. In this scheme, last words become more like curtain lines of plays, carefully staged: entirely artifacts, works of literature, aesthetic objects, even artifice, possibly even disengaged from the life of which they are the concluding note. One has only to remember that some people have become more famous for their dying words than for anything they said before, more famous for their deaths than for their lives.[24] Ohlmarks provides the example of figures mentioned in Icelandic sagas for no reason other than that they died in perfect good style, with a laconic comment, a bon mot of indifference, or a word of rough humor. He adds that during certain epochs the Japanese upper class cultivated a similar art of what Strindberg called "dying tastefully" (p. 94).

An aesthetics of last words is also implied in Brian O'Kill's thoughtful and sophisticated introduction to his anthology

Exit Lines: Famous (and Not-So-Famous) Last Words (Harlow, Essex, 1986) as well as in the anthology itself. Here the aesthetic entity or object is emphatically not merely the last word itself, disengaged from the life, as it tended to be in some of Conrad's remarks, but both the life and the last word, both the play and its concluding line, together—more specifically, as in Fadiman's aesthetics, the relationship between the two as the constituent elements that form the totality. O'Kill is of course aware that "the widespread appeal of the subject" has many facets. Last words reveal "a kaleidoscope of human attitudes and dilemmas"; they inspire morbidity, solemnity, as well as jokes; they provide a deliberate summary, a confession, or wisdom; and in some major religions they are believed to determine the dying person's "eternal fate" (p. v). But O'Kill's interest is kindled particularly by that type of last word that lends itself less well to such appeals. For he excludes from his collection such formal "last addresses" as suicide notes and the last words of victims of executions, concentrating instead, unlike Fadiman, on those final words—the majority, according to him—that are "not intended as definitive statements but happened to become the last. . . . It is their unselfconscious, accidental, almost ironic quality which makes them so fascinating, so richly human, and so amenable to whatever significance we may impute to them" (pp. v–vi). O'Kill continues: "They may form, unknowingly, a striking summary of a person's career and beliefs." (This, of course, had always been maintained, but specifically of the more deliberate variety of last words where the summary is made knowingly.) "Or they may have a cryptic or symbolic quality which gives them a haunting resonance—as with Goethe's request for light" (p. vi). This is not a particularly good example, as it is haunted by the suspicions of either inauthenticity or innocence of intended symbolic meaning (see above, pp. 81–88). Still, the point is hard to dismiss out of hand. A "seemingly inappropriate time" of death with a correspondingly in-

appropriate exit line (i.e., one not intended as an exit line)—
Samuel Butler's question about the checkbook, Thomas Mann's
inquiry about his glasses—may, on sympathetic consideration, yield some significance: not significance in the sense of
revelation from the borders of existence or even revelation of
the hitherto unknown true self, but a significance giving what
may loosely be called aesthetic or stylistic satisfaction.

> Whether these [unexpected, trivial, "insignificant"] ends are
> really inappropriate may be doubted. Such moments are so
> characteristic of everyday lives, and so touchingly evocative of
> human frailty, that—although pious biographers have tended
> to disguise them—they sure do not belittle the people con-
> cerned. (P. vi)

In the anthology itself each dying word is accordingly followed by a brief essay, and here O'Kill goes much further
than these bare abstractions or understatements of the introduction suggest. In each of the one- or two-page essays, he
tries to show how the last word picks up a motif from the life,
how it echoes details or dominant concerns, so that the last
word becomes part of a pattern—or even establishes a pattern—comprising the entire life. It becomes an exit line that
gives the kind of aesthetic pleasure of realization suggested by
the theater metaphor: the last word is seen as the last line of
a play; life and death are revealed as a work of art or the analogue of a work of art. From this perspective it is eminently
fitting that Lord Chesterfield, concerned with manners no
matter how seemingly trivial throughout his life, died asking
that a chair be offered to Dayrolles, who had the courtesy to
pay him a deathbed visit; Wagner's asking about his watch
brings to an appropriate conclusion a life in which time had
always been a major concern. Napoleon's "broken utterances" as the curtain fell in St. Helena "manage to combine
[his] chief preoccupations" (p. 119); so do Thoreau's "moose"
and "Indian" (p. 172). Gertrude Stein's "self-questioning was

a most appropriate final utterance" (p. 162); and Ibsen's "On the contrary!" "came appropriately from one who had devoted his life to the correction of lies" (p. 86). Aesthetics in this sense are clearly O'Kill's principle of selection of last words, and yet he also delights in the sheer richness and infinite variety—of life and death—revealed in those words that are, or are believed to be, the last.

This may be a hint that the aesthetic detachment, and the lighter tone that tends to accompany it, are hard to sustain for long. They might remind one of Ibsen's poem "Paa vidderne," in which a house burning to the ground is viewed from a deliberate distance as a spectacle of rare beauty, as a painting as it were, a work of art. It may therefore be no coincidence that the anthology that luxuriates the most in the "infinite" *stylistic* variety of last words "of some two thousand two hundred dead [!] people," Jonathon Green's *Famous Last Words* (London and New York, 1979), also joins ranks with the latter-day Sterbehilfen in expressing the hope that it may offer some comfort to those whose last words are still to come. To be sure, the arrangement of this collection is guided by stylistic principles: "Certain moods, certain styles do persist, and this book has been divided into eighteen loosely generalised sections that show these ranges of feeling." Though the compiler regrets that we have no last words of many of the famous, not to mention the less famous, he is satisfied that "fortunately" there have always been many "who did remember to sign off in style," and who are therefore included in his anthology (p. 5). So Green is able to offer his readers a survey according to stylistic categories, some of which are circumscribed in the chapter headings as follows: "Across the great divide," "Holier than thou," "Dulce et decorum," "The tough get going," "Gallows humor," "The show must go on," and "Look back in anger." And yet, in spite of its jocular tone and interest in stylistics, the introduction ends on a different note: "We can draw some comfort in the way these men and women have coped with their impending demise. . . . When the inevitable arrives, all that one can hope, like so many of the people included here, is at least to do it well." A faint echo again of the late-medieval art of dying well, even though "well" in this context has the overtone of *"aesthetically* perfect," of *style.*

Other anthologies of the forties, fifties, sixties, and seventies are less coy about their intention to provide aid to the dying (as well as the living, among whom one may expect more readers). Most straightforwardly in the ars moriendi and memento mori tradition is John Myers's *Voices from the Edge of Eternity* (Northridge, Calif.: Voice Publications, 1968). "Death is a subject no one can treat lightly," we are warned at the outset, and the index finger seems to be raised throughout the rest of the preface. For Myers is interested in last words only to the extent that they convey "glimpses into eternity." The dying "quite clearly" see beyond the grave, and what they see proves our immortality and the truth of the biblical account of life after death, "etc." The evidence is believed to be "scientific," and as such will provide readers with "the dawn of what the prophets of old called 'hope.'"

Less specialized in its prospects but no less forthcoming in its promise of Christian wisdom for the living and the dying is the Rev. Herbert Lockyer's *Last Words of Saints and Sinners* (1969; see above, p. 63). The religious nature of Lockyer's interest in the subject is undisguised, and yet, remarkably, his collection is nonproselytizing in parts, while in others it revives the old schema of saints dying happily and infidels dying in agony (pp. 130, 155). He gives us a full range of last words, not just of saints and sinners, organized, again, according to the profession of the dying and with only intermittent evangelical commentary. As a result, this collection can be, as Lockyer delicately puts it, "both informative and inspirational," leaving, however, no doubt about which is better: "The dying testimonies . . . can animate us to renewed zeal and fresh activity in life and to say in humble trust, yet with holy boldness, 'To depart and be with Christ, is better'" (p. 13). And, lest we forget, "our end may be nearer than we realize" (p. 17).

More secular in outlook, yet just as strongly motivated by the desire to offer help, orientation, and even consolation, are four Continental anthologies. Most heavy-handed is Lotte Zielesch's compilation *Das Herz steht still* (Munich, 1946), which promises the consolation that only those who have come closest to the "solution of the enigma of existence" and have become "knowing" can offer (p. 5). Another book in this category is Friedrich Laubscher's *Letzte Worte: Mahnung und Trost, Erinnerung und Vermächtnis* (Stuttgart: Verlag Junge Gemeinde, 1973; first publ. ca. 1953). From antiquity and the Old Testament to the post–World War II period, "heathens and Christians" confirm with their last words—be they "the sum total of the life-time wisdom of a man" or "greetings . . . already from another land"—that "at the gate of eternity" our life will yield "decisive words," even though it may up to that point have been no more than idle talk. Such words show us life in "the right light," give us the "right measure." This of course jeopardizes the whole enterprise, for if "we" are the dying, such wisdom arrives rather late, and if "we" are the survivors, we are apparently constitutionally unable to see that light until we ourselves reach that all-important gate.[25]

Claude Aveline is more sophisticated. In the introduction to his collection *Les Mots de la fin* (Paris, 1957), he insists somewhat defensively that this genre's appeal is neither macabre nor anecdotal. He is at pains to point out that the inspiration of any—particularly scholarly—interest in last words is of a much more serious nature (pp. 11–12), especially serious— and this marks the distance from thinkers such as Lockyer— in a world without God. For if it is guidance that is expected of last words, it is particularly the kind of guidance that was formerly provided by religious institutions. The light imagery in the following quotation suggests the context in intellectual history: What was once the gift of God is now derived from the ultimate human borderline situation:

> For the man without God it is not death that is the enigma, it is life. And what one can gain from the dead is that they put it into words. They have achieved *their* destiny; we perhaps still have the time to improve ours. May their experience help us with it. Sudden death, unconscious death, is egotistical, it offers us nothing. What we need is enlightenment from the lights that are about to be extinguished.[26]

The advice becomes more practical, as Aveline hastens to add that just as a similarity between masters and disciples is necessary for the "lessons" of the masters to be effective, so any given last words can help only those listeners or readers who are predisposed to "hear" them. And if one does not know which "type" one is in this respect, one will, we are assured, soon find out while leafing through the collection— or rather collections (p. 19). For, curiously, the 150 most important "mots de la fin" are presented in one section of the book, each accompanied by a brief background essay, while 600 "other" last words are simply listed, second-class style. "Instruction" is offered in both sections, but the author is careful to point out that the lessons may not always be in accordance with commonly accepted ideas of "vertu" and that his book is not a manual of morality (p. 19). The basic lesson, however, is "Vivez!"—which should appeal to most.

Such high expectations for what last words can accomplish imply that high standards are employed to determine what qualifies as a last word. Like most of us in our last-word civilization, Aveline is aware that last words, as an institution, may be the objects of intellectual frivolity. He recalls a character in a Balzac novel who accuses another of filling his diary with the last words of all the great men who died without saying anything and reminisces about a film about Pancho Villa where the dying hero asked a journalist: "Tell me, what shall be my last word. . . ." Tied up with this precarious status of last words is, naturally, the whole problem of authenticity (p. 159). So, given his emphasis on the substantive quality of last words, Aveline is careful to weed out last words that are under suspicion of having been "fabricated" by the dying themselves in order to die true to their career, reputation, or personality. "To have its true value, a last word must emanate from a reaction, conscious or not, against the imminence of the event" (p. 160).[27] This sounds a bit like the old legalistic language of Anglo-Saxon common law concerning "dying declarations." But what the Frenchman has in mind in 1957 is something far more "existential." We cannot be sure that we know who we are; shattering experiences teach us something new about ourselves; we need them to get to know ourselves, "and death will be the last one, if the opportunity has not presented itself earlier" (p. 161).[28] What is passed on in last words, and what is learned from them, is an individual's ultimate knowledge about himself and, thus, about the human condition. It follows that the handing down, the tradition of last words, is a humanizing cultural activity of a very high order.

Similar in orientation and ambition, though not as heavily existential, is Herbert Nette's collection of last words, *Adieu les belles choses* (Düsseldorf, 1971; 2d ed., Munich, 1983 as *"Hier kann ich doch nicht bleiben"*). Messages from the border, treasured for so long in so many cultures, enhance the life of the living. The reader "may hear in all these voices an encouragement to live, an appeal to enriched, fulfilled existence (p. 5).[29] Hence, Nette too selects only those statements that derive from "genuine confrontation with death" (as far as that can be made out), discarding anything but that which has the ring of the most credible. The arrangement (which was quite haphazard in Aveline) here is systematic according to the "inner attitude" of the dying as revealed in the actual last words. So we hear from the believers, the skeptics, the bonmotists, those who maintain composure ("Haltung") to the last (as was often the case with victims of the French Revolution, even if their style did get cramped some of the time), from those who think of their loved ones or, again, of their life's work—guidance in all cases.

❖ ❖ ❖ ❖ ❖

Reading these anthologists—or the "serious" ones among them—along with their introductions, one does come away with the feeling that last words are part of the legacy of mankind to itself, that they are, or have for some time been considered, a valuable part of our civilization, an element of our cultural self-awareness and our humanistic tradition. As last words are passed on from generation to generation, a civilization affirms and perpetuates itself.

This conclusion conflicts with the view expressed most memorably, if impressionistically, by George Santayana in his essay "English Death-Bed Manners," written during the First World War and published in his *Soliloquies in England and Later Soliloquies* (New York, 1922). Santayana pointedly minimizes and even trivializes the significance of the moment of death and of last words, and he finds that Protestant and particularly English deathbed manners (the very word is revealing) are an appropriate reflection of this view. "Death is a fact; and we had better accept it as such as we do the weather"; that is, by attaching no particular importance to it.

> No summoning of priests, no great concourse of friends and relations, no loud grief, no passionate embraces and poignant farewells; no endless confabulations in the antechamber . . . no tearful reconciliation of old family feuds nor whisperings about the division of the property. (P. 91)

While this may be true of "English manners" as far as bystanders are concerned, one does wonder about the astonishing insight that the Spanish-born philosopher claims to have into the English soul when it approaches the end:

> In the departing soul, too, probably dulness and indifference. No repentance, no anxiety, no definite hopes or desires either for this life or for the next. Perhaps old memories returning, old loves automatically reviving; possibly a vision, by anticipation, of some reunion in the other world: but how pale, how ghostly, how impotent this death-dream is! I seem to overhear the last words, the last thoughts of a mother: "Dear children, you know I love you. Provision has been made. I should be of little use to you any longer. How pleasant to look out of that window into the park! Be sure they don't forget to give Pup some meat with his dog-biscuit." It is all very simple, very much repressed, the pattering echo of daily words. Death, it is felt, is not important. What matters is the part we have played in the world, or may still play there by our influence. We are not going to a melodramatic Last Judgement. . . . We have tried to do right here. If there is any Beyond, we shall try to do right there also. (Pp. 91–92)

The sentiment is strikingly commonsensical, and as a personal attitude it is enviable. But it is highly doubtful that Santayana's words describe with any degree of accuracy the attitude that has prevailed through the centuries, even, and especially, in the English-speaking world. And much the same might be said about a more recent devaluation of last words on grounds that had previously been touched upon by Kaines, Mark Twain, Walt Whitman, Herbert Spencer, and Ret Marut. In *Mirrors of Mortality*, John McManners remarks at the conclusion of his review of "Death and the French Historians":

> Dying is the loneliest, and therefore the most highly individual thing we do. It is also the moment when we are least likely to be able to reveal our true sentiments, whether through weak-

ness or, if we are strong, through respect for the conventions
that make the event bearable for others. (P. 130)

Again, although there may be some truth in this, to be determined case by case, this is not how the living and the dying
have felt about the matter for several centuries.

It seems, on the contrary, that Joseph Addison evinces, if
not the last word on the matter, at least a more correct historical insight, not to mention a different quality of wisdom
when he says:

> There is nothing in history which is so improving to the reader
> as those accounts which we meet with of the deaths of eminent
> persons, and of their behaviour in that dreadful season. I may
> also add, that there are no parts in history which affect and
> please the reader in so sensible a manner. The reason I take to
> be this, because there is no other single circumstance in the
> story of any person, which can possibly be the case of every
> one who reads it. (*Spectator*, no. 289, 1712)

Nothing, said Richard Steele in the same periodical, makes a
stronger impression on us than "reflexions upon the exits of
great and excellent men" (*Spectator*, no. 133, 1711).

This conviction, our tour d'horizon suggests, also underlies
most anthologies of last words, whether sectarian or not. The
question they do not answer, though they pose it in a most
challenging manner, is whether what can be called the legacy
of mankind to itself has a discernible history. In the just-
quoted passage, Addison ascribes the interest that death and
last words command to a universal fact of human nature that
is beyond history—namely, our mortality—and yet he refers
to "history" twice in this context. Could we take this as our
cue?

5

AN INTELLECTUAL HISTORY OF LAST WORDS? Landmarks in Uncharted Terrain

Is there, as the German novelist Jean Paul put it, a "world history of the dying"[1] in the sense of manners or "styles" of dying differing from epoch to epoch? And would last words be indicators of such styles and their change? Would an anthology of last words be "an intellectual, cultural and literary history in miniature," as the German weekly *Die Zeit* put it on 6 January 1984 (p. 36)? Our survey of anthologies suggests that this question implies confidence in the concept of Zeitgeist. This is the underlying assumption of Charles D. Stewart's essayistic historical overview "The Art of Dying" in his *Fellow Creatures* (Boston, 1935) as well as of Walther Rehm's magisterial book *Der Todesgedanke in der deutschen Dichtung vom Mittelalter bis zur Romantik* (Halle, 1928). The Weltanschauung of a period, Rehm believes, is encapsulated in its attitude toward death, and history shows the change of such attitudes—or, rather, an alternation of just two such attitudes (p. 4)—which, however, is not to deny that "the core of man always remains the same" (p. 7).

Due to the historical nature of this chapter, publication information will be given in the text rather than in the Notes where appropriate.

Such a formulation reveals the tenuousness of this view. Ariès's sweeping sketch of a history of attitudes toward death in *L'Homme devant la mort* (Paris, 1977) has proved even more susceptible to the critical suspicion that there really is no such history of attitudes and that there could be none. Instead one would have to count on the simultaneous presence of a number of possible attitudes in any era, corresponding to the social and intellectual particularities of the dying, and this multiplicity would not demonstrably have changed in ways fundamental enough to allow us to speak of a period's distinct style of dying, prevalent throughout Europe, for instance.[2] A reasonably distinct and sufficiently widespread change in norms and expectations from one period to another would be one thing; the realities of the deathbed would be quite another. Even funeral sermons, a significant Lutheran institution from the sixteenth to the eighteenth century, tend to standardize the demise in their all but obligatory description of the circumstances of the "individual" death: it almost always comes out as "gentle and peaceful." No wonder funeral sermons were sometimes denounced as "lying sermons" (see above, p. 117).

It remains doubtful how quantifying social history in the manner of Michel Vovelle's *La Mort et l'occident* (Paris, 1983) would get around these difficulties.[3] The evidence it uses, its "indicators" of changes in the collective attitude toward death, are gravestones, epitaphs, last wills, votive plaques, funeral orations and sermons, etc.—tracks, of course, but aren't they "cold tracks," removed from the moment of dying that Jean Paul had in mind when he spoke of a world history of the dying?[4] Last words, on the other hand, come closer to the reality of dying—if they are authentic. But even if last words are accepted as valid indicators of an alleged change in the attitude toward death, there is still the objection of those historians who have their doubts, in principle, about collective *mentalités*, about Zeitgeist. And finally there remains the suspicion (indicated in our comments on historically oriented anthologies of last words) that nothing *new* could be established through this line of inquiry.[5]

One cannot significantly simplify the problem of a history of last words by limiting the inquiry to Western history since the Christian culture of the Middle Ages, as is common in the attempts to write a "History of Death." Nonetheless, this chapter will largely disregard pre-Christian and non-Western civilizations in order to put some limits on the topic. This is not to suggest that last words play a less prominent role in those civilizations; the opposite is true in the entire range from the so-called "primitive" to the "high" cultures. In some otherwise diverse cultures, one finds, for example, the belief in the magical power or prophetic truth of the dying word. Egypt, China, and Japan developed written and spoken formulas for the farewell to life. Antiquity perfected the literary genre of *exitus illustrium virorum*, the description of the demise of important personalities, tyrants and sages in particular, and cultivated moreover the genre of the "farewell speech." Both are gold mines for last words; last words were exploited in antiquity by the schools of rhetoric, which made them the common currency of the educated, who passed them on like heirlooms from generation to generation. Ultima verba were treasured because they were believed to put the entire life of the person in a nutshell, the life as seen either by friend or by foe, of course—which made the authenticity of last words dubious by definition, though that did not make them any less useful or indispensible for biographical or historiographical writing.[6] The Old Testament too is a reservoir of last words in the form of dying speeches that seal the legacy of the moriturus with the emphasis of finality. Among the most memorable are the deaths of Jacob (1 Moses 49), Moses (5 Moses 33), David (2 Samuel 23; 1 Kings 2) and Isaac (1 Moses 27). Rabbinic literature continues the tradition with the legacy-like dying speeches of rabbis, which follow a pattern allowing few variations.[7]

If, then, in considering the feasibility of a history of last words, one leaves aside this "pre-history" and the "parallel history" in non-Western cultures, the problem narrows to the question of whether there is such a history in the "Christian era." As the objections against a "History of Death," mentioned above, can, in principle, be raised against a history of last words as well, one is faced with the problem of the "simultaneity of the non-simultaneous" that troubles any historian of mentalités or of Zeitgeist, Ariès included. Claiming that essentially the same ensemble of attitudes prevailed at all times is no solution. For this kind of reductionism, in denying that there is a history of death, denies the possibility of a history of life, of civilization, and indeed of man. This position is hardly more appealing or tenable than a rigorous schema of a historical sequence of attitudes. What might be worth exploring, however, is a middle path between history-denying anthropological reductionism and the all-too-"constructive" designs of an accurate history of "the" mind or of well-defined mentalités following each other in a neat sequence. In other words, there may be historical landmarks: orientation points in a historical flow or in a plethora of events. At such points a certain view (in our case a view of the nature, significance, and function of last words) may crystallize—not necessarily as a novel one, "overcoming" the previous one and in its turn to be "superseded" by the next landmark. Such marks would also not necessarily signal an attitude shared by "all," but they would still be orientation points having a certain pre-history and post-history and signaling a certain width of consensus. In chronological order, such landmarks would be the artes moriendi; the (primarily Elizabethan and Jacobean) dying speech formally pronounced under the gallows or in front of the executioner's block; the polemical confrontation of the death of the "believer" and the "unbeliever"; the criticism of the view, propounded by the artes moriendi, that assigns categorical importance to the last moment and the last word; and finally (as suggested by some of the nineteenth- and twentieth-century anthologies of last words), the claim, stated or implied, that last words qualify as ersatz religion, as a secularized substitute for formal religious guidance.

The *Grandes Heures de Rohan*, a manuscript book of hours in folio from the first quarter of the fifteenth century preserved in the Bibliothèque Nationale in Paris, shows a full-page illustration of "the death of a Christian." The dying man, almost a corpse himself, already among skulls and bones scattered all about, exhales his soul into a bubble containing the words: "In manus tuas, domine, commendo spiritum meum." God, depicted above, replies in French that the repenting sinner would be "avec moi" on the day of judgment.[8] The dying word is of course an echo of the last words of Christ on the cross: "Father, into your hands I commend my spirit!" (Luke 23:46)—the most significant and most imitated last word of the New Testament. Untold Christians have departed this life with these words, whether directed to the Father or the Son, including Saint Augustine, Charlemagne, John Huss, Thomas Becket, and Cardinal Newman.[9] This verbal imitatio Christi was canonized as the optimal exit line in those "dying books" designed for clerics (and later for laymen as well), that emerged in the fifteenth century and became generally known as *Arts of Dying Well, artes moriendi,* following the title of the first printed version, dated around 1450 (the year printing with movable type originated). By the end of the fifteenth century, some three hundred manuscripts of these late-medieval artes moriendi had been written, and over one hundred had been published in various versions (which are believed to put into words an understanding of the significance of the hour of death which had been widespread earlier).[10] "Uncounted" numbers of such books kept appearing well into the seventeenth century; their impact on devotional tracts and sermons, Moral Weeklies, dramas, and novels is noticeable as late as the eighteenth century, even though by that time there

was also criticism, even in theological circles, of the ars moriendi mentality.[11] Protestants and Christian Humanists found
the genre no less useful than did orthodox Catholics, each
adapting it to their particular convictions.[12]

This attractiveness of the artes moriendi, making them one
of the most popular genres of consumer literature, is not difficult to understand. Devils and angels vie at the deathbed for
the soul of the dying man with their temptations and promises, or so we are told (and often shown, as in numerous illus-
trations from the early days of this tradition). Characteristically, the drama of the moriturus being questioned by the
cleric ends with a confession of sins, repentance, the offering
of the sacraments, and that reaffirmation of Christian faith
which culminates in words that guarantee admission to
heaven: prayers or, ideally, the repetition of Christ's last
words on the cross.[13] The alternative would be eternal damnation.[14] One way or the other, it is the last moment, the last
word, that decides the fate of the soul—as Hamlet knows
when he refrains from stabbing Claudius in the back while he
is at prayer. As the well-known German Lutheran pastor and
hymn writer Johann Heermann put it in his *Güldene Sterbe-
kunst* (1628): "If only the final [hour] is good, everything is
good. . . . He, however, whose end is unholy [*unselig*] would
be a thousand times better off if he had not been born" (2d
ed., Leipzig, 1659, pp. 287, 290). Daniel Schaller had said the
same in 1604 in his *Supellex mortis* (Magdeburg, pp. 613–618);
the echo is still unimpaired in 1673 in Edward Pearse's *Great
Concern: or, A Serious Warning to a Timely and Thorough Preparation for Death* in which Pearse keeps warning that at the
moment of death "the Battel is to be won or lost for ever"—
salvation or damnation will be "immediately determined by
. . . God" (21st ed., Boston, 1705, ch. 2). And this refrain is
still loud and clear in the distant followers of the ars moriendi
theology in the eighteenth century. Abbé Barthélemy Baudrand, rather liberal himself, stated as late as 1784 in his *L'Âme*

sur le Calvaire: "The moment of death will decide everything for ever."[15]

One should of course keep in mind here that Catholic and Protestant convictions may give different weight to the last word depending on the relative merit attributed to a life of godliness and good works vs. to salvation by faith alone, which might come about, though not with great probability in the view of orthodox Protestants, in a last-minute or last-word conversion of a moriturus who had lived his sinful life to the hilt.[16] But differences are by no means clear cut. Lutherans do tend to suspect last-minute repentance as an act of bad faith and to polemicize against Catholics, who allegedly validate the last word routinely, no matter how despicable the life it concludes (see below, pp. 177–180). Yet in Dante's *Divina Commedia*—a pre-ars moriendi compendium of Catholic belief, to be sure—the sinners who repented with their last breath are found not in paradise but in purgatory (*Purgatorio*, III–V). Protestants could not accept this "way out," this intermediate and revisable solution, as they liked to point out in their Arts of Dying Well with all the anti-Catholic fervor of which early reformers were capable: for them it was either-or; no prayer, no mass, can revise the decision made with an unsatisfactory last word.[17] But again, even Protestants, could in a pinch consider a God-fearing life an adequate substitute for the proper last word, as their funeral sermons reveal (see below, pp. 175–176). Indeed, the question whether sudden death (without an opportunity for the saving last word) would invariably open the gates of hell was controversial among Protestants in the early eighteenth century at the latest (see below, pp. 172–177).

The dispute between the denominations is somewhat unresolved even today, with both Protestant hymns ("Für einen bösen schnellen Tod/ Behüt uns, lieber Herre Gott") and the Catholic litany ("A subitanea et improvisa morte libera nos, Domine") still inciting fear of sudden death as the greatest of all evils. In the mid-twentieth century, a Catholic priest states matter-of-factly: "Man's eternal fate . . . depends on his moral condition in the hour of his death."[18] Secularized and transformed, this time-honored attitude lives on in Freud's famous remark in "Thoughts for the Times on War and Death," "If you want to endure life, prepare yourself for death," as well as in Elias Canetti's aphorism, "How many will consider life worth living once one does not die any more?"[19]

The death of the Christian was canonically programmed in the Art of Dying Well; dying was either holy or unholy. Accordingly, when anthologies of last words feature Christian deaths, they have overwhelming edifying potential but also the ring of monotony, even when the preferred "in manus tuas . . ." was not pronounced. The artes moriendi themselves sometimes offer "examples";[20] indeed, in some cases the ars moriendi merges into an anthology of last words of exemplary Christians, or at least an anthology in the formative stage. This development is understandable from the premise that "a good end is all-important." So one reads in the preface to the ars moriendi of the Lutheran schoolteacher Martin Mylius, *Sterbenßkunst/ Gefasset in/ Schöne außerlesene Exempel/ etlicher fromen Christen/ welche seliglich von dieser Welt abgeschieden/ Daraus man zu lernen/ wie man sich zu einem/ Christlichen Ende bereyten/ und seliglich von hinnen fahren sol* (Görlitz, 1593). It is a companion piece to his Latin *Apophthegmata morientium* (Görlitz, preface dated 1592) which brought together only the final utterances themselves, of over one hundred persons, with at the most a very brief description of the circumstances of death: "consoling speeches with which many pious people . . . concluded this temporal life and commenced eternal life," as the subtitle specifies.[21] The *Sterbenß-kunst* for its part assembles only about three dozen "swan songs" of "pious, holy people" from Old Testament times on, but those fewer cases are presented with their "entire last acts and histories" (preface) taken from a variety of sources, for the most part reports of the clerics officiating at the deathbed. Mylius's exemplary Christians are of "high and low estate" (*Stand*)—St. Jerome, King Frederick II of Denmark, duchesses and counts, jurists, physicians, councillors, and ordinary men and women. What their death is to teach us is signaled in the very title of the collection: holy dying, of course. Yet while the *Sterbenßkunst* contains only its cases or examples, the *Apophthegmata* conclude with a section containing meditations on eternal life, consolation for the bereft, memento mori prayers, and similar aids to living and dying. This appendix throws into relief the closeness of Mylius's anthology to the ars moriendi; it is in fact a variation on it even though its selection of examples is not limited to Christians: in addition to church fathers, martyrs, Christian theologians, doctors, scholars, and even theater directors, there are Old Testament figures as well as Roman emperors.

Mylius's books, the best-known works of this kind at the time, had been preceded by *Legenda pie defunctorum, das ist/ Fürbild und Exempel etlicher/ sterbenden Heiligen und Christgläubigen Menschen/ von Christi Geburt an biß auf diese Zeit*, a collection of exemplary last words put together by the Lutheran Wilhelm Wille (Frankfurt a.M., 1569)[22] and by *Disce mori. Oder Sterbekunst . . .* , a similar anthology by the prolific Lutheran preacher Bruno Quinos (Bautzen, 1580). The echo of the ars moriendi is unmistakable: it is self-evident that "the last hour is all-important and that the Art of Dying Well is the most necessary of all arts." Indeed, the last word is more important than temporal life itself, as a bad life can be improved and turned around even at the last moment, through the grace of God, but not after death, through masses and prayers—the anti-Catholic polemics again (Quinos's preface). His fourteen "Christian farewells," all culled from funeral sermons, serve as models. A Calvinist companion piece is Johann Jacob Grynaeus's *Apophthegmata morientium*, also published prior to Mylius's volumes (Basel, 1588). Taking as his cue Seneca's sentiment that the dying day is the judge of all preceding days (as did Montaigne and Charron at about this time), Grynaeus attempts a chronological survey ranging from emperors and philosophers of antiquity and Old Testament figures to the usual assortment of church fathers, martyrs, Catholic kings, and leading Reformers (Luther *and* Calvin *and* Zwingli, *plus* Erasmus and Melanchthon!).

Contemporaneous with Mylius's efforts are the book dealer Paul Cretzer's three tomes of "Christian Farewells," *Christliche Abschiede* (Hamburg, 1593), again identified in the preface as an "Art of Dying Well" (*Sterbenskunst*). While the first part features "patriarchs and other god-fearing men, along with emperors, kings, electors, and princes," the second specializes in "women and spinsters," with the third contributing theologians and martyrs; almost 700 examples of memorable last words altogether. This compilation is followed by Johann Groß's Calvinist anthology of some 400 last words, *Morientium apophthegmata. Geistlich Schwanen-gesang* (Basel, 1622), and *Tremenda mortis hora, Oder das böse Stündlein* by the Lutheran pastor Wenceslaus Bergmann (Görlitz, 1651), both artes moriendi in the form of a collection of exemplary last words.

Groß, who acknowledges his indebtedness to Grynaeus, includes the full range of candidates from antiquity and the Old Testament, via the thief on the cross, to Barbarossa, Huss, and contemporaneous princes and church wardens, with special consideration of the common man. Surprisingly for a Calvinist, he harps on the thief on the cross, converted in the eleventh hour, as a model case: no matter how evil a life may have been, a good death ensures salvation. "All's well that ends well" (he quotes the proverb), and, referring to his subtitle, he reminds his readers to emulate "the birds" and even heathens in this regard—who, again surprisingly, are known to have redeemed themselves with their last words. Still, he warns against the example of Bileam who had aspired to the death of the righteous, but not to their more demanding, godly life. A subject index of "doctrinal points" throws into relief the close amalgamation of ars moriendi and anthology of last words in these *Morientium apophthegmata*.

Bergmann's volume appears to have been one of the most successful of such works. From 154 exempla in the first edition, it grew to 450 in the fourth (in 2 parts, Wittenberg, 1708). "At the close of a man's life his deeds will be revealed" (Sir. 11:27), warns the preface to the fourth edition with all the intimidation familiar from the *ars moriendi*; and, once again, it is "mostly" funeral sermons that provide the collection's material, ominously enough. The arrangement of the cases is worth noting. The examples of each chapter illustrate with their last words a specific theological point generally made by the artes moriendi: how to overcome the temptation of the devil in extremis; intimations of eternal life; reconciliation with God; confession of faith, etc. Everybody dies a holy death. But even with the grand total of 450 cases advertised as early as the title page, there never can be enough examples. It is suggested that "young, prospective students" might wish to start their own collection.

The series of artes moriendi cum anthology of last words continues with Joachim Hildebrand's *Veteris ecclesiae, martyrum imprimis et SS. patrum Ars bene moriendi variis morientium dictis* . . . (Helmstedt, 1661), which speaks for itself, and Christoph Sommer's *Epilogi pie demortuorum, Oder: Exemplarische Sterbe-Schule/ in sich haltend Denckwürdige letzte Reden und Seufzer Christi und über vierhundert seiner Gläubigen* (Leipzig und Jena, 1676). Sommer thinks nothing of quoting Cicero in the preface ("appropinquante morte multo animus est divinior"), but he hastens to give the *vaticinatio morientium* a Christian interpretation: it is inspired by the Holy Ghost ("hence they say more than they understand"). Given this impeccable source of the "prophetic" last words of the dying, the Rudolstadt deacon, who collected them "with much trouble and dedication," as he praises himself on the title page, need not feel shy about polemically calling last words the *true* relics. His relics themselves have little to offer that is new, except perhaps the "child in its mother's womb": stillborn, with its hands folded. Sommer's meticulous index, a specialty of several of these works, contains many classes between the extremes of saints on the one hand and students on the other; women have their own index. The chapters again correspond thematically to the phases and varieties of dying specified in the artes moriendi, with headings such as "Last words of consolation and faith," "Last words of penitence," "Last admonitions," "Last words of those who overcame great temptations at their end," "Last words of those who had strange heavenly visions at the end of their lives," etc. Finally, there is the collection *Erbauliche Todes-Stunden viler Gottseeliger Personen* by Christoph Gottlieb Erdmann (i.e., the influential Swabian political philosopher Johann Jakob Moser; pt. 1, Tübingen, 1730). At this late date—the Enlightenment had reached Germany by this time—one still hears the teaching of the ars moriendi, its orthodoxy undiluted: "Our eternal salvation or damnation depends" on the "moment" of dying, the preface states in no uncertain terms (p. 4). One also hears a note that is much rarer in the German territories than in England: the cliché that the last moment will reveal the "truth" (rather than faith or faithlessness),

> because it is not to be assumed that persons who are really standing at the gates of eternity and are to appear before the chair of the great judge will utter anything but what truth, their conscience and experience will force on their lips. (P. 7)

The entire social range of the enlightened age is represented in this anthology of last words—the baron rubbing shoulders with the pastor, the duke with the chamberlain.

These anthologies cum ars moriendi, much like many of the collections discussed in the previous chapter, take their last words from the—predominantly Lutheran—funeral sermons that were popular for some two hundred years, from the age of Reformation to the Enlightenment. These funeral sermons themselves (many thousands have been preserved in the Herzog-August-Bibliothek in Wolfenbüttel) regularly conform to the precepts of the ars moriendi: a Christian life properly ends with "Into your hands I commend my soul" or an equivalent prayer or confession of faith.

Corresponding to these Lutheran and Calvinist Arts of Dying Well in the form of anthologies of last words, we find on the Catholic side an anthology, identified as an ars moriendi on the title page, compiled by Pierre Lalemant, prior of Ste. Geneviève and chancellor of the University of Paris, entitled *La Mort des justes, ou Recueil des dernieres actions & des dernieres paroles de quelques Personnes illustres en Sainteté, de l'ancienne & de la nouvelle Loy*, "Pour servir de modele à ceux qui veulent aprendre à bien mourir" (Paris, 1672; frequently reprinted until 1722; a Spanish translation, *La muerte de los justos*, came out in Madrid as late as 1793). The forty-three "just men" whose last years, days, hours, and, as a rule, words are memorialized here are without exception "Heroes of Christendom"—saints, church fathers, popes, Charlemagne, Louis the Pious, etc.—even though the illustrious line that extends into the fourteenth century starts with Moses, David, and Ezekiel. Strangely, however, Lalemant deviates from the mind-set of the artes moriendi (in the manner of Catholic justification through works, Protestants might have said) in that he puts less emphasis on the decisive power of the last word, be it the standard formula or some other pious utterance, than on the idea that holy death would follow from holy living— and unholy death from unholy living. It is "frivolous," says the "Avertissement," to hope that one would die in a manner different from the way one lived; hence the most reliable path to holy dying would be holy living. And nothing could better teach us such a life than the deaths of the saints. We should study them "a quarter of an hour a day. . . ." Those who live piously, with an eye on death at all times, would not be taken by surprise when death strikes. There is still, then, the horror of death, but the reason usually given by the artes moriendi for such fear of death, the possibility that one might be taken "unprepared," is played down by Lalemant.

By this time, however, while the artes moriendi did continue to demonstrate their vitality, a new landmark had come into view, a very different and yet similar one. That is the "dying speech" customarily made by the condemned—traitors, highwaymen, crowned heads, horse thieves, murderers, counterfeiters, burglars, dissenters, etc.—at the place of execution, literally under the gallows or in front of the executioner's block (this occurred primarily in the British Isles and North America, and to a lesser extent in France as well, though very rarely in the German territories). The dying speech was "the most important part of the execution"[23] until the eighteenth and sporadically even in the nineteenth century. The speech could be improvised or read from a manuscript prepared in prison. One way or the other, taken down in shorthand or the authentic version handed to the sheriff or the family in its authentic wording, the text of the farewell was printed in countless cases as a broadside, a small pamphlet, or a chapbook, sometimes with an introductory section on the trial and a concluding note on the circumstances of the execution, not infrequently with gruesome details or even a picture of the culprit dangling from the gallows or kneeling before the block. In virtually all instances the execution was a public event, a drama with well-defined roles to live up to, which the masses loved. The printed texts of the "gallows' speeches" that constituted an execution's high point were usually entitled *Last Words* . . . or *Last Speech* . . . or *Dying Speech of* . . . . Hundreds, perhaps thousands, have been preserved in the archives of the English-speaking world; frequently they were also collected in entire volumes (see above, pp. 106–109, 111–115).

The appeal of such texts derives from the general conviction that the truth will be spoken at the moment of inescapable death. "Nemo moriturus praesumitur mentiri," as the old maxim of common law has it, which Shakespeare eloquently paraphrased so often (see above, pp. 37–38). The horse thief James Dunn alludes to this common view as late as 1792 when he concludes his *Last Speech and Voluntary Confession* (Carlisle, Ireland) with a statement that requires no further explanation: "This I declare to be true as a dying man." By this time, to be sure, there had been numerous controversies about precisely this point, especially in the cases of English traitors as well as Jesuits and other "papists," who were at least suspect as enemies of the state in England. Early eighteenth-century anthologies of last speeches of criminals had categorically warned against taking such last statements concerning guilt or innocence at face value (see above, pp. 107–109); and as early as 1679 not only *The Tragical History of Jetzer* (see above, p. 20) but also *The Last Speeches of the Five Notorious Traitors and Jesuits . . . who were Justly Executed at Tyburn, June 20, 1679* recommended scepticism: like everybody else, we are told in *Last Speeches*, the culprits were aware—and we hear an echo of this in several of the "Last Words" broadsides—"that the last Words of dying Men bear a great sway amongst the Living" (p. 1). The prisoners about to meet their Maker confirm this in no uncertain terms. John Fenwick, one of the five in *The Last Speeches* of 1679, reminds the spectators: "I hope Christian Charity will not let you think, that by the last act of my Life, I would cast away my Soul, by sealing up my last Breath with a damnable Lye" (p. 5); likewise his coconspirator William Harcourt: "The words of dying persons have been always esteem'd as of greatest Authority, because uttered then, when shortly after they are to be cited before the high Tribunal of Almighty God" (p. 2). But this is exactly why the editor of these *Last Speeches* warns against taking at face value the last speeches of these (and not only these) convicted traitors, who one and all denied complicity in the assassination attempt on the king of which they were accused. In fact, he adds, just because belief in the truth of the last word was so widespread, these culprits could do more harm in their moment of dying than they could have done all their lives (p. 1).

The convicted were not expected to lay bare steadfastness in their heretical religious or political views; what was expected was a change of heart, confession of guilt, and recantation. For only in this manner, and in a public show of the culprits' contrition, could the religious and political values and norms of the people and the state be confirmed emphatically, almost ritually; only in this manner could the solidarity of society be reinforced[24]—especially in England, where politics and religion were most intimately intertwined in these centuries. Judging by the printed speeches, it was rather the exception that the prisoner to be executed did not confess the crime he was accused of and failed to recant his fundamental convictions; most frequently this happened in cases of religious heresy, which were sometimes memorialized by interested parties in separate anthologies of last words (see above, pp. 106, 115). Most unusual, however, at least until the early eighteenth century, were cases in which no last words were reported at all in the broadsides or chapbooks that have survived. Failure to pronounce or record the last word of a criminal executed in public is apparently a later development, as are the reports about some victims of the French Revolution who supposedly went to their death laughing.[25]

Sympathy for formal "Last Speeches" seems to have disappeared entirely in the twentieth century, if Count Harry Keßler's observation is any indication at all: the Mexican soldier's typical eagerness to make a speech before his execution was just a matter of satisfying his "vanity."[26] Still, the tradition lived on in the prisoners whose final patriotic exclamations so irritated the Nazi execution commandos on the eastern front, that they reportedly sealed their victims' lips with tape; and the *Jerusalem Post* in its International Edition of 12 May 1990 reminds its readers that the Jewish historian Simon Dubnow, seconds before being shot in Riga in December 1941, shouted the memorable words: "Write and record!" (p. 9).

But to return to the "Last Words" or "Dernières Paroles" of the sixteenth and seventeenth centuries: regardless of whether guilt was admitted or denied in hora mortis, the final speech at the place of execution developed a certain pattern which became de rigueur. As in the Christian deathbed scene, the moment before execution—perhaps with the loop already around the prisoner's neck, as is sometimes seen in illustrated broadsides—was not a moment for originality. Moreover, the standard formulas of the farewell to life correspond, even verbatim, to the thematic repertory of last words recommended by the artes moriendi.[27] The one difference is that the culprit about to be dispatched into eternity was not formally confronted, at least not in so many words, with the alternative of heaven or hell.[28] For among the typical topics of these speeches and of the reports of eye and ear witnesses on the execution itself, which were often printed as a sequel to the prisoner's last speech, there is no mention of the rivalry between devils and angels for the soul of the moriturus. Instead, the constitutive elements of the speech and the report on the last moments include, not necessarily in this order and not always in such completeness, confession of sins or admission of guilt (or protestation of innocence, followed, however, by the stereotypical admission of that sinfulness which is the lot of Christendom); forgiveness for enemies, witnesses, and the prosecuting attorney; the request for forgiveness from God and man, especially from the victims of the crime; the self-presentation as a deterring example, often followed by a plea for God's mercy; a prayer and, finally, the commendation of the spirit or the soul into the hands of the Lord or the Son. In this concluding formula the overlap of the broadsides and chapbooks with the artes moriendi becomes complete. Small-time frauds and assassins of crowned heads, pickpockets and martyrs of their faith, highwaymen and political rebels, pirates, spouse murderers, clerics, arsonists—what they all have in common is that in their last moments on earth they turn their thoughts to God and eternity, for which they desperately hope to qualify, if only in the manner of the thief on the cross. Such hope is nourished in these texts, as well as in the ballads about executions that were often published under similar titles, above all by the exit line long canonized in the Christian world: "Into Thy hands I commend my spirit," or, "O Lord, receive my soul!" These time-honored words occur rather stereotypically, no matter how different the cases.[29] In one "Last Words" pamphlet, the words' highly unusual absence is what the three exclamation marks following the concluding statement that three of several pirates to be hanged had presented themselves under the gallows so drunk "in the last moment of their earthly existence, as to be launched almost in a state of stupid insensibility into eternity"[30] might be understood to point to.

That was in 1830. By this time, however, the exit line canonized by the artes moriendi and the gallows speeches no longer universally commanded the decisive power over the destination of the soul that it had once had. Three lines of thought had been instrumental in bringing about this change.

1. The last words commending the soul into the hands of the Lord sealed the dying man's reconciliation with the Creator. As man was sinful by definition, such reconciliation was necessary in all cases. But what if death occurred suddenly, without allowing the generically sinful Christian an opportunity for a last word and hence for that preparation which determined the future of the soul? Some orthodox theologians thought nothing of interpreting the litany's "mors subita et improvisa" as anything *but* a matter of chance: it was an indi-

cation of God's displeasure, indeed punishment for a sinful life, for sudden death would open the gates of hell. Early on, Protestants were no less severe in this respect than Catholics such as Cardinal Roberto Bellarmino in his *De arte moriendi libri duo* (Rome, 1620, book II, ch. 14); and there was method to the rumors spread immediately after Luther's death by his opponents to the effect that the Reformer had been found "dead in his bed"—had gone to the flames eternal in other words—which of course called for agitated denials from his followers, who avowed that he had departed this life with a proper confession of Protestant faith.[31]

So great was the fear of death in a state of unpreparedness that theologians during the Reformation and earlier went so far as to devise a veritable insurance against the wrong last word, spoken in a state of weakness or dementia. It took the form of a "before need" manifesto of faith. In the hour of death itself one might profess unbelief or be

> deluded into arguing with God or blaspheming. . . . The confession of faith written in advance was therefore to be like an unassailable will, made in the spirit of cautiousness and in foresight of a possible defeat in the [final] battle with the devil, stipulating that any changes introduced later and any expression of conflicting sentiment would not in the least change its authority and validity.[32]

Luther, for example, formally declared any blasphemy he might conceivably pronounce on his deathbed invalid a priori and "inspired by the devil."[33]

However, in the course of the seventeenth and eighteenth centuries, at the latest, common sense gained ground here, even within theology. The sea change is signaled by Benjamin Grosvenor's treatise *Observations on Sudden Death* (London, 1720). To be sure, there had earlier been somewhat half-hearted deviations from the standard view on the evil of sudden death. As early as 1597, Richard Hooker, in the fifth book of his *Laws of Ecclesiastical Polity*, had downplayed the theological risk, but he had still taken seriously such factors as orthodox public opinion, which would slander the suddenly deceased as a hell-bound sinner of quality, and the practical inconvenience of dying without the time needed to attend to the "disposition of worldly things." His conclusion was that while sudden death was not a spiritual disaster, non-sudden death would certainly be "a blessing of God" (§ 46). And a century after Hooker, the minister John Dunton, reminding readers in his *House of Weeping* of the many famous cases beginning with Tarquinius and the fishbone, had considered an unprepared demise unfortunate at least when it occurred in a state of flagrant impiety (1692; 2d ed. 1692, pt. 2, p. 107). Grosvenor opposed the orthodox view with more wholehearted determination, going so far as to declare—some five generations after Montaigne—that unforeseen death would in many instances be nothing short of a blessing: "a Mercy to the good Man" (p. 11), its "advantages" being "more considerable" than its "disadvantages" (p. 23). Indeed, the general drift of Grosvenor's argument is that the whole question is no longer of great interest. A little later, the enlightened philosopher St. Evremond, in the fourteenth of his *Lettres morales et critiques* (Amsterdam, 1737), quoted Montaigne on this subject: "The quickest death is best" (p. 129), a view that antiquity, down to Pliny's *Natural History* (Book 7, ch. 54), had taken as all but self-evident.

Sudden death would, of course, not categorically preclude last words, but under its auspices they would just "happen" to be last words, subject to "chance"—and as such they might, in some cases, be seen to be not totally irrelevant but significant or telling in a way inconceivable from the point of view of the cult of the standardized last word; at the very least, such accidental last words might become the object of original, perhaps creative thoughtfulness. Similar reflection on the last word might suggest itself in those circumstances where there is no surprise about the moment of death, but still no opportunity for pronouncing the normative formula that ensured the soul's departure in the general direction of Abraham's bosom—either because the dying Christian lost his ability to speak or because his mental faculties had become impaired. In such cases, too, theologians took a more broad-minded position in the course of the seventeenth and eighteenth centuries. A Christian life was not automatically devalued if, through no fault of the dying person, the required line could not be spoken as the curtain fell. The biblical phrase that a tree would lie as it fell (Eccl. 11:3) thus lost its absolute validity, although clever theologians like John Donne hit upon the sophism that the tree could fall only in the direction determined by its lifelong growth: that death and life would necessarily correspond to each other.[34]

It follows that sudden, unprepared death endangers the afterlife of the soul only if it concludes a sinful life. This is what many generations of Lutheran preachers reiterated in their funeral sermons from the seventeenth century on, with sporadic precursors even in the century of the Reformation itself, usually with a reference to St. Augustine's statement in *De doctrina Christiana* that a death preceded by a "good" life could not be considered "bad." Pastors officiating at the funeral would consequently strain to point out that the suddenly deceased parishioner said a prayer shortly before his demise, or that he had demonstrated Christian virtues, of which there are arguably more than the few standard ones that customarily receive good press. Of course, a suitable last word would be preferable even in such cases—the murdered or the drowned, soldiers killed on the battlefield, or burghers felled by a fatal stroke in their sleep. In the various collections of printed funeral sermons housed in the Herzog-August-Bibliothek in Wolfenbüttel, there are some very curious examples of the preachers' recklessly well meant efforts to interpret a last word, dutifully reported even in cases of sudden death, as a

valid equivalent of "I commend my spirit into your hands."
Even the most versatile preacher, however, could not do
much to improve the chances of a woman who died on the
evening of her wedding complaining about "great pain"
(Stolberg Collection, no. 3433; 1651). More conducive to be-
nevolent interpretation was a drowning man's "O God, help"
(Stolberg Collection, no. 3394a; 1604) or even the last gasp of
a fallen officer: "O Lord Jesus! I am shot!" for "there can be no
doubt that Lord Jesus, to whom he complained of his physical
suffering, forthwith took his soul to his bosom and admitted
it to heaven" (Xa 4° 1: 5[2]; 1676). Even the last shriek "O no"
of a woman slain with a log of firewood by her daughter-in-
law could be interpreted imaginatively and purposefully as
that godfearing tranquility of mind which readily accepts
death in the confidence that Jesus will save the soul (Stolberg
Collection, no. 3403; 1684). There is no need for such theological acrobatics in Pastor Johann Caspar Reynacher's funeral
sermon for the twenty-seven parishioners drowned in a Swiss
lake when their boat capsized in a sudden storm. They had
just been to church, and some of the bodies were fished out of
the water still holding their hymnbooks in their hands—
showing for all who were willing to see that this sudden death
was not *mala mors* (Stolberg Collection, nos. 3361–3387; 1732).

Such theological contortions do, however, refer back to the
general view that unprepared death was something to be
feared. This is rubbed in by Hieronymus Weller, for example,
in his book on sudden demise, *Von denen so des gehlingen tods
sterben* (Leipzig, 1549), even though he is, in principle, convinced that "the god-fearing cannot fall out of God's hand"
(unpag.). Sixteenth- to eighteenth-century funeral sermons
abound with descriptions of the horrors of unforeseen death
as exemplified by notorious cases; Valerius Herberger in one
of his many funeral sermons regaled the faithful with no
fewer than forty-eight such unfortunate cases, ranging from
Sophocles to Barbarossa.[32] Such listings, though without the

raised index finger of the Christian moralist, were in fact topoi of classical antiquity, collected not in the spirit of memento mori but primarily for their curiosity value, for instance in Pliny's *Natural History* (Book 7, ch. 54) and, most notably, in Valerius Maximus's *Dictorum factorumque memorabilium libri novem*, which in chapter twelve of its ninth book offers a compendium of "unusual deaths," featuring bizarre cases such as Aeschylus dying after an eagle dropped a turtle on his bald head and Anacreon choking on a grape. First compiled in the first century A.D., it was a steady seller into the seventeenth and eighteenth centuries. As late as the dawn of the Enlightenment, this classical lore was appropriated under preacherly auspices, e.g., by the anonymous *Parentator Tragicus* (Leipzig, 1720), an assortment of twenty-seven funeral sermons occasioned by sudden deaths (p. 79).

This and other instances show, then, that fear of sudden death not only persisted in the seventeenth and eighteenth centuries but continued to be inculcated, even though a less rigorous, more "philanthropic" theology was gaining ground by that time which, typically citing St. Augustine, gave weight to the consideration that a Christian life would foreshadow happiness in the beyond. Both lines of thought—warning and reassurance—are ubiquitous in the funeral sermons that flourished at the time, indicating that unforeseen demise continued to be a matter of concern.

2. On the other hand, there could be concern in the diametrically opposite situation—the impeccably "correct" last word, pronounced loud and clear, could be suspect if it concluded an unquestionably sinful life: did it indicate a sincere change of heart or fear of death, or was it even cynical, calculating lip service, far removed from Pascal's "wager"? Commonsensical doubt is expressed, for example, in the pamphlet *The Trial, Condemnation, & Execution of Richard Patch, for the Murder of Mr. Isaac Blight* . . . (Boston, 1807). The anonymous author re-

ports that when the culprit, who had steadfastly refused to admit the crime, already had his head in the noose, he gestured to indicate that he wanted to speak, and finally confessed his guilt; "most probably, when he found all hopes were vain, he then confessed" (p. 35). A candidate for salvation? The author clearly doubts it. A long time earlier, before the wave of artes moriendi, Dante had had his doubts when he assigned the late repentant, as distinguished from the unrepentant who went straight to hell, not to heaven but to purgatory (see above, p. 161); after all, one could not prove the truthfulness of their contrition.

In the seventeenth and eighteenth centuries, discussion about the sincerity of the last word became more agitated.[36] Primarily it was of course the Protestants in the age of the Reformation who (like the zealous author of the Faust book of 1587, incidentally [ch. 68]) kept slandering or at least suspecting deathbed repentance as mere "Catholic" lip service, as the "rue of Judas" or of Cain—contrition not issuing from true faith but from fear. But even a Catholic Counter-Reformation theologian like Cardinal Bellarmino was very strict and sceptical on this point in his *De arte bene moriendi* of 1620 (book I, ch. 13): nothing short of sincere rue and contrition would do. "*Sincere* rue (*poenitentia vera*)," his Lutheran confrère Nicolaus Haas agrees with him as late as 1700 in *Der getreue Seelenhirte*, "is never late."[37] Nonetheless it was common for Protestants to rail against the Catholic view that the routine last unction "removed the sins"; on the contrary, only a last word issuing from sincere piety and belief could bring about such a change.[38]

So the last word remained suspect and controversial; in effect it could imply the very opposite of what it said. For this reason the notorious sinner's deathbed recantation became a prominent, not to say popular, genre in the seventeenth and eighteenth centuries, playing a considerable role not only in theological but also in literary and public life. The most sensational case was that of the Earl of Rochester, the Restoration libertine. The circumstances of his death aroused widespread interest and controversy. Gilbert Burnet's biography, published in the year of Rochester's death (1680) and devoting five times as many pages to the earl's dying as to his life, became an enormously popular book. It engendered a far-reaching public debate about the effectiveness and theological validity of the change of heart on the deathbed, with feelings continuing to run high on the issue until the late eighteenth century. Could the repentant libertine claim as a model the thief on the cross who had discovered faith in the eleventh hour, or could he not? In other words: Did the thief's case demonstrate an extraordinary act of sovereign grace on which one could by no means *rely*? In the course of the decades, enlightenment and generosity gained ground, also among theologians, who, however, rarely failed to point out the *risk* of repentance so shortly before the gates were closing and the *need* for a Christian life from early on.[39]

A good German example is Johann Jacob Moser's labored preface (dated 1740) to his frequently re-edited collection of accounts of the last hours of criminals, *[Seelige] lezte Stunden einiger dem zeitlichen Tode übergebener Missethäter* (Stuttgart, 1767). He gingerly treads the line between the extreme positions: no, the mere fact of verbal repentance does not necessarily indicate the true contrition—as distinguished from fear—that is a prerequisite for salvation; but yes, it is not at all impossible, indeed more likely than not, that God will bestow his grace on a criminal about to be executed when he turns to his Savior in the spirit of regret and with a change of heart—as did the thief on the cross. Still, Moser tips his hand when he selects only cases that strongly suggest that the culprit is not destined for the flames of hell. But again, he feels obliged to add, in the "new preface" dated Christmas, 1752, that his edifying examples should by no means encourage anyone to commit a capital crime in hopes of dying an edifying death in the state of grace! In eighteenth-century France, as John McManners has observed, a more political consideration came into play as well: the conflict between the clergy and public anticlericalism, which left its conspicuous mark on the Grand Siècle, often came to a head on the deathbed (and, given the dying conventions of the time, this meant that it came to a head virtually in public)—Was there to be explicit genuflection or equally explicit persistence in error? Religious and political loyalty were accordingly put to the test at this irrevocably final and indeed mandatory opportunity to show one's true colors.[40]

3. This widespread convention of ennobling the moment of death as the moment of truth did not, of course, exclude the most disturbing of all possibilities: unbelief steadfastly reaffirming itself in extremis. Everyone was familiar with the terrifying and edifying polemical confrontation of what Jeremy Taylor, in his bestselling eponymous tract, called holy dying and the horrors of the final hour of the unbeliever who panics at the last moment as he sees the gates of hell opening wide to receive his soul (see above, p. 122). Edward Godwin says it all on the title page of his book, *The Death-Bed: A Poem Containing the Joyful Death of a Believer, and the Awful Death of an Unbeliever* (Bristol, 1744); so does John Collett Ryland in *The Death-Bed Terrors of an Infidel: Or, a Modern Freethinker Exemplified in the Last Awful Hours of a Young Gentleman, Who Departed from the Principles of Christianity, and turned Deist. To Which is Added, as a Contrast, the Glorious Salvation of Baron Dyherrn*, who recanted his deism and died a "happy death."[41] But what if the anti-Christian freethinker did not depart this life screaming at his visions of horror, but instead stood by his credo, serenely defiant and confident even in his last words? Deslandes (1712) and G. W. Foote (1886), to mention just two, used their anthologies of the last words of *esprits forts* to round up virtually everybody of rank and name outside the domain of the

Church. When it came time for the most conspicuous philosophical unbelievers of the Age of Reason to speak their last word, the intellectual world waited with bated breath for the moment of truth. All manner of rumors were afloat about the circumstances of Voltaire's demise—he called for the curé, but did he die a Christian?[42] The most sensational death without a change of heart was no doubt David Hume's in 1776.[43] "Le bon David" himself knew what was at stake, as did his circle of like-minded friends. If he panicked into a revocation of his convictions, self-righteous clerics would rejoice and freethinkers would suffer a serious setback, not just in Edinburgh. If he died in a state of serene confidence in the rightness of his chosen path, the "philosophical age," the "siècle des lumières," would be vindicated. Friends and others, standing by his bedside or monitoring the gossip from afar, were waiting tensely. Hume's deathbed had "propaganda value."[44] Not surprisingly, his "philosophical" death—without a last-minute conversion or recantation—brought about a flood of argumentative literature, Christian and otherwise, just as Voltaire's was to do on the eve of the Revolution.

> After the death of Hume both Christians and anti-Christians recognized more clearly than ever before the potential impact of news about the deaths of famous people, and both sides began to compete for that news in a way that may finally have led to the end of the phenomenon.[45]

The last significant test case of this nature was the death of Thomas Paine in 1809—again, contrary to rumors spread by interested parties, it was a victory for enlightened reason; neither recantation nor panic were recorded.[46]

To be sure, in accordance with the principle of the "simultaneity of the non-simultaneous," the artes moriendi maintain an impact of sorts well into the Age of Reason. Nonetheless, the widening of the three circles of thought discussed (the

downplaying of the gravity of sudden death; generosity about
the sincerity of the sinner's last-minute change of heart; steadfastness of the unbeliever on his deathbed) does signal an intellectual sea change, and its relaxing effect becomes unmistakable by the middle of the eighteenth century.[47]

Symptomatic of the changed intellectual climate is the
versified "Guide to Happy and Serene Dying"[48] by the leading German poet of the early Enlightenment, the Hamburg
burgher Barthold Hinrich Brockes. It was published in 1748,
one year after Brockes's death, as an appendix to the ninth
volume of his chef-d'oeuvre, the prosy verse theodicy *Irdisches
Vergnügen in Gott*. All "causes" of fear of death are "demonstrated" here to be irrelevant, and among these products of a
misguided theological imagination there is, most prominently, the doctrine of the artes moriendi, not mentioned by
name, which "makes death the most fearful and horrible experience of all":

> They speak of all eternity. Whether you'll be saved
> Or will be tortured,
> All depends on this one moment.
>
> (P. 571)

Countering such—traditionally honorable—anxiety, Brockes
is confident that he can "prove" (as he puts it in one of his
brief interspersed passages of unabashed prose which make
their point without the charm of poetry, such as it is in his
case) "that one would not even need to fear death with a view
to salvation or damnation and that on that account there was
no need to know the time of death beforehand" (p. 604). And
why not?

> Our death would be shocking, and the most bitter evil,
> Indeed contrary to nature, if, after our life,
> Troubling itself with vanity,
> We had no hope of a better one.
>
> (P. 604)

Even those "ambushed" by the grim reaper "unexpectedly," "in the midst of [their] sins," would have nothing to fear (pp. 612, 614). For, one way or the other, the circumstances of death reflect the will of God—who could not help but mean well (we are in the age of Enlightenment). "So be calm, whoever you may be, and unconcerned about the hour," "So let us be reasonable/ And do what we should do, be decent as long as we live" (pp. 617, 618)—in support of which Brockes quotes Seneca as well as the church fathers. A "good," "willing," "serene," and even "cheerful" death would invariably ensue; or, pressing Hamburg imagery into service: one could be assured that the ship would finally sail into port (p. 620). All the more surprising is the about-face at the book's end: Brockes returns verbatim to the formula of the ars moriendi, hallowed over the centuries: "At the end I commend / My spirit into thy hands" (p. 624). Coming as it does in the wake of Brockes's reflections about the categorical insignificance of the last "point in time" on this earth, such a conclusion cannot even be considered an attempt to secure old-fashioned soul insurance; it is no more than a phrase whose former meaning has been totally devalued.

In effect, then, Brockes's "Art of Dying" of 1748 reads like an anti–ars moriendi. It may serve as a barometer indicating a decisive change of climate that has taken place since the fifteenth century. In light of this reading, a number of other relevant eighteenth-century phenomena may plausibly be seen as further indications that in a hypothetical history of last words, an epoch is coming to an end. They are admittedly heterogeneous phenomena, and yet they point in the same direction: parodies of last words, the dying formula "We shall meet again!" and the last words of leading figures of the French Revolution immortalized as part of a national or even international highbrow folklore.

Just as "Last Word" broadsides were essentially an English genre, parodies of last words—often taking the form of broadsides and thus reminiscent, even typographically, of a familiar sight—are likewise more at home in the English-speaking world than anywhere else. Both genres initially overlap chronologically, as parodies sporadically make their appearance in the seventeenth century; but in the course of the eighteenth century, parodies become ever more plentiful (Pope's series of ludicrous last words in his "Epistle to Lord Cobham" [1733] may even have the makings of a parody of such parodies); still, in sheer numbers, parodies do not catch up with the serious "Last Word" broadsides and chapbooks of the English tradition. These parodies use the convention of last words before execution or on the deathbed primarily for the purpose of political, religious, and social satire, the precise meaning of which escapes the present-day reader more often than not. Occasionally there are even pointed remarks calling attention to the fact that specific features of the traditional English gallows speech are being lampooned. Thematically, there are no limitations: there are parodistic "last words" of Thomas Pride, who signed the death sentence of Charles I (1659?); of the Whore of Babylon (an anti papist pamphlet of 1673); of the Bank of Ireland (1721); of Parliament (1722); of an underweight Queen Anne's guinea (1774?); of retailers crippled by a new tax (1785); of "Sir John Barleycorn," who rails against less-than-conscientious beer brewers (in the year of the French Revolution, oddly enough); of the eighteenth century (1800); of Napoleon (1803!); of a potato merchant who manipulated the market (1824); etc.[49] Straggling behind these English parodies is a rare German one, a broadside entitled *Die letzten Worte eines sterbenden Arbeiters im Spital und dessen Testament* (Vienna, 1848), which rails against political conservatism with the verve of a fighter on the barricades *and* the traditional claim to prophetic powers ("a dying person turns visionary"). France was equally deficient in this area—its only contribution, and a half-hearted one at that, appears to be a parodistic satire dated 1649 on the institution of last words, which has an English topic: *Les Dernières Paroles du roy d'Angleterre* (Charles I).

Like the overwhelming majority of the prose parodies, the far-fewer poetical ones also come from the English-speaking world. Their themes, however, are nonpolitical and rather eccentric, as their titles reveal at first glance: *The Last Sayings of a Mouse Lately Starved in a Cup-Board. As they were Taken, in Short-Hand, by a Zealous Rat-Catcher, who List'ned at the Key-Hole of the Cup-Board Door* (n.p., 1681), "The Last Dying Words of Bonnie Heck, a Famous Grey-Hound in the Shire of Fife" by William Hamilton (ca. 1750), and Robert Burns's well-known poem "The Death and Dying Words of Poor Mailie, the Author's Only Pet Yowe" (1786).

Parodies of last words signal in their way that the centuries-long Christian tradition of the more or less formulaic farewell to life and the corresponding heaven-directed mind-set have been losing their grip in the course of "secularization." A complementary phenomenon is the widespread presence in eighteenth-century literature of a rival formula, which can be seen as the secularized counterpoint to the Christian exit line (which the artes moriendi made obligatory or at least highly desirable) and, at the same time, as a specific, almost parodistic counterpoint to the assurance given to the thief on the cross that he would join the Savior in paradise after death. This is the lovers' dying formula: "We shall meet again!" In one variation or another, but remarkably resistant to textual change, it occurs, for example, in *La Nouvelle Héloise*, in *Werther*, and in *Faust*. As a last word, as the final validation of an all-important love relationship, this formulaic farewell of the dying lover is a sort of cipher of Enlightened belief in a secularized heaven where the perfection vainly hoped for on earth will be achieved.[50]

Since the flourishing of the English gallows speech in the sixteenth and seventeenth centuries, apparently only one other coherent complex of last words has retained a certain currency in the folklore of the educated: the curtain lines of leading figures of the French Revolution and its aftermath. An entire chapter is reserved for them in Claude Aveline's anthology of last words *Les Mots de la fin* (Paris, 1957); Herbert Nette likewise groups them together in his collection of famous farewells to life, *"Hier kann ich doch nicht bleiben"* (Munich, 1983), and understandably they form the most distinct cluster of last words in the first French post-Revolutionary anthology of last words, Léon Thiessé's *Derniers Moments* of 1818. Also, mention of the final utterances of the victims is a sine qua non, and indeed a narrative asset, in any account of the main event in French history, from Carlyle's *French Revolution* of 1837 to Simon Schama's *Citizens* of 1989; even tourist guides will call attention to them because of their anecdotal charm.[51]

Unlike the "Last Speech" or "Death and Dying Words" pamphlets of the Elizabethan and post-Elizabethan ages, the final utterances of victims of the French Revolution typically are not formal Christian *speeches* and summations but succinct remarks, often aphoristic, definitely this-worldly, not infrequently even witty and frivolous or all-too-human and down-to-earth. For example, Marie-Antoinette's poignantly mundane *"Pardonnez-moi"* when she stepped on the executioner's foot, or the alleged last word of Malesherbes, Louis XVI's loyal secretary of the interior, who, stumbling as he ascended the steps to the guillotine, observed to Sanson, the executioner: "A bad omen. A Roman would turn back." Not surprisingly, such remarks made it with flying colors into the lore of "familiar quotations," into the collective memory or the "mythology" of the nation and, to some extent, the world. It is certainly telling that what was apparently the one French attempt at the time to launch into a formal speech in front of the guillotine was drowned out by a roll of drums ordered with revolutionary presence of mind: Louis XVI's pathetically pompous "Frenchmen! I die innocent, posterity will no doubt revenge me, I pardon my enemies . . . "[52]

What follows in this paragraph is a small selection from Aveline's anthology (which, of course, also includes the various famous last words of Danton who in one version, his head on the block, reminds the spectators to take advantage of the last opportunity to look at his face because "it's worth it"): Madame Roland, Goethe's favorite (after offering precedence to a scared fellow victim so that he would be spared the sight of her blood, coaxing the hesitant executioner with the flirtatious reminder that he could not very well deny a lady her last request): "O Liberty! How are you mocked!"; Marie Joseph Chalier, the Jacobin: "Give me my cocarde and attach it to me, for I am dying for liberty"; Charlotte Corday, Marat's assassin, giving Jean Jacques Hauer, the young officer guarding her, a lock of her hair: "Sir, I do not know how to thank you for the trouble you have taken: I can only offer you this, keep it to remember me by"; General Adam Philippe de Custine advising the executioner's assistants that it would be easier to pull his boots off *after* his death; Madame du Barry: "Just one moment, Mr. Executioner! Help! Help!"; General Armand Louis de Gontant-Biron, offering the executioner a glass of wine: "Take it, you do, after all, need courage to do your job"; Camille Desmoulins: "O my poor wife!"; and *her* last word when she was guillotined in her turn a week later: "In a few hours I am going to see my Camille again!"—a variant of "We'll meet again!" which in its way points to the same secularization of the formulaic last word that had been standardized in the realm of Christianity and had maintained its authority unimpaired for several centuries.

This sort of admittedly sketchy survey of historical landmarks may be convincing at first sight. But one should keep in reserve a general reminder that these phases are not chronologically isolated. Christian deathbed conventions survive in the eighteenth century, as funeral sermons reveal (see note 34). Parodies of last words may be found side by side with serious "gallows speeches." The "We shall meet again" mentality was anticipated in the seventeenth century (see note 50). The worldly-wise and witty remarks in view of the French guillotine were "rehearsed" with similarly spirited final bons mots at the time of Queen Elizabeth, her predecessors, and her immediate successors. Thomas More's famous, witty plea for his beard, which had not committed treason, may come to mind, or Anne Boleyn's helpful hint to the executioner that it would be easy to behead her as her neck was very thin, or Sir Walter Raleigh's testing of the blade of the executioner's sword and pronouncing it a severe cure but effective against all ailments, etc. And yet this was the time when the commendation of the soul into the hands of God was routine, as we hear about the death not only of Essex and Mary Stuart, but also of Anne Boleyn.

One may have even more doubts about the logic of history—or more joy in the face of the seemingly inexhaustible variety of last words possible if not in all, then in many, periods—if one looks ahead from the "secularizing" eighteenth century (which encouraged us to posit a historical threshold) to the following periods. Do last words now assume the function of religion, becoming ersatz religion (in a good sense of the word)? Surely there is something to this, as the anthologies of last words discussed earlier suggest. But could one be more specific? Scholarly studies on "Death Sentences" in nineteenth- and twentieth-century literature have as yet been far too selective to allow convincing generalizations about the "intellectual climate."[53] Of course it is easy and tempting to make sweeping claims. It has been stated, for example, and not unexpectedly, that the concept of "dying beautifully" becomes dominant in turn-of-the-century literature: "Decadence . . . is the art of dying beautifully" (Verlaine), with correspondingly beautiful last words; Maeterlinck, d'Annuncio, Claudel, Barrès, Keyserling, Rilke, Hofmannsthal, and even Walter Pater may come to mind.[54] But even if one could document this view, just how "representative" would such a finding be? The critical objections that have been raised against Ariès's concept of a coherent history of styles of dying, objections based on the conviction that the immense variety of the ways of dying, constant over the centuries, cannot be pigeon-holed into neat historical phases, might also be mobilized against the hypothesis of a history of last words, and these objections become particularly persuasive for the years between the end of the eighteenth century and the progressive disappearance of deliberate last words in the wake of the modern "medicalization" of death.

Or so it seems at this point. One could be tempted to abandon all hope for any historical pattern to emerge and to plunge jubilantly into the overwhelming variety of possibilities believed to offer itself, essentially unchanged, everywhere and at all times. But before pleading for the historian's *salto mortale*, one might explore a possible way out of the dilemma—a way that, while acknowledging some degree of multiplicity, would nonetheless allow us to perceive historically changing "dominants" or landmarks that would command respect. Or maybe even two ways out. They can be described here only in the form of questions.

For one thing, doesn't the history of *biography*—from the pious conclusion of saints' lives via the construction of the guiding figure dispensing wisdom on his deathbed all the way to the triumphant debunking of the "hero" through a disappointing last word that "takes back everything"[55]—reveal changes over the centuries in the manner in which last words were seen as a sigillum veri, as a key to the "ruling passion strong in death"? This question gains interest and meaning—even urgency—at the crossroads where typical biographical opposites meet, creating productive tensions and challenges: didactic intention (religious or secular) vs. "realistic" debunking in the manner of Lytton Strachey; literary and artistic "shaping" vs. "scientific" historiographic ambition; factual documentation of a life in its social contexts vs. the exploration of psychic "realities"; grandiose "total vision" in the manner of Stefan George vs. the technique, perfected by Boswell, of making telling details speak.[56]

The other key to a hypothetical history of last words might

be *literary works*, which would, however, have to be examined much more extensively for their thematics of "death sentences" than has been attempted so far.[57] Sceptical prejudgment (that there cannot be a *history* of last words in this terrain) would demonstrate enviable decisiveness, but "anthropological curiosity" would not be satisfied, and it too is not dishonorable or entirely without proven merit.

This essay chose as its starting point Socrates' remark that the unexamined life is not worth living. Would, then, the examined life be worth living? A life aware of itself until the last moment, when it sums up its "worth" in a final word? Last but not least, it is the aura of jocularity not infrequently enveloping last words in our culture that points to the fact that the question may be worth thinking about, no matter how irresistible it may be to cynics. Montaigne thought it worth pondering, not just in general terms, but in a manner that reveals the historical aspect. For so long as only *one* (well-prepared and preferably formulaic) exit line is acceptable and prevalent, Montaigne's reflection about *"various* deaths" and the *different* final words that he would like to collect and study would be meaningless; it would not really have an object on which to focus. But it is precisely this reflection on the various deaths to which Montaigne—who for his part hoped to die not in the traditional way, with normative last words, but while planting cabbages—pays such serious attention. Why? The philosopher, for whom "to philosophize is to learn to die" (*Essais* 1:20), would like to learn from it what at his historical juncture tradition can apparently no longer teach him, and that is not a little: "He who would teach men to die would teach them to live." Others, following Montaigne over the centuries, have had the same expectation—and would have been content with less.

Notes

PREFACE

1. On the controversy about Haller's last words, see Karl S. Guthke, *Das Abenteuer der Literatur* (Bern and Munich, 1981), p. 10.
2. *Jahrbuch der Deutschen Schiller-Gesellschaft* 31 (1987): 162.

CHAPTER 1

LAST WORDS IN EVERYDAY CULTURE

1. Letter to Charlotte von Stein, 8 March 1808.
2. *Boswell's Life of Johnson*, ed. G. B. Hill, rev. L. F. Powell (Oxford, 1934–1950), 2:228.
3. *Lachen und Weinen* (Arnhem, 1941).
4. *Schriften*, vol. 2, pt. 2 (Frankfurt, 1977), pp. 449–450.
5. Hugo von Hofmannsthal, *Der Tor und der Tod*, in *Gedichte und lyrische Dramen*, ed. Herbert Steiner (Stockholm, 1946), pp. 291–292:

> Warum, du Tod,
> Mußt du mich lehren, erst das Leben sehen,
> Nicht wie durch einen Schleier, wach und ganz,—
> Erst, da ich sterbe, spür ich, daß ich bin.

6. See Harriet C. Frazier, "'Like a Liar Gone to Burning Hell': Shakespeare and Dying Declarations," *Comparative Drama* 19 (1985): 166–180; Morris Palmer Tilley, *A Dictionary of the Proverbs in England in the Sixteenth and Seventeenth Centuries* (Ann Arbor, Mich., 1950), p. 434, cites several examples from Shakespeare.
7. Quoted from Thomas B. Harbottle and P. H. Dalbiac, *Dictionary of Quotations (French and Italian)* (London, 1901): "Qui n'a plus qu'un moment à vivre n'a plus rien à dissimuler" (Quinault); "La sagesse est sur les lèvres de ceux qui vont mourir" (Lamartine).
8. *Newsweek*, 28 March 1983, p. 60.
9. Unless otherwise indicated, (supposed) last words have been

taken, throughout the book, from the anthologies discussed in Ch. 4; especially useful among them are those of Le Comte and Nette. Additional sources for the cases cited here: Michael Meyer, *Ibsen* (Garden City, N.Y., 1971) p. 807; Ernst Pawel, *The Nightmare of Reason: A Life of Franz Kafka* (New York, 1984), p. 446; Diderot, *Œuvres complètes*, ed. J. Assézat, vol. 1 (Paris, 1875), p. LVII; sources of last words of Swedish kings: Åke Ohlmarks, *Sista Sucken* (Stockholm, 1970); Robert I. Rotberg, *The Founder: Cecil Rhodes and the Pursuit of Power* (New York, 1988), p. 674; Brian Roberts, *Cecil Rhodes* (New York, 1987), p. 295; source of last words of Frederick William I: Friedrich von Oppeln-Bronowski, *Der Baumeister des preußischen Staates* (Jena, 1934), p. 324 (the statement, as is often the case, is not the dying word it is customarily made out to be, but a remark from one of the last days of the king's life). In the rest of the book, specialized sources of last words will occasionally be cited where this seems desirable.

10. On this "quotational" aspect of the currency of last words, see Richard Macksey, "Last Words: The *Artes Moriendi* and a Transtextual Genre," *Genre* 16 (1983): 493–516. Horst Rüdiger calls attention to a remark of Montherlant's to the effect that for a Frenchman about to be shot it was all but obligatory to shout "Vive la France!" (*Neue Zürcher Zeitung*, 21 October 1971, p. 35). Analogous conventions exist in other countries and situations. See pp. 5, 14, 15. One example is the resistance fighter's "Es lebe Holland!" in Grete Weil's *Tramhalte Beethovenstraat* (Frankfurt, 1963; 1983), p. 128.

11. Gyles Brandreth, *The Last Word* (New York, 1979), p. 6.

12. Edward Le Comte, *Dictionary of Last Words* (New York, 1955), p. vii. For similar statements on the age-old fascination with last words, see Anon., "Exit Lines," *Time*, 17 January 1955, p. 53; Anon., "Last Words," *Every Saturday* 2 (8 September 1866): 276–277; Thomas D. Bedell, "The Tongues of Dying Men," *Reader's Digest* 115 (July 1979): 122–125; Rodger Kamenetz, "Last Words," *North American Review* 269, pt. 2 (1984): 61–63; and Wilhelm Waetzoldt, "Die letzten Worte," in *Schöpferische Phantasie* (Wiesbaden, 1947), pp. 84–87.

13. Carlos Fuentes, *The Old Gringo* (New York, 1985), p. 92.

14. This appears in Jörg von Uthmann's *Paris für Fortgeschrittene* (Hamburg, 1981), p. 117.

15. January-February 1990, p. 80. Cp. Donald Spoto, *Laurence Olivier* (London, 1991), p. 353.

16. *Newsweek*, 28 May 1990, p. 17. See also *Newsweek*, 24 February 1992, p. 21: " 'I'd like to thank my family for loving me and taking care of me. And the rest of the world can kiss my ass.' The last words of convicted killer Johnny Frank Garrett, who was executed last week in Texas for killing a Catholic nun in 1981." *Newsweek*, 4 May 1991, p. 21.

17. New York, 1987.

18. 22 August 1988, p. 36; 7 January 1985, p. 19.

19. 27 October 1988, p. 83.

20. Vol. 16 (1983): 512, 516.

21. Ohlmarks, *Sista Sucken*, p. 93. See also Stith Thompson, *Motif-Index of Folk-Literature*, vol. 2 (Bloomington, Ind., 1956), D 1715; Tilley, *Dictionary of Proverbs*, p. 434: "Dying Men speak true (prophesy)"; *Handwörterbuch des deutschen Aberglaubens*, ed. E. Hoffmann-Krayer, vol. 8 (1936–1937), p. 454: "The dying also have the gift of prophesy. Their words have power." Antiquity had a technical term for it: *morientium vaticinatio*. Examples from antiquity and the Bible are cited in H. Martensen-Larsen, *An der Pforte des Todes*, 2d ed. (Berlin, [1931]), p. 130. See also below, Ch. 5, note 6.

22. Wolfgang Hildesheimer, *Mozart*, tr. Marion Faber (New York, 1982), p. 359.

23. See August Stahl, "Rilkes Rede über den Tod," in *Perspektiven des Todes*, ed. Reiner Marx and Gerhard Stebner (Heidelberg, 1990), pp. 91–93.

24. L. L. Schücking, *Die Familie im Puritanismus* (Leipzig and Berlin, 1929), p. 184. See also above, p. 96. On the significance of the dying scene in cultural history from the late Middle Ages to the seventeenth century, see Robert Kastenbaum, "Deathbed Scenes," in *Encyclopedia of Death*, ed. Robert Kastenbaum and Beatrice Kastenbaum (Phoenix, Ariz.: Oryx Press, 1989), pp. 97–101.

25. For confirmation by a medical authority, see *The Dying Patient*, ed. Orville G. Brim Jr. (New York, 1970), p. xv. See also Nina Auerbach, "Death Scenes," in *Private Theatricals: The Lives of the Victorians* (Cambridge, Mass., 1990); Michael Wheeler, *Death and the Future Life in Victorian Literature and Theology* (Cambridge, England, 1990); John R. Reed, "Deathbeds," in *Victorian Conventions* (Athens: Ohio University Press, 1975); Margarete Holubetz, "Death-Bed Scenes in Victorian Fiction," *English Studies* 67 (1986): 14–35; Elisabeth Jay, *The Religion of the Heart: Anglican Evangelicalism and the Nineteenth-Century*

Novel (Oxford, 1979), pp. 154–168; R. Cecil, "Holy Dying: Evangelical Attitudes to Death," *History Today* 32, no. 8 (August 1982): 30–34.

26. Willa Cather, *Death Comes for the Archbishop* (New York, 1927), pp. 172–173.

27. Jay, *Religion of the Heart*, p. 159.

28. London, 1838. See also Matthew Poole, *His Late Sayings, a Little Before his Death, Concerning the Most Material Points of the Popish Party, Charged Against the Protestants* (West-Smithfield, 1679); John McManners, *Death and the Enlightenment* (Oxford, 1981), p. 238.

29. *Nation*, 24 September 1973, p. 282.

30. Claude Aveline, *Les Mots de la fin* (Paris, 1957), p. 162: "La phrase la plus banale devient considérable quand rien au monde ni en soi- même n'est plus assez fort pour qu'une autre la suive. Dans la perspective de chaque être, qui n'a pas tout dit n'a rien dit."

31. *Fragments d'un discours amoureux* (Paris, 1977), pp. 247–248: "C'est le dernier coup de dés qui compte. . . . La victoire est à qui capturera ce petit animal, dont la possession assurera la toute-puissance: la dernière réplique. . . . Qu'est-ce qu'un héros? Celui qui a la dernière replique. Voit-on un héros qui ne parlerait pas avant de mourir?"

32. 22 February 1988, p. 63, on Paul M. Kennedy's *Rise and Fall of Great Powers* (New York, 1987); see Heinrich Drimmel, *Franz von Österreich* (Vienna, 1952), p. 324.

33. *New York Times Book Review*, 22 May 1988, p. 43, quoting from Janet Flanner's account in the *New Yorker* (1932), reprinted in her book *Paris Was Yesterday* (New York, 1972; 1988), p. 83.

34. 31 August 1988, p. 20. Similar cases: "Crash Tape Tells of Contacts With Heinz Plane and Copter," *New York Times*, 24 April 1991, p. A22; "Last Words of Challenger Crew," *Weekly World News*, 5 February 1991, front page.

35. E. J. Gold, *The Lazy Man's Guide to Death and Dying* (Nevada City, Calif., 1983), p. 2.

36. Nietzsche, *Fröhliche Wissenschaft*, no. 36; Willibald Schmidt, *De ultimis morientium verbis* (diss., Marburg, 1914); see also the last words of Jacob and Moses: 1 Moses 49; 5 Moses 33. See also above, p. 157.

37. Vallee's last words, "You know how I love a party," were printed in the *Washington Post*, 5 July 1986, p. B6.

38. 29 October 1990, p. 80.

39. 12 February 1990, p. 88.

40. *Dreiser-Mencken Letters*, ed. Thomas P. Riggio (Philadelphia, 1986), 2: 450–451; see also below, Ch. 5, note 55. Another curious case: When Flaubert died in 1880, newspapers stated that his last words had been about Avenue d'Eylan where Victor Hugo lived, while Maupassant understood Flaubert's servant to have reported "Hellot" (a Rouen physician) to be his final word, according to Herbert Lottman, *Flaubert* (Boston, 1989), p. 335.

41. 20 April 1988, p. 32.

42. 21 September 1987, p. 37. See also "Officer's Last Words Recalled at Murder Trial," *New York Times*, 16 September 1990, Metropolitan section, p. 43; news stories in the *Boston Globe*, 3 December 1989, p. 12, and 14 December 1989, p. 12. Andy Warhol satirized the convention in his drawing "Journal American," in *Andy Warhol: Death and Disasters. The Menil Collection* (Houston, 1988), p. 13.

43. 31 May 1991, p. 15.

44. Vol. 20, no. 9 (1990): 81.

45. *The Citizen Kane Book* (Boston, 1971); quotation on p. 123 (from the script). Other films that come to mind include *Drowning by Numbers*, *Miller's Crossing*, *Harold and Maude*, and *My Own Private Idaho*.

46. *Boston Globe*, 23 July 1989.

47. Jim Davis, *Garfield Stepping Out* (Melbourne, 1985).

48. Matt Groening, *Work Is Hell* (New York, 1986).

49. Santa Barbara, 1985.

50. 1991, no. 3:10.

51. "Some Passing Remarks on Some Passing Remarks," in Fadiman, *Party of One* (Cleveland, 1955), p. 466 (originally in *Holiday*, November 1952); see also Fadiman's foreword to Barnaby Conrad, *Famous Last Words* (New York, 1961), p. 7.

52. 17 July 1981, p. 814.

53. *National Review*, 14 June 1985, p. 50.

54. I found these contests following up a hint given by Fadiman (in Conrad, *Famous Last Words*, p. 14). *New Statesman*, 27 October 1934; 25 March 1939; 8 August 1942 (animals); 26 February 1944.

55. 11 October 1987, p. 27. See also "The Quiz," *New York Times*, 8 April 1990, Education section, pp. 24–25, 60.

56. Ich würde gern wissen, was man im nächsten Jahrtausend über den Tod und die 'letzten Worte' Heideggers und seiner Anhänger berichten wird, und hielte einen Wettbewerb für unbedenklich, der Vorschläge an die Tradition weiterzureichen hätte.

Ich nähme es gern aus privater Indiskretion, habe es aber nicht. Dann hieße es: Was kann einer, den die Existentialanalytik ebenso getroffen hat wie die Frage nach dem 'Wesen des Grundes', zum Schluß noch gesagt haben? Im günstigsten Fall von Evidenz: Was muß er gesagt haben? Etwa: *Kein Grund mehr zur Sorge. (Die Sorge geht über den Fluß* [Frankfurt, 1987], p. 222)

57. See above, note 12; see also Ch. 4.

58. E.g., Karl Petit, *Dictionnaire des citations du monde entier* (Verviers, 1960; 3d ed., 1984), pp. 276–277; Burton E. Stevenson, *Home Book of Quotations* (New York, 1937), pp. 413–417; Ebenezer Cobham Brewer, *Dictionary of Phrase and Fable* (1870; London, 1971), pp. 355–357; Gorton Carruth and Eugene Ehrlich, *The Harper Book of American Quotations* (New York, 1988), pp. 323–325. See also the index ("Last Words") in Walter Fogg, *One Thousand Sayings of History* (Boston, 1929), and George Seldes, *The Great Thoughts* (New York, 1985). Gilles Henry, *Dictionnaire des phrases qui on fait l'histoire* (Paris, 1991), ch. 13: "Le Mot de la fin."

59. *Library Review* 24 (1974): 255.

60. Fourth ed., New York, 1981, p. 374.

61. *The Last Word* (New York, 1986).

62. In *Perspektiven des Todes*, pp. 113–114.

63. Toronto, 1985, pp. 147–148, 155.

64. New York, 1989, 414.

65. London, 1986, pp. 152–153.

66. See also below, note 74. All these cases can be verified by browsing in the catalogue of any major library.

67. 8 September 1866, p. 276.

68. Thomas Finkenstaedt, "Galgenliteratur: Zur Auffassung des Todes im England des 16. und 17. Jahrhunderts," *Deutsche Vierteljahrsschrift für Literaturwissenschaft und Geistesgeschichte* 34 (1960): 527–553; Lincoln B. Faller, *Turned to Account* (Cambridge, England, 1987). See also Chs. 4 and 5.

69. Johannes C. Sacher, *[Hyazinth] Bayers letzte Worte vor und während dem Hingange zur Richtstätte* (Liestal, 1851).

70. See Ch. 4.

71. *A Collection of Scarce and Valuable Tracts* . . ., 2d ed. (London, 1810), 4:254–260.

72. William Waller, *The Tragical History of Jetzer* (London, 1679).

73. Or: "Monsieur, je vous demande excuse, je ne l'ai pas fait exprès." This anecdote does not go back to a written or oral statement by the executioner, Sanson; hence it is of doubtful authenticity. See G. Lenotre, *La Guillotine et les exécuteurs des arrêts criminels pendant la Révolution* (Paris, 1893), p. 166. See above, pp. 185–187, and Aveline, *Les Mots de la fin*, pp. 41–47.

74. Byron E. Eshelman, *Death Row Chaplain* (Englewood Cliffs, N.J., 1962), e.g., p. 26; August Mencken, *By the Neck* (New York, 1942). See also Clinton T. Duffy, *88 Men and 2 Women* (Garden City, N.Y., 1962). On 13 January 1928, the "extra edition" of the New York *Daily News* featured on its front page a photo of Ruth Snyder's execution in the electric chair: " 'Father, forgive them, for they don't know what they are doing' were Ruth's last words" (Carl Glassman, *Hocus Focus* [New York and London, 1976], p. 26). Books: e.g., Eduardo Molina Fajardo, *Los últimos días de García Lorca* (Barcelona, 1983). Anthologies: Leon Prochnik, *Endings: Death, Glorious and Otherwise, As Faced by Ten Outstanding Figures of Our Time* (New York, 1980); Homer F. Cunningham, *The Presidents' Last Year* (Jefferson, N.C., 1989); as a rule, last words are reported in these "case histories."

75. Ira Bruce Nadel, *Biography: Fiction, Fact and Form* (New York, 1984), esp. pp. 181–182. See also Desmond MacCarthy's definition of the biographer as "an artist who is on oath" (*Memories* [London, 1953], p. 32). See my essay "Life from the End: Last Words in Narrative Biography," in *Reading Stories*, ed. Raymond A. Prier (Albany, N.Y., 1993).

76. Herbert Nette, *"Hier kann ich doch nicht bleiben": Eine Sammlung letzter Worte* (Munich, 1983), p. 10; Aveline, *Les Mots de la fin*, p. 162; Donald A. Stauffer, *The Art of Biography in Eighteenth-Century England* (Oxford, 1941), pp. 515–517: Christian biographies, Stauffer claims, are the exception, so much so that life fades into insignificance compared with the dignity of death. This is an overstatement; Christian

biographies would seem to be the rule rather than the exception as far as attention to last words is concerned. Biography would be hard put to do without them. This may explain why so often in the history of "life writing" last words have in fact been invented (see Brian O'Kill, *Exit Lines* [Harlow, Essex, 1986], p. vii). E. M. Forster, on the other hand, came out strongly against attributing biographical significance to last words: "The *end* is not of supreme importance in life. We do not judge a man by the words he gasps on his death bed" (*Albergo Empedocle and Other Writings* [New York, 1971], p. 134); see also Garrett Stewart, *Death Sentences: Styles of Dying in British Fiction* (Cambridge, Mass., 1984), ch. 5; and Hildesheimer, *Mozart*, p. 359.

77. Michael Holroyd, *Lytton Strachey: A Critical Biography*, vol. 2 (London, 1968), p. 391; see also p. 431. In Strachey's biography of Victoria, however, we are not treated to actual last words but to a fictive stream of consciousness at the point of death.

78. *Boswell's Life of Johnson*, ed. Hill, 3:192.

79. Holroyd, *Lytton Strachey*, 2:709.

80. Wilson, *Tolstoy* (London, 1988), esp. p. 57.

81. Gerhart Pohl, *Gerhart Hauptman and Silesia* (Grand Forks, N.D., 1962), p. 67.

82. Van Wyck Brooks, *Scenes and Portraits* (New York, 1954), p. 188.

83. *The Development of English Biography* (London, 1959), pp. 141–142.

84. No. 349; 1712.

85. The most useful observations on this subject are in A.O.J. Cockshut, *Truth to Life: The Art of Biography in the Nineteenth Century* (London, 1974), ch. 3.

86. *Harvard University Gazette*, 22 April 1988, p. 6.

87. Hannah Pakula, *The Last Romantic: A Biography of Queen Marie of Roumania* (London, 1985), p. 182. Queen Elisabeth died on 2 March 1916.

88. Lael Tucker Wertenbaker, *Death of a Man* (New York, 1957), p. 177.

89. Letter from Houghton to me.

90. Robert G. Walker, "Public Death in the Eighteenth Century," *Research Studies of the State College of Washington* 48 (1980): 11–24; "Rochester and the Issue of Deathbed Repentance in Restoration

and Eighteenth-Century England," *South Atlantic Review* 47 (1982): 21–37.

91. Das letzte Wort eines Sterbenden: Macht kein Wesens davon und haltet es nicht etwa heilig. Denn das letzte Wort ist nicht mehr sein eigenes Wort; es ist zur Hälfte schon das Hauchen aus einem anderen Zustand, der nichts mit Euch und Eurem Leben zu schaffen hat. Das letzte Wort eines Sterbenden hat noch nie jemand verstanden. Und noch nie jemand gehört. Aber dennoch hat es schon mehr Unheil angerichtet als die Worte Lebender. Und hütet Euch bei Menschen, die Ihr schätzt und hochachtet, ihr letztes Wort zu vernehmen! Es kann ihre ganze Lebensweisheit mit einer Silbe umwerfen und Ihr steht hülflos da. Das letzte Wort eines Sterbenden ist noch weniger wichtig als das eines Mannes, der sinnlos betrunken ist. (*Der Ziegelbrenner* 2, no. 3 [1918]: 51)

92. Mark Twain, *The Curious Republic of Gondour* (New York, 1919), pp. 132–133, 135–136. Similar sentiments will be quoted in Ch. 4. See also Herder's *Ossian* essay: "Impersonal, indistinct speech as in the final mental confusion of the dying" (*Sämmtliche Werke*, ed. B. Suphan, vol. 5 [Berlin, 1891], p. 182). Karl Marx is said to have remarked that last words are for fools who had had nothing to say (Macksey, "Last Words," p. 514).

93. *The Writings of Mark Twain*, Definitive Edition, vol. 9 (New York, 1923), pp. 51, 60. See also "The Story of the Good Little Boy" (1870), a grotesque short story about missing the opportunity to pronounce well-thought-out last words designed to be the triumphant culmination of a virtuous life.

94. Chambers's *Encyclopædia*, vol. 3 (London and Edinburgh, 1878), p. 722.

95. See S. S. Peloubet, *A Collection of Legal Maxims in Law and Equity* (New York, 1884; Littleton, Colo., 1985), p. 181. The admission of "dying declarations" as evidence in certain types of cases, still prevalent today, is based on the view that a Christian would not tell a lie in extremis, as he would soon have to face his Maker and his judge. This raises the question of the justifiability of the practice when it is the dying declaration of a non-Christian whose religion does not include

a doctrine of a similar judgment in the beyond—all the more so, as in the case of nominal Christians there is no inquiry into whether they in fact believe in such a judgment and punishment in the afterlife. See M. S. Tosswill, "Religious Belief in Dying Declarations," *New Law Journal* 131 (11 June 1981): 617–618; P. Brazil, "A Matter of Theology," *Australian Law Journal* 34 (24 November 1960): 195–199.

96. On the *artes moriendi*, see Ch. 5, pp. 161–168. Ferdinandus Jacobus van Ingen, *Vanitas und Memento mori in der deutschen Barocklyrik* (Groningen, 1966), pp. 120–130.

97. Walther Rehm, *Der Todesgedanke in der deutschen Dichtung vom Mittelalter bis zur Romantik* (Halle, 1928), pp. 150–153.

98. Rudolf Böhm, *Wesen und Funktion der Sterberede im elisabethanischen Drama* (Hamburg, 1964); Theodore Spencer, *Death and Elizabethan Tragedy* (Cambridge, Mass., 1936).

99. Graham Greene, "The Last Word," in *The Last Word* (London, 1990).

100. *Death-Scene of an Inebriate* (Philadelphia, ca. 1860).

101. *The Dying Sailor: Or, the Victim of Parental Neglect*, ed. Daniel P. Kidder (New York, 1850).

102. Anon., *The Dying Words of Ockanickon* (London, 1682).

103. Juan León Mera, *Últimos momentos de Bolívar* (Quito, 1883).

104. Leone Fortis, *Le ultime ore di Camoens* (Padua, 1854).

105. Peretti, *Ultimi momenti del Padre Ugo Bassi, fucilato dagli Austriaci in Bologna* (Florence, 1873).

106. 23 April 1973, p. 93; see Paul Gambaccini, *Paul McCartney in His Own Words* (New York, 1976), p. 79. I have also been told about a vignette featuring a last word on Ice Cube's rap album *Amerikkka's Most Wanted*.

107. Allen B. Skei, "'Dulces exuviae': Renaissance Settings of Dido's Last Words," *Music Review* 37 (1976): 77–91.

108. Ch. 45; see also Njals Saga, ch. 77; Egils Saga, ch. 22; Gisli Saga, ch. 13.

109. New York, 1946, p. 103.

110. Bernard Malamud, *A New Life* (New York, 1961), p. 304. I owe this gem to Macksey's "Last Words."

111. *The Homecoming* (New York, 1966), p. 39; *Loot* (New York, 1967), p. 64; also Sterne, *Tristram Shandy*, book 5, chs. 3–4.

112. Garden City, N.Y., 1944, p. 197.

113. *Love Story* (New York, 1970), p. 170; Kafka, *Gesammelte Schriften*, vol. 1 (New York, 1946), p. 240.

114. David Marr, *Patrick White* (London, 1991), p. 588.

115. Patrick White, *The Twyborn Affair* (London, 1979), p. 126.

116. Vladimir Nobokov, *Speak, Memory* (New York: Paragon Books, 1979), p. 68.

117. Ralph Ellison, *Invisible Man* (New York, 1952), p. 13.

118. Joseph Heller, *Picture This* (New York, 1988), esp. ch. 34.

119. Johanna Gilhof, "Wie man in der norddeutschen Literatur stirbt," *Niedersachsen* 13 (1907–1908): 359–361.

120. 25 November 1991, p. 56.

121. Ed. Ross C. Murfin (New York: St. Martin's Press, 1989), pp. 85, 93.

122. Quotations are from *The Complete Works*, ed. Stanley Wells and Gary Taylor (Oxford: Clarendon, 1986).

123. On the significance of the last word in the *ars moriendi*, see above, pp. 161–168.

124. Thomas Finkenstaedt, "Galgenliteratur," p. 355. See above, pp. 19, 168–170.

125. See the citation from the 1679 *Last Speeches of the Five Notorious Traitors* . . . above, p. 169.

126. Frazier, "'Like a Liar Gone to Burning Hell,'" esp. pp. 166–170. See above, pp. 27–28.

127. See Tosswill, "Religious Belief in Dying Declarations," and Brazil, "A Matter of Theology."

128. T. F. Thiselton Dyer, *Folk Lore of Shakespeare* (London, n.d. [c. 1883]), pp. 340–341; Tilley, *Dictionary of Proverbs*, p. 434.

129. A survey of the many ways of dying is Martin Spevack's "Art of Dying in Shakespeare," *Jahrbuch der Deutschen-Shakespeare-Gesellschaft West* (1989), pp. 169–173. On the cult of the death scene in Elizabethan drama see, above all, Spencer, *Death and Elizabethan Tragedy*. Harry C. Bauer's "Shakespeare's Last Words," *Library Review* 24 (1974): 255–261, is an uncritical listing (except for Bauer's claim that he is impressed by Shakespeare's "realism"). Two recent books have no bearing on my subject: Walter C. Foreman Jr., *The Music of the Close: The Final Scenes of Shakespeare's Tragedies* (Lexington, Ken., 1978); Robert F. Willson Jr., *Shakespeare's Reflexive Endings* (Dyfed, Wales, 1990).

130. A telling detail: When Luther died, his enemies could think of

no better way to discredit him than to float the rumor that he had been found dead in his bed. See above, p. 173.

131. For an unexpected confirmation, see Botho Strauß above, pp. 65–66.

132. As a curiosity one might mention that Julius Caesar's last words, familiar to everyone in the form of "Et tu, Brute," are most likely a coinage of Shakespeare's. See O'Kill's *Exit Lines*, p. 23.

133. Hugo von Hofmannsthal, *Elektra*, in *Dramen*, vol. 2, ed. Herbert Steiner (Frankfurt, 1954), p. 41.

134. Frazier, who points out the irony of the "futility of Edmund's deathbed truthfulness" in this scene, sees Lear dying "of the grief of knowing 'She's dead as earth' " ("'Like a Liar Gone to Burning Hell,'" p. 172).

135. Frazier, fixated on the pragmatic and legalistic aspect of last words rather than the powerful *ars moriendi* tradition, misses the point in an otherwise perceptive reading when she concludes that Shakespeare wished "to subject to ironic contemplation . . . a superstitious [!] belief of his day" in posing the question of whether Desdemona should indeed go to hell. Beside the point is her general conclusion: "Shakespeare's intention is surely to qualify the Renaissance proverb [!] that the dying speak the truth through Desdemona's final words" ("'Like a Liar Gone to Burning Hell,'" pp. 172–176).

136. See esp. *Mirrors of Mortality: Studies in the Social History of Death*, ed. Joachim Whaley (London, 1981), pp. 8–10 (Whaley), and pp. 117–121, 129 (John McManners); Werner Friedrich Kümmel, "Der sanfte und selige Tod," *Leichenpredigten als Quelle historischer Wissenschaften*, ed. Rudolf Lenz, vol. 3 (Marburg, 1984), pp. 199–226, esp. pp. 199–200; Philippe Ariès, *The Hour of Our Death* (New York, 1982), pp. 297–315.

CHAPTER 2
WHY THE INTEREST IN LAST WORDS?

1. *Time*, 25 July 1988, p. 17. "First words" belong with anecdotes of childhood, whose biographical value is inversely proportionate to their charm.

2. Quoted from Daniel P. Kidder, *The Dying Hours of Good and Bad*

Men Contrasted (New York, 1848; 1853), preface. Sharpin (see p. 119) makes a similar point. On Addison, see above, p. 154.

3. What follows is further supported by the introductions to anthologies of last words discussed, with special attention to this aspect, in Ch. 4, as well as by a few essays for the general reader about the convention of the last word, though these hardly go beyond listings of last words; in addition to the articles cited in Ch. 1, note 12, they are: Anon., "Last Words of Poets," *Talks and Tales Magazine*, November 1899, pp. 30–32; Lance Morrow, "A Dying Art: The Classy Exit Line," *Time*, 16 January 1984, p. 76; E. V. Lucas, "Last Words," in *Luck of the Year* (New York, 1923), pp. 180–184; Fadiman, *Party of One* (Cleveland, 1955), p. 466 (originally in *Holiday*, November 1952); see also Fadiman's foreword to Barnaby Conrad, *Famous Last Words* (New York, 1961), p. 7; Charles D. Stewart, "The Art of Dying," in *Fellow Creatures* (Boston, 1935), pp. 268–278; Anon., "Exit Lines," *Time*, 17 January 1955, p. 53; Anon., "Last Words," *Musical America*, December 1954, p. 9; James Lindsay, "Last Words," *The Outlook*, 14 April 1928, pp. 470–471; Rolf Michaelis, "Wörterbuch des Todes," *Die Zeit*, 6 January 1984, p. 36.

4. On Victorian accounts, see R. Cecil, "Holy Dying: Evangelical Attitudes to Death," *History Today* 32, no. 8 (August 1982): 30–34; Hugo von Hofmannsthal, *Elektra*, in *Dramen*, vol. 2, ed. Herbert Steiner (Frankfurt, 1954), p. 41.

5. The quote, by Horst Rüdiger, appeared on the back cover of Nette, *"Hier kann ich doch nicht bleiben": Eine Sammlung letzter Worte* (Munich, 1983); it was first published in *Neue Zürcher Zeitung*, 21 October 1971, p. 35.

6. Octavio Paz, "The Day of the Dead," in *The Labyrinth of Solitude* (New York, 1961), p. 54.

7. Quoted from Edward Le Comte, *Dictionary of Last Words* (New York, 1955), p. viii.

8. Goethe, *Dichtung und Wahrheit*, Hamburg edition, vol. 9, p. 9; Weimar edition, pt. 4, vol. 23, p. 313.

9. Thomas Mann, *Adel des Geistes*, Stockholm edition (Frankfurt, 1955), p. 127.

10. Arthur and Barbara Gelb, *O'Neill* (New York, 1962), p. 939.

11. 6 January 1984, p. 36, by Rolf Michaelis.

12. See, e.g., Thomas M. Kettle, "On Saying Good-Bye," in *The*

Day's Burden (Dublin, 1918), p. 105; Jay Weiss, "Last Words," *The Humanist* 36, no.6 (1976): 27–29; Morrow, "A Dying Art: The Classy Exit Line," p. 76. Earlier examples: *Spectator*, no. 153 (1711; Steele) and no. 349 (1712; Addison).

13. See Kenneth A. Chandler, "Three Processes of Dying and Their Behavioral Effects," *Journal of Consulting Psychology* 29 (1965): 296–301; Lyn H. Lofland, *The Craft of Dying: The Modern Face of Death* (Beverly Hills and London, 1979); Philippe Ariès, *L'Homme devant la mort* (Paris, 1977). In the rare cases of a physician's report on last words, nothing of significance seems to turn up; see René Burnand, "L'Homme devant la mort," *Concours médical*, October 1959, pp. 4113–4118. The hospice movement has changed the situation somewhat in recent years; see Elisabeth Kübler-Ross, *On Death and Dying* (New York, 1968).

14. Richard Curle, *Joseph Conrad's Last Day* (London, 1924), pp. 33–34.

15. "Die Spur von meinen Erdetagen nicht in Äonen untergeht."

16. Robert Jay Lifton, *The Broken Connection: On Death and the Continuity of Life* (New York, 1979), p. 277; see also Marguérite Yourcenar, *Mishima: A Vision of the Void* (Henley-on-Thames, 1986), p. 143. On Mishima's final speech and the circumstances of his death, see John Nathan, *Mishima: A Biography* (Boston, 1974), pp. 278–281; on the figures of Old Norse sagas, see Lars Lönnroth, "Hjalmar's Death-Song and the Delivery of Eddic Poetry," *Speculum* 46 (1971): 1–20.

17. New York, 1966, p. 220. I owe this quotation to John S. Dunne, *Time and Myth* (Garden City, N.Y., 1973), p. 5.

18.   ¿Sólo así he de irme?
      ¿Como las flores que perecieron?
      ¿Nada quedará en mi nombre?
      ¿Nada de mi fama aquí en la tierra?
      ¡Al menos flores, al menos cantos!

                    (*Cantos y crónicas del México antiguo*, ed.
                    M. León-Portilla [Madrid, 1986], p. 154)

19. See *Symposion*, 209.

20. Heneage Ogilvie, *No Miracles Among Friends* (London, 1959), p. 164.

21. Theodore Spencer, *Death and Elizabethan Tragedy* (Cambridge, Mass., 1936), pp. 22–24; Carl Burckhardt, *Die Kultur der Renaissance in Italien*, sect. 2, ch. 3 ("Der moderne Ruhm").

22. R. C. Finucane, "Sacred Corpse, Profane Carrion: Social Ideals and Death Rituals in the Later Middle Ages," in *Mirrors of Mortality: Studies in the Social History of Death*, ed. Joachim Whaley (London, 1981), p. 51.

23. On Bergson, see Garrett Stewart, *Death Sentences: Styles of Dying in British Fiction* (Cambridge, Mass., 1984), p. 370 n. 35. On reports of physicians on last words, see above, note 13. On the "panoramic vision" (which is also reported of falling mountaineers) there are many remarks, but no detailed summaries, in the psychological literature; see, e.g., Carol Zaleski, *Otherworld Journeys* (Oxford, 1987), pp. 128–129; Hermann Nothnagel, *Das Sterben*, 2d ed. (Vienna, 1908), pp. 40–41; R.C.A. Hunter, "On the Experience of Nearly Dying," *American Journal of Psychiatry* 124 (1967): 84–88; Russell Noyes Jr., "The Experience of Dying," *Psychiatry* 35 (1972): 178–179. The extensive literature on other visions of the dying is incorporated into Zaleski's study.

24. *Dichtungen und Schriften*, ed. Friedhelm Kemp (Munich, 1956), p. 853. Also quoted in Stewart's *Dying Sentences*.

25. Charles J. Thurmond, "Last Thoughts before Drowning," *Journal of Abnormal and Social Psychology* 38, Clinical Supplement (1943): 165–184. For the banality of the "last" thoughts of the drowning, of falling mountaineers, etc., see also Gwynne Nettler, "The Quality of Crisis," *Psychology Today* (April 1985): 54–55.

26. *The Savage God* (London, 1971), pp. 234–235.

27. Boswell quoted Johnson as saying, "The act of dying is not of importance" and "It matters not how a man dies," in *Boswell's Life of Johnson*, ed. G. B. Hill, rev. L. F. Powell, (Oxford, 1934–1950), 2:106–107.

28. See William Fletcher Barrett, *Death-Bed Visions* (London, 1926); Raymond A. Moody Jr., *Life after Life* (Atlanta, 1975); and Zaleski, *Otherworld Journeys*.

29. Goethe, *Maximen und Reflexionen*, Hamburg edition, vol. 12, p. 415:

Madame Roland, auf dem Blutgerüste, verlangte Schreibzeug, um die ganz besonderen Gedanken aufzuschreiben, die ihr auf dem letzten

Wege vorgeschwebt. Schade, daß man ihr's versagte; denn am Ende des Lebens gehen dem gefaßten Geiste Gedanken auf, bisher undenkbare; sie sind wie selige Dämonen, die sich auf den Gipfel der Vergangenheit glänzend niederlassen.

30. Herman Melville, *Moby Dick* (New York, 1952), p. 473 (ch. 110).

31. Kenneth Burke, "Thanatopsis for Critics: A Brief Thesaurus of Deaths and Dying," *Essays in Criticism* 2 (1952): 369–375; Robert Detweiler, "The Moment of Death in Modern Fiction," *Contemporary Literature* 13 (1972): 269–294.

32. "The Closing Hours," in Herbert Spencer, *Facts and Comments* (New York, 1902), pp. 95–96.

33. 1642, pt. 2, sect. 11. I owe this quotation to Edward Le Comte.

34. In *The Meaning of Death*, ed. Herman Feifel (New York, 1959), p. 237.

35. Edward Young, *Night Thoughts* (London, 1742–1745), book II, line 639.

36. "Treatment of the Dying Person," in *The Meaning of Death*, ed. Feifel, p. 252.

37. 21 February 1984, p. 16.

38. K. R. Eissler, *The Psychiatrist and the Dying Patient* (New York, 1955), pp. 51, 263.

39. See Heidegger, *Sein und Zeit* (Tübingen, 1957), p. 240.

40. Grand Rapids, Mich., 1969, p. 12.

41. Karl Lehmann, *Der Tod bei Heidegger und Jaspers* (diss., Heidelberg, 1938), p. 39: "Angesichts des Todes entspringt Existenz aus ihrer eigentlichen Tiefe zu ihrer wesentlichen Möglichkeit." See also *Death: The Final Stage of Growth*, ed. E. Kübler-Ross (Englewood Cliffs, N.J., 1975); Lofland, *The Craft of Dying*, pp. 96–100; and Noyes, "Experience of Dying," pp. 182–183.

42. New York, 1927, p. 172. This quotation comes from Frederick J. Hoffmann, "Mortality and Modern Literature," in *The Meaning of Death*, ed. Feifel, p. 154.

43. *Max and the Cats* (New York, 1990), p. 15. The original, *Max Os Felinos*, appeared in 1981.

44. Munich, 1981, p. 55: "die allmächtige Kraft dessen, was ein Mann zuletzt gesagt hat . . . ewig . . ." Karl Corino capitalized on the aura of the last word when he chose *Lauter letzte Worte* as the title for

the collected poems of Dieter Leisegang, who committed suicide after a long illness (Frankfurt, 1980).

45. *The Death and Letters of Alice James*, ed. Ruth B. Yeazell (Berkeley, Calif., 1981), p. 43. I owe this quotation to Garrett Stewart, *Death Sentences*, pp. 367–368.

46. Hugo von Hofmannsthal, *Der Tor und der Tod*, in *Gedichte und lyrische Dramen*, ed. Herbert Steiner (Stockholm, 1946), pp. 291–292.

CHAPTER 3

PORK-PIE OR FATHERLAND?

1. Stephen Macdonald, *Not About Heroes* (London, 1983), p. 75.

2. V. S. Pritchett, *Chekhov* (New York, 1988), p. 227.

3. William Beatty, *Authentic Narrative of the Death of Lord Nelson* (London, 1807), pp. 48, 50.

4. The generally known rival version was for a long time "Bugger Bognor," as listed, e.g., in J. Bryan III, *Hodgepodge* (New York, 1986), p. 117, and casually referred to in Judith Grossman's novel *Her Own Terms* (New York, 1988), p. 162. The recently published diary of the physician attending the king reveals that his last words were "God damn you," in reaction to being given an injection of morphine (Francis Watson, "The Death of George V," *History Today* 36, no. 12 [December 1986]: 28). The king may have gathered, if not accepted, the decision that it would be in the interest of the Empire that his demise be announced in the morning papers rather than the scandal-mongering evening papers.

5. "Love/leave" appears to be due to different decipherings of James Stanhope's notes on Pitt's death; the popular anecdote about Bellamy's meat-pie ("pork") is said to have been floated by Disraeli following the "recollection" of a porter in the House of Commons several years after Pitt's death—incredible, if only because Pitt was unable to have solid food for a considerable time before his death, as Robin Reilly comments in his *Pitt the Younger, 1759–1806* (London, 1978), p. 367.

6. Arthur M. Wilson offers the remark about "incrédulité" as the first step to philosophy (see above, p. 5) along with his hope that this

perfect exit line, spoken on the eve of Diderot's death, might indeed be authentic (*Diderot* [Oxford, 1972], p. 712; André Billy reports on Diderot's quarrel with Madame Diderot at lunch on the day he died, quoting Diderot as saying as his last words: "What harm do you think that will do me?" (*Diderot* [Paris, 1932], p. 602: "Quel mal veux-tu que cela me fasse?").

On Schiller's controversial last words, see my essay " 'Richter' oder 'Leuchtöl'? Schillers letzte Worte in der Biographie," in *Jahrbuch des Freien Deutschen Hochstifts*, 1992.

7. According to Nigel Dennis, "Arthur from the Barge: A Study of Last Words," *Encounter* 98 (November 1961): 27–31.

8. See also Gerda E. Bell, "Georg Büchner's Last Words," *German Life and Letters* 27 (1973): 17–22. Paul Gerhardt's long-controversial last word, a quotation from one of his hymns, has recently been shown to be plausible; see Christian Bunners, " 'Kann uns doch kein Tod nicht töten': Paul Gerhardts letzte Worte," *Musik und Kirche* 59 (1989): 1–11.

9. F. K. Donnelly, "A Possible Source for Nathan Hale's Dying Words," *William and Mary Quarterly* 42 (1985): 394–396. Commentary in *William and Mary Quarterly* 43 (1986): 327–330. The most commonly heard version is: "I only regret that I have but one life to lose for my country."

10. Paul Egon Hübinger, *Die letzten Worte Papst Gregors VII* (Opladen, 1973). ("I have loved justice and hated injustice; therefore I die in exile.")

11. William Lewis Hertslet et al., *Der Treppenwitz der Weltgeschichte* (Berlin, 1967), p. 16. First published in 1882, with many editions since.

12. Edward Le Comte, *Dictionary of Last Words* (New York, 1955).

13. This can be learned, for example, from Alphonse Aulard's study "Derniers moments et exécution de Danton," in *Etudes et leçons sur la Révolution française*, 9th ser. (Paris, 1924), pp. 45–70.

14. *North American Review* 269, no. 2 (1984): 62.

15. See, e.g., Frank T. Zumbach, *Edgar Allan Poe* (Munich, 1986), p. 685.

16. Vol. I, pp. 335–336.

17. Kenneth Silverman, *Edgar Allen Poe* (New York, 1991), pp. 435, 518.

18. J. G. Lockhart, *Memoirs of Sir Walter Scott* (Edinburgh, 1838), VIII:393- 394.

19. Carola Oman, *The Wizard of the North* (London, 1973), p. 356.

20. Sir Herbert J. C. Grierson, *Sir Walter Scott, Bart.* (Oxford, 1938), pp. 299–300.

21. Edgar Johnson, *Sir Walter Scott: The Great Unknown* (New York, 1970), 2:1337–1338.

22. See Alan Shelston, *Biography* (London, 1977), p. 14.

23. Richard Ellmann, *Oscar Wilde* (New York, 1988), pp. 580–581.

24. Jean Richepin, *Morts bizarres* (Paris, 1876).

25. Richard Marius, *Thomas More* (New York, 1984), pp. 513–514.

26. Paul J. Korshin, "Johnson's Last Words," *Times Literary Supplement*, 29 January 1982, p. 108.

27. Mary Jane Hurst, "Samuel Johnson's Dying Words," *English Language Notes* 23 (1985): 45.

28. Walter Jackson Bate, *Samuel Johnson* (New York, 1977), p. 599.

29. Walter Jackson Bate, *The Achievement of Samuel Johnson* (New York, 1955), p. 61.

30. G. H. Lewes, *Life of Goethe* (1855; New York, 1965), p. 563.

31. *Insel-Almanach auf das Goethe-Jahr 1932* (Leipzig, [1931]), pp. 207–208.

32. *Goethe: Leben und Werk*, vol. 2 (Königstein, 1985), p. 569.

33. Carl Schüddekopf, *Goethes Tod* (Leipzig, 1907), pp. 100–101.

34. Houston Stewart Chamberlain, *Goethe* (Munich, 1912), p. 78.

35. Schüddekopf, *Goethes Tod*, p. 26; see also pp. 72, 81, 85, 92.

36. Weimar edition, pt. 4, vol. 45, p. 222.

37. *Goethes Gespräche*, ed. Wolfgang Herwig (Zurich and Stuttgart: Artemis, 1972), vol. 3, pt. 2, p. 889.

38. Dolf Sternberger, "Goethes letzte Worte," in *Schriften*, vol. 1 (Frankfurt, 1977), p. 44.

39. Gedenkausgabe, *Werke, Briefe und Gespräche*, ed. Ernst Beutler, vol. 23 (*Gespräche*, pt. 2) (Zurich, 1950), no. 2316, p. 867.

40. Bettina von Arnim, *Tagebuch* (Berlin, 1835), p. 232.

41. Sarah Austin, *Characteristics of Goethe*, vol. 3 (London, 1833), p. 93; cp. Schüddekopf, *Goethes Tod*, p. 166.

42. *Goethes Gespräche*, vol. 5 (1987), p. 634; vol. 3, pt. 2, p. 902.

43. *Jahrbuch der Goethe-Gesellschaft*, vol. 14 (1928), p. 209.

44. See my essay, " 'Gipsabgüsse von Leichenmasken'? Goethe

und der Kult des letzten Worts," *Jahrbuch der Deutschen Schiller-Ge-sellschaft* 35 (1991): 73–95, esp. 88–94.

45. *Goethes Gespräche*, ed. Herwig, vol. 3, pt. 2 (Zurich and Stutt-gart, 1972), p. 889 (Krause's note was first published in 1928).

46. Stets des Lebens dunkler Seite
Abgewendet wie Apoll;
Daß er Licht um sich verbreite,
War der Ruf, der ihm erscholl.
Und so stand er jung im Streite
Bis ins Alter würdevoll,
Gegen Drachen-Nachtgeleite,
Das aus allen Ecken schwoll,
Das er bald mit Scherz beiseite
Schob, bald niederschlug mit Groll.
Als er abtrat nun vom Streite,
War das letzte Wort, das quoll
Aus der Brust erhobner Weite:
"Mehr Licht!" Nun, o Vorhang, roll
Auf, daß er hinüber schreite,
Wo mehr Licht ihm werden soll!

(Friedrich Rückert, "Goethes letztes Wort,"
in *Gesammelte Gedichte*, vol. 6
[Erlangen, 1838], pp. 112–113)

47. Lawrence Perrine, *Sound and Sense: An Introduction to Poetry*, 5th ed. (New York, 1977).

48. *Mehr Licht/More Light*, ed. Achim Lipp and Peter Zec (Ham-burg, 1985).

49. Ein Mann aus Augsburg ist allein deshalb in die Augsburger Ir-renanstalt eingeliefert worden, weil er sein ganzes Leben bei jeder Gelegenheit behauptet hatte, Goethe habe als Letztes *mehr nicht!* und nicht *mehr Licht!* gesagt, was allen mit ihm in Be-rührung gekommenen Leuten mit der Zeit und auf die Dauer der-artig auf die Nerven gegangen sei, daß sie sich zusammengetan hatten, um die Einweisung dieses auf so unglückliche Weise von seiner Behauptung besessenen Augsburgers in die Irrenanstalt zu erwirken. Sechs Ärzte hätten sich geweigert, den Unglücklichen

in die Irrenanstalt einzuweisen, der siebente habe eine solche Einweisung sofort veranlaßt. Dieser Arzt ist, wie ich aus der *Frankfurter Allgemeinen Zeitung* erfahren habe, dafür mit der Goetheplakette der Stadt Frankfurt ausgezeichnet worden. (Frankfurt, 1978), p. 58.

There is also a "Mehr Licht!" cartoon in the satirical magazine *Fliegende Blätter* ([12 May 1938], p. 297), as well as a book by Hermann Ahlwardt, *Mehr Licht!*, subtitled *Der Orden Jesu in seiner wahren Gestalt und in seinem Verhältnis zum Freimaurer- und Judentum*, 2d. ed. (Dresden, 1910; later editions in 1925 and 1928). Wolfgang Mieder, to whom I owe the *Fliegende Blätter* reference, also called my attention to Stephen Scobie's poem "The rooms we are" in the eponymous collection (Victoria, B.C., 1974; the poem begins: "More light! screamed / Goethe, dying."

50. Burton E. Stevenson, *Home Book of Quotations* (New York, 1937), p. 414. *Miscellaneous Works of the Late Philip Dormer Stanhope, Earl of Chesterfield . . . to Which is Prefixed Memoirs of his Life . . . by M. Maty, M.D.* (London, 1777), 1:224.

51. Theo Aronson, *Crowns in Conflict* (London, 1986), p. 101.

52. Ernest Newman, *The Life of Richard Wagner*, vol. 4 (New York, 1946), p. 712. Henri Bordillon, *Gestes et opinions d'Alfred Jarry, Ecrivain* (Laval, 1986), p. 195 (the physician's report). Keith Beaumont wonders whether Jarry could have meant "cureton"; see his *Alfred Jarry: A Critical and Biographical Study* (New York, 1984), p. 290 and note. The final utterance Beaumont relates ("je cherche, je cherche . . . j'ch, j'ch") goes back to Paul Léautand's *Journal littéraire*; Léautand does not, however, claim to have been an ear-witness; besides, the alleged repetition of "je cherche"—a hundred times(!)—does not jibe with the physician's report (*Journal littéraire*, vol. 2 [Paris, 1955], p. 75). Erika Mann, *Das letzte Jahr* (Frankfurt, 1956), p. 71. These authors are referred to here only as sources, not as examples of any interpretation of the last words in question.

53. About such last words Lawrence L. Langer says: "Nor do we know whether the condemned men were able to sustain [the sentiments expressed in their last words] when they stood alone before the final silence of extinction" (*The Age of Atrocity: Death in Modern Literature* [Boston, 1978], p. 39).

54. *Die letzten Worte einer Heiligen* (Kirnach-Villingen, 1928); *The World's Great Letters*, ed. M. Lincoln Schuster (New York, 1940), pp. 458–460; *Last Words: Letters and Statements of the Leaders Executed after the Rising at Easter 1916*, ed. Piaras F. MacLochlainn (Dublin, 1971); *Der letzte Brief*, ed. Friedrich Reck-Malleczewen (Frankfurt, 1949); Olivier Blanc, *La Dernière Lettre: Prisons et condamnés de la Révolution 1793–1794* (Paris, 1984).

55. *Fear and Trembling. Repetition*, vol. 6 of *Kierkegaard's Writings*, ed. and tr. Howard V. Hong and Edna H. Hong (Princeton, 1983), pp. 116–117.

56. *Boswell's Life of Johnson*, ed. Hill, 3:167.

57. E. Förster-Nietzsche, *Das Leben Friedrich Nietzsches*, vol. 2, pt. 2 (Leipzig, 1904), p. 932.

58. See esp. Edward Le Comte, *Dictionary of Last Words* (New York, 1955), and James Lindsay, "Last Words," *The Outlook*, 14 April 1928, pp. 470–471. Rolf Michaelis calls the doubtfulness of their authenticity "one of the main problems of 'last words'" (*Die Zeit*, 6 January 1984, p. 36). See also Horst Rüdiger, *Neue Zürcher Zeitung*, 21 October 1971, p. 35.

59. See Stevenson, *Home Book of Quotations*, p. 413.

60. *The Oxford Book of Death*, ed. D. J. Enright (Oxford, 1983), p. 314; Dennis, "Arthur from the Barge," p. 29.

61. See Shelston, *Biography*, p. 14.

62. That "dying behavior" corresponds to such social expectations is pointed out by Glenn M. Vernon, in *Sociology of Death* (New York, 1970), pp. 92–94.

CHAPTER 4

GUIDANCE, ENTERTAINMENT, AND FRISSON

1. *Vie de Rancé* (1844), ed. Jacques Chastenet (Paris, 1971), p. 16.

2. "Der Tod der Ärzte": J. R. de Salis, *Rainer Maria Rilkes Schweizer Jahre* (Frauenfeld, 1936), p. 200. Today it is, among others, Ariès who polemicizes against this "denial of death"; see his chapter entitled "Death Denied" in *The Hour of our Death* in which he quotes a typical case: "Eventually [the dying person] left without saying anything.

. . . 'She didn't even say good-bye to us'" ([New York, 1982], p. 563; cp. p. 572).

3. *Time*, 5 September 1988, p. 58; Elisabeth Kübler-Ross, *On Death and Dying* (New York, 1968); Daniel Berrigan, *We Die Before We Live: Talking with the Very Ill* (New York, 1980).

4. *The Essayes*, rev. ed., ed. Michael Kiernan (Oxford, 1985), p. 10. Orthography modernized.

5. *Death and Western Thought* (New York, 1963), p. 101.

6. *The Complete Essays of Montaigne*, trans. Donald M. Frame (Stanford, Calif., 1965), p. 62. *Essais*, ed. Albert Thibaudet (Paris, 1950), p. 114:

> Et n'est rien dequoy je m'informe si volontiers, que de la mort des hommes: quelle parole, quel visage, quelle contenance ils y ont eu; ny endroit des histoires, que je remarque si attantifvement. Il y paroist à la farcissure de mes exemples: et que j'ay en particuliere affection cette matiere. Si j'estoy faiseur de livres, je feroy un registre commenté des morts diverses. Qui apprendroit les hommes à mourir, leur apprendroit à vivre. (1580; from "il y paroist" manuscript addition, first published in 1595. Montaigne died in 1592.)

7. Pierre Charron, *De la Sagesse* (1601), book 2, ch. 11, first paragraph: "Pour juger de la vie, il faut regarder comment s'en est porté le bout; car la fin couronne l'oeuvre, la bonne mort honore toute la vie, la mauvaise diffame." Cp. Montaigne, *Essais*, 1:19.

8. See Charron, *De la Sagesse*, book 2, ch. 11, par. 4.

9. On the "post-history" of the collection, see Samuel Pickering Jr., "The Grave Leads But to Paths of Glory: Deathbed Scenes in American Children's Books, 1800–1860," *Dalhousie Review* 59 (1979): 452–464.

10. According to the catalog of the National Library of Scotland, *A Cloud of Witnesses* is the work of Hugh Clark, Alexander Marshall, and John McMain.

11. See Maximillian E. Novak, "Defoe's Authorship of *A Collection of Dying Speeches* (1718)," *Philological Quarterly* 61 (1982): 92–97.

12. Preface. For traditional doubts about the truthfulness of last words, especially in the case of Sir Walter Raleigh, see also L. B. Smith, "English Treason Trials," *Journal of the History of Ideas* 15 (1954): 471–498. On Jetzer, mentioned subsequently, see above, p. 20.

13. On the Continent these were preceded, in a manner of speaking, by the bizarrely comprehensive chamber of horrors furnished by Henning Grosse, which, however, does not feature last words in all cases: *Tragica, seu tristium historiarum de poenis criminalibus et exitu horribili eorum qui Impietate, Blasphemia, Contemptu & Abnegatione Dei, Haeresi, Magia, Execratione, Maledicentia, Periurio, & alio quovis Nominis Divini rerumque Deo sacrarum abusu: Impietate erga Parentes, caeterosque sanguine junctos: Parricidio, Tyrannicide, Homicidio, Adulterio, Incestu atque aliis nefariis libidinibus: Sacrilegio, Furto, Avaritia, Latrocinio, Rapina, Manducio, Fraude, & omnis generis illicita atque excrabili vite turpitudine ultionem divinam provocarunt, & mirabiliter perpessi sunt libri II* (Eisleben, 1597). In German territories, criminals about to be executed only rarely launched into a dying speech. See above, p. 112; Richard van Dülmen, *Theatre of Horror* (Oxford, 1990); and Johann Samuel Patzke, *Aufrichtige Nachricht von der Bekehrung und den letzten Stunden einer Kindermörderin, Nahmens Anna Elisabeth Blumin . . .* (Magdeburg, 1767).

14. See Frank Wadleigh Chandler, *The Literature of Roguery* (Boston, 1907), vol. 1, ch. 4, esp. pp. 179–181, on some of the references in the next paragraph. A bibliography of individual English criminal biographies and of anthologies of such biographies is found in Lincoln B. Faller, *Turned to Account: The Forms and Functions of Criminal Biography in Seventeenth- and Early Eighteenth-Century England* (Cambridge, England, 1987). See especially *A Compleat Collection of State-Tryals, and Proceedings upon Impeachments for High Treason, and other Crimes and Misdemeanors; From the Reign of King Henry the Fourth, to the End of the Reign of Queen Anne . . .* , 4 vols. (London, 1719).

15. Recueil de Pieces pour servir à l'Histoire du Cœur humain. . . .
cette force héroïque & . . . cette intrépidité que le Ciel départit
aux grands ames. . . . Aussi, nous ne craignons pas de le dire, le
tableau que nous présentons dans cet Ouvrage est l'Histoire, bien
honorable à l'humanité, des luttes du cœur de l'homme contre les
horreurs de la mort la plus cruelle. . . . cet air d'assurance &
dignité qui les élève au dessus de l'humanité. . . . Mais ce qui
donne la plus grande idée de l'homme, c'est de l'entendre se
livrer sur l'échafaud à des saillies, à des jeux de mots. . . . C'est
du sein de la Religion que tous les illustres malheureux tiroient

cette force & cette élevation de sentiments qui nous étonnent. . . .
le crime le plus affreux & le plus impardonable contre l'humanité. . . . qui ne leur est confié que pour travailler à la gloire du
Prince, à le faire aimer [sic] des Sujets, & à les rendre heureux.

16. Herbert Lockyer, *Last Words of Saints and Sinners* (Grand Rapids, Mich., 1983), p. 174. (Earlier editions published in 1969 and
1975.)

17. Caspar Titius, *Loci theologiae historici, oder Theologisches Exempel-
Buch* (Wittenberg, 1633), ch. 31; Heinrich Junghans, *Evangelische und
historische Sterbe-Kunst* (Leipzig, 1665), index; Johannes Stieffler, *Loci
theologiae historici* (Jena, 1668), pp. 1938ff., 1949ff. The periodical
*Neues und Altes aus dem Reiche Gottes und der übrigen guten und bösen
Geister* (Frankfurt and Leipzig, 1733–1739; pts. 1–19 [of 24] edited by
the political philosopher Johann Jakob Moser) features a regular section on "edifying and terrifying last hours." The most grotesque example of this strange genre is Johann Samuel Adami's *Misanders
Theatrum tragicum* (Dresden, 1695), which collects the weirdest cases
of uncommon death, among them those just cited in the text. All have
their moral and theological use explained in sufficient detail.

18. Lockyer, *Last Words of Saints and Sinners*.

19. In Geoffrey Gorer, *Death, Grief, and Mourning* (New York,
1965), pp. 195–196.

20. See below, note 23.

21. Absurd as it is, this line of inquiry was seriously pursued, on
the basis of a number of anthologies of last words and other "most
reliable" sources of last words, in "Death Psychology of Historical
Personages" by Arthur MacDonald, *American Journal of Psychology* 32
(1921): 552–556. This seems to be the only attempt to evaluate last
words by quantifying them, and the results are curious. The psychologist, rigorously ahistorical in his calculations, finds that death is a
great equalizer in the sense that there is "regularity" and "uniformity" in the way members of certain professions have died over the
centuries, no matter how different the "conditions." MacDonald is
convinced that dying words are "a mental and moral test of the real
character" of individuals as members of certain professional groups.
The implication is a quasi-scientific predictability of the kinds and
number of last words that a given distinguished individual will speak

as he dies. (Only men are divided into professional groups: "Religious, Royalty, Military, Philosophers, Litterateurs, Physicians and Scientists, Artists, Poets, Statesmen"; women—70 out of the 794 case histories—form a professionally undifferentiated group by themselves.)

The statistical details are even more curious. As the survey is, in the nature of things, limited to the famous (others die without their last words being recorded), it is instructive to hear that in most cases men must live to be at least fifty to become eminent, with royalty and military showing the lowest average age, "due in part to the large number of deaths by violence, which is the case also with Religious, Statesmen and Women." But if this factor of death by violence is eliminated, the statistics reveal that poets and artists die youngest. As for the mental state at the point of death, as indicated by the last words, we learn that, taking all categories together, 17 percent were sarcastic or jocose, "indicating a high degree of mental control." ("In fact some of the dying complained that it was taking too long and they were getting tired.") Litterateurs (or "writers and authors") die with words of sarcasm or jocularity "or both" on their lips more often than all other groups (24 out of 106; 37 percent of those dying with sarcastic or jocose last words are writers and authors). "They were also relatively the freest of pain," as column 10 of this intricate statistical survey reveals. "The Military show much the relatively highest number of requests, directions or admonitions in their last words. The Philosophers stand relatively high in questions, answers and exclamations." And so on. More than twice as many of all categories expressed content in their last words than expressed discontent (46 vs. 19 percent). Yet the average number of their last words was exactly the same, namely 16. "While relatively few of the Statesmen and Women were sarcastic [in their last words], they [the ones dying sarcastically] took many more words to express themselves than the others; the Poets [dying sarcastically] also had as high an average as 24 words." On the other hand, poets who died with "Question, Answer, Exclamation" used only 3 words. Women in this category used the highest number, 8. However, women dying with "Request, Directions, Admonition" used a staggering average of 63 words, "which is three times as great as that of any of the others, except Royalty, which has 23"; artists in this category score an average of zero words, with physicians and scientists being the next most taciturn group, making do with an average of 8 words. Among those dying contented, philosophers use the fewest words (8), the religious types the most (25). Among those dying discontented, philosophers again get by with the smallest number of words (11), while royalty uses the most (23, which is one more than the religious figures need on average). Among those dying with indifference, however, artists and scientists are most economical—9 and 10 words respectively.

22. See, e.g., *Mirrors of Mortality: Studies in the Social History of Death*, ed. Joachim Whaley (London, 1981), pp. 117–121, and Norbert Elias, *The Loneliness of the Dying* (Oxford, 1985), pp. 12–16. See also Ch. 5, note 2.

23. J. Bryan III, *Hodgepodge* (New York, 1986), pp. 116–119; Robert Hendrickson, *The Literary Life and Other Curiosities* (New York, 1981), pp. 105–109. See also Nigel Rees, *"Quote . . . Unquote"* (London, 1978), the section entitled "Famous Last Words"; Scott Slater and Alec Solomita, *Exits: Stories of Dying Moments and Parting Words* (New York, 1980); Bob Arnebeck, *Proust's Last Beer: A History of Curious Demises* (Harmondsworth and New York, 1980), which includes, alongside Mozart and Calamity Jane, the author's parakeet, and promises "a redeeming touch of absurdity" to boot; Robert Ramsay and Randall Toye, *The Goodbye Book* (New York, 1979) chs. 5 and 7 of which offer "an amusing potpourri" of last words; Henry Lauritzen, *Berømtheders sidste Ord* (Aalborg, 1967); Gyles Brandreth, *The Last Word* (New York, 1979), *871 Famous Last Words, and Put-Downs, Insults, Squelches . . .* (New York, 1982), and *Famous Last Words and Tombstone Humor* (New York, 1989); Norman and Betty Donaldson, *How Did They Die?* (New York, 1980), which in addition to last words offers a variety of curious "facts . . . difficult to unearth elsewhere"; *The Oxford Book of Death*, ed. D. J. Enright (Oxford, 1983); Richard De'ath, *Died Laughing* (London and Boston, 1985), whose chapter "Exit Lines" promises "a laugh a page" (p. 12); Leon Prochnik, *Endings: Death, Glorious and Otherwise, As Faced by Ten Outstanding Figures of Our Time* (New York, 1980).

24. See also Edward Le Comte, *Dictionary of Last Words* (New York, 1955), p. vii; Jonathon Green, *Famous Last Words* (London and New York, 1979), p. 5.

25. See also the somewhat similar collection of Hans Jürgen

Schulz, *Letzte Tage: Sterbegeschichten aus zwei Jahrtausenden* (Berlin, 1983).

26. Pour l'homme sans Dieu, l'énigme n'est donc plus dans la mort, mais dans la vie. Et ce qui peut être obtenu des mourants, c'est qu'ils en fournissent le mot. Ils ont accompli *leur* destinée; nous disposons peut-être encore du temps nécessaire pour améliorer la nôtre. Que leur experience nous y aide! La mort subite, la mort inconsciente sont des morts égoïstes, elles ne nous apportent rien. Nous avons besoin de nous éclairer aux lumières qui vont s'éteindre.

27. "Pour avoir son véritable prix, un mot de la fin doit émaner d'une réaction, consciente ou non, devant l'imminence de l'événement."

28. ". . . et la mort sera la dernière, si l'occasion ne s'est pas présenté plus tôt."

29. ". . . kann aus all diesen Stimmen eine Ermutigung zum Leben heraushören, einen Appell zu vertieftem, ausgefülltem Dasein."

CHAPTER 5

AN INTELLECTUAL HISTORY OF LAST WORDS?

1. "Erinnerungen aus den schönsten Stunden für die letzten" (1815) in *Herbstblumine* (*Sämtliche Werke*, ed. Norbert Miller, pt. 2, vol. 3 [Munich: Hanser, 1978], p. 351).

2. See Detlev Illmer's review of Ariès in *Zeitschrift für historische Forschung* 6 (1979): 215; Norbert Elias, *The Loneliness of the Dying* (Oxford, 1985), pp. 12–16; Joachim Whaley, Introduction to *Mirrors of Mortality: Studies in the Social History of Death*, ed. Joachim Whaley (London, 1981), pp. 8–10; John McManners, "Death and the French Historians," in *Mirrors of Mortality*, ed. Whaley, pp. 117–121, 129; Arno Borst, "Zwei mittelalterliche Sterbefälle," *Merkur* 390 (November 1980): 1081–1098; Kümmel, "Der sanfte und selige Tod," *Leichenpredigten als Quelle historischer Wissenschaften*, ed. Rudolf Lenz, vol. 3 (Marburg, 1984), pp. 199–226.

3. See Whaley's criticism (of an earlier work of Vovelle's) in *Mirrors of Mortality*, p. 13.

4. See Michel Vovelle, *La Mort et l'occident* (Paris, 1983), pp. 15–16.

5. See also the somewhat uncritical historical overview in Richard Macksey's essay "Last Words: The *Artes Moriendi* and a Transtextual Genre," *Genre* 16 (1983): 493–516.

6. On antiquity: A. Ronconi, "Exitus illustrium virorum," *Reallexikon für Antike und Christentum*, vol. 6 (1966): 1258–1268; E. Stauffer, "Abschiedsreden," *Reallexikon für Antike und Christentum*, vol. 1 (1950): 29–35; Willibald Schmidt, *De ultimis morientium verbis* (diss., Marburg, 1914). See also Ch. 1, note 21.

On Egypt: Michael Grant refers to formulaic dying words in the Egyptian Book of the Dead in his *Ancient Mediterranean* (London, 1969), p. 41.

On Japan: Åke Ohlmarks, *Sista Sucken* (Stockholm, 1970), p. 94; *Japanese Death Poems, Written by Zen Monks and Haiku Poets on the Verge of Death*, ed. Yoel Hoffmann (Rutland, Vermont, 1986), about the centuries-old tradition of writing or pronouncing a poem at the last. There is also a Buddhist sect in Japan that believes that the pronunciation of the name of the Savior-Buddha Amida at the point of death ensures entry into "Paradise" (exhibition catalog *Courtly Splendor of Japan: Twelve Centuries of Treasure from Japan*, Boston Museum of Fine Arts, 1990, p. 58; see also "Amida" in the *Encyclopedia Brittanica*, Micropedia, vol. 1 [1974]). On the importance of "dying well" in present-day Japanese culture, see Robert Jay Lifton et al., *Six Lives, Six Deaths* (New Haven, 1979), pp. 14–23. The vitality of the last-word tradition in mid-twentieth-century Japan may be gathered from a casual reference in Yasunari Kawabata's novel *The Sound of the Mountain* (New York, 1981), pp. 206–207 (first published in 1954 as *Yama no Oto*).

On China: Paul Demiéville, "Stances de la fin," *Mélanges offerts à M. Charles Haguenauer* (Paris, 1980), pp. 11–29 (sixteenth through eighteenth centuries) and *Poèmes chinois dèvant la mort* (Paris, 1984). See also *The Analects of Confucius*, ed. William Edward Soothill (Yokohama, 1910), p. 387: "When a bird is dying, its song is sad. When a man is dying, what he says is worth listening to" (book 8, ch. 4); cp. *The Analects of Confucius*, trans. Arthur Waley (New York: Vintage Books, 1989), p. 133: ". . . his words are of note." Even in the late twentieth century, Japanese and Chinese anthologies of last words continue to appear; e.g., Susumu Nakanishi's *Jisei no Kotoba* (Tokyo: Chuo Koronsha, 1986).

The Rapanui, the indigenous population of Easter Island, are among the many peoples who believe in the prophetic power of dying words; to hear them, family members think nothing of taking the five-hour jet flight from Santiago to the island, as Grant McCall reports in his *Rapanui: Tradition and Survival on Easter Island* (Sydney, 1980), pp. 118–119.

7. Anthony J. Saldarini, "Last Words and Deathbed Scenes in Rabbinic Literature," *The Jewish Quarterly Review* 68 (1977): 28–45; Jacob Neusner, "Death-Scenes and Farewell Stories: An aspect of the Master-Disciple Relationship in Mark and in Some Talmudic Tales," *Harvard Theological Review* 79 (1986): 187–197. I am told that to this day written records of last words will be inserted in the Wailing Wall in Jerusalem by relatives of the deceased.

8. Illustration no. 8 in Alberto Tenenti, *Il senso della morte e l'amore della vita nel Rinascimento* (Turin, 1957). Cp. Tenenti, *La Vie et la mort à travers l'art du XVe siècle* (Paris, 1952), p. 49.

9. John Dover, *The Words of the Crucified* (London, 1967), pp. 60–61. See above, p. 50.

10. Rainer Rudolf, *Ars moriendi* (Cologne and Graz, 1957), pp. 56–61.

11. "Uncounted" according to Rudolf, *Ars moriendi*, p. 113; Mary Catherine O'Connor, *The Art of Dying Well: The Development of the Ars Moriendi* (New York, 1942), pp. 1–2; Franz Falk, *Die deutschen Sterbebücher* (Köln, 1890); Henri Brémond, "L'art de mourir," in *Histoire littéraire du sentiment religieux en France*, vol. 9 (Paris, 1932); François Lebrun, *Les Hommes et la mort en Anjou aux 17e et 18e siècles* (Paris, 1971), pp. 436–441; D. Roche, "La Mémoire de la mort: Recherches sur la place des arts de mourir dans la librairie et la lecture en France au XVIIe et XVIIIe siècles," *Annales* (1976): 76–119; Roger Chartier, "Les Arts de mourir, 1450–1600," *Annales* (1976): 51–75; Robert Favre, *La Mort dans la littérature et la pensée françaises au siècle des lumières* (Lyon, 1978), pp. 83–86, 94–97, 128–131 (theological critique); O. M. Brack Jr., "The Death of Samuel Johnson and the Ars Moriendi Tradition," *Cithara* 20 (1980): 3–15. The impact of the artes moriendi on the eighteenth-century novel has been shown in detail in a case study by Margaret Anne Doody, "Holy and Unholy Dying: The Deathbed Theme in *Clarissa*," in *A Natural Passion: A Study of the Novels of Samuel Richardson* (Oxford, 1974).

12. See especially Nancy Lee Beaty, *The Craft of Dying* (New Haven, 1970).

13. E.g., Beaty, *The Craft of Dying*, p. 21; Rudolf, *Ars moriendi*, pp. 65, 98; A. Freybe, *Das Memento Mori in deutscher Sitte* . . . (Gotha, 1909), pp. 239, 255; *The Book of the Craft of Dying*, ed. Frances Comper (London, 1917), pp. 23, 28.

14. E.g., *The Book of the Craft of Dying*, ed. Comper, pp. 33, 35.

15. Quoted from Robert Favre, *La Mort . . . au siècle des lumières*, p. 83; see also p. 130 in the same volume.

16. See Beaty, *The Craft of Dying*, pp. 191–193; Favre, *La Mort . . . au siècle des lumières*, pp. 128–130.

17. E.g., Johann Heermann, *Güldene Sterbekunst* (1628) (2d ed. Leipzig, 1659), p. 296; Heinrich Junghans, *Evangelische und historische Sterbe-Kunst* (Leipzig, 1665), pp. 36, 39–40; Junghans also rails against the Catholic notion of salvation by works (p. 48). See also the discussion of Quinos, above, p. 163.

18. Rudolf, *Ars moriendi*, p. 56.

19. *The Standard Edition of the Complete Psychological Works of Sigmund Freud*, vol. 14 (London, 1957), p. 300; Elias Canetti, *Die Provinz des Menschen* (Munich, 1973), p. 53.

20. Freybe, *Das Memento Mori*, p. 241. It is worth noting in this context that John Dunton's anthology of last words (see above, pp. 105–106) was published in his miscellany *House of Weeping*, which, at least in its second edition (1692), also contains a guide to holy dying. (This Dunton was an Anglican minister; see below, note 36, for the other John Dunton.)

21. There is also a German translation, *Apophthegmata morientium*, by Hermann Rätel (Görlitz, preface dated 1593) and a short version in Latin, *Homo disce mori*, published in Hamburg in 1593.

22. Title and date according to Bergmann, discussed a few lines further down.

23. Thomas Finkenstaedt, "Galgenliteratur: Zur Auffassung des Todes im England des 16. und 17. Jahrhunderts," *Deutsche Vierteljahrsschrift für Literaturwissenschaft und Geistesgeschichte* 34 (1960): 535. My remarks are based primarily on the extensive collections of broadsides and pamphlets in Houghton Library and the Harvard Law School Library; copies of dozens of additional texts of this kind were obtained from several other, primarily British, libraries.

24. See Lincoln B. Faller, *Turned to Account: The Forms and Functions of Criminal Biography in Seventeenth- and Early Eighteenth-Century England* (Cambridge, England, 1987), esp. pp. 85–90, 106–107, 115; J. A. Sharpe, " 'Last Dying Speeches': Religion, Ideology and Public Execution in Seventeenth-Century England," *Past and Present* 107 (1985): esp. 158–167; Daniel Szechi, "The Jacobite Theatre of Death," in *The Jacobite Challenge*, ed. Eveline Cruickshanks and Jeremy Black (Edinburgh, 1988), pp. 57–73.

25. Olivier Blanc, *La Dernière Lettre: Prisons et condamnés de la Révolution 1793–1794* (Paris, 1984), pp. 82–87; Sharpe, " 'Last Dying Speeches,' " p. 165; Finkenstaedt, "Galgenliteratur," p. 547.

26. Harry Keßler, *Notizen über Mexico* (Berlin, 1898), p. 37.

27. This hard-to-miss fact is mentioned, e.g., by Finkenstaedt, "Galgenliteratur," p. 549, as well as by Beach Langston, "Essex and the Art of Dying," *The Huntington Library Quarterly* 13 (1950): 109–129.

28. An exception may be *The Last Speech and Confession of Oliver Plunket*: ". . . if he did not now speak the Truth he should be Damned to all Eternity" (London, 1681, p. 1).

29. E.g., a traitor: *The Dying Speech of James Shepheard* (London, 1718); a murderer: *The Last Speech, Confession, and Dying Declaration of James McKaen* (Glasgow, 1797); a burglar: *The Last Speech and Confession of Charles Dunn* (London, 1688); a queen: *The Entertaining Life and Death of the Amiable Lady Jean [sic] Gray* (Edinburgh, n.d.); a king: *Massacre of the French King [. . .] Louis XVI* (London, [1793?]).

30. *Dying Declaration of Nicholas Fernandez* [and nine other pirates] (New York, 1830), p. 24.

31. Christof Schubart, *Die Berichte über Luthers Tod und Begräbnis* (Weimar, 1917), esp. p. 37; Horst Schmidt-Grave, *Leichenreden und Leichenpredigten Tübinger Professoren (1550–1750)* (Tübingen, 1974), pp. 35–36.

32. Rudolf Mohr, *Protestantische Theologie und Frömmigkeit* (diss., Marburg, 1964), p. 247.

33. Weimar edition, vol. 26 (Weimar, 1909), p. 509; cp. Rudolf Mohr, *Der unverhoffte Tod* (Marburg, 1982), p. 177.

34. See Favre, *La Mort . . . au siècle des lumières*, pp. 83–87, 128–131; John McManners, *Death and the Enlightenment* (Oxford, 1981), pp. 252–255; *The Sermons of John Donne*, ed. E. M. Simpson and G. R. Potter, vol. 6 (Berkeley, Calif., 1953), p. 202 (1624); for a similar view, see

Abbé Baudrand (1765) as quoted in Favre, p. 130, John Dunton in *The House of Weeping*, 2d ed. (1692), pt. 2, p. 231, and Thomas Beverley, *The General Inefficacy and Insincerity of a Late, or Death-Bed Repentance* (London, 1670; 2d ed. 1692), foreword. See also above, p. 167, on Lalemant.

Ariès dates the relaxation of the ars moriendi-induced anxiety about the last hour and the concomitant unconcern about sudden death, along with the devaluation of the moment of dying, from the sixteenth century, if not earlier (*The Hour of Our Death* [New York, 1982], pp. 297–315). Specialists in German sixteenth-to-eighteenth-century funeral sermons have opposed this view, stating that on the level of the average believer, the artes moriendi maintained their power well into the Age of Reason, as evidenced by the description of the deathbed in funeral sermons; see Kümmel, "Der sanfte und selige Tod." In defense of Ariès, it may be pointed out that he is quite aware of the "simultaneity of the non-simultaneous." On funeral sermons occasioned by sudden death, see Rudolf Mohr, *Der unverhoffte Tod* (Marburg, 1982); Mohr bases his conclusions about the abandonment of the interpretation of sudden death as an indication of damnation on far too few examples; a wealth of confirming material is found in the collections of funeral sermons in the Herzog-August-Bibliothek, Wolfenbüttel; see also Schmidt-Grave, *Leichenreden und Leichenpredigten Tübinger Professoren*, pp. 36–39: following Augustine, only sudden death following an ungodly life is to be considered *mala*.

35. Valerius Herberger, *Traurbinden*, vol. 5 (Leipzig, 1618), pp. 210–215.

36. Favre, *La Mort . . . au siècle des lumière*, pp. 84–87, 94–97. See also [Henry Hammond's] *Of a Late, or, a Death-Bed Repentance* (Oxford, 1645). See also below, note 39. On the following sentence, see especially Jeremy Taylor, "The Invalidity of a Late or Death-Bed Repentance" (1651), in *The Whole Works*, ed. Reginald Heber, rev. Charles Page Eden, vol. 4 (London, 1861), pp. 381–407; Beverley, *The General Inefficacy . . . of a Death-Bed Repentance*; and John Dunton, *The Hazard of a Death-Bed Repentance* (London, 1708). (This John Dunton is identified in the British Library Catalogue as a book dealer.)

37. Leipzig, 1700, p. 155.

38. Junghans, *Evangelische und historische Sterbe-Kunst*, pp. 36, 56.

39. See Robert G. Walker, "Public Death in the Eighteenth Cen-

tury," *Research Studies of the State College of Washington* 48 (1980): 11–24, and "Rochester and the Issue of Deathbed Repentance in Restoration and Eighteenth-Century England," *South Atlantic Review* 47 (1982): 21–37. The imitation of the thief on the cross is called for in Dunton's *House of Weeping,* pt. 2, p. 278; the opposite position is taken by Beverley in *The General Inefficacy . . . of a Death-Bed Repentance,* pp. 13, 51, and by the John Dunton cited above in note 36.

40. McManners, "Death and the French Historians," pp. 107–109. Robert Cooper attempted to bring the entire debate to an end in his *Death-Bed Repentance, Its Inconclusiveness and Absurdity* (Leeds, 1841; 2d ed. London, 1845); he argued that, on the one hand, unbelievers (Paine, Voltaire, Rousseau, Hume, Gibbon, etc.) had not left this life in terror, as Christian propaganda claimed; on the other, the hour of death was, for biological reasons, not the right moment for the confirmation or refutation of any intellectual credo.

41. London, 1770, p. 32. See also *The Contrast: or, The Death-Bed of a Free-Thinker, and the Death-Bed of a Christian . . .* (Middlebury, 1807). Preface:

> The death-beds of those, who live in the contempt of religion, and in the practice of sin, generally exhibit a scene of wretchedness and despair; while the Christian, whose heart has been brought into unison with the divine law, and whose faith apprehends an atoning sacrifice, with an eye of serene lustre views the messenger of death, and with a hope full of immortality bids the world adieu.

42. McManners, *Death and the Enlightenment,* pp. 261–269; Favre, *La Mort . . . au siècle des lumière,* pp. 163–167, on the death of other *esprits forts.*

43. Walker, "Public Death in the Eighteenth Century," pp. 11–24; and Ernest C. Mossner, *The Life of David Hume* (Austin, Tex., 1954), ch. 40.

44. Walker, "Public Death," p. 19.

45. Ibid., p. 21

46. Ibid., pp. 21–23.

47. W. Rehm does not discuss these three themes, though he does introduce his chapter, "The Enlightenment" with the following statement:

Gates open to a different world when one enters the eighteenth century to investigate the idea of death there. One feels one is dealing with
entirely different people, whose intellectual orientation and moral
stance are quite different, whose creative awareness and feeling for life
and attention to all problems of this world rather than the beyond are
something novel.
[Es öffnen sich neue Tore zu einer anderen Welt, wenn man in das 18.
Jahrhundert eintritt, um dort nach dem Todesgedanken zu forschen.
Man meint, völlig andere Menschen vor sich zu haben mit ganz an-
derer geistiger Richtung und sittlicher Einstellung, mit einem neu ge-
arteten schöpferischen Lebensbewußtsein und Lebensgefühl und
einem neuen Verhältnis zu allen Fragen des Diesseits mehr noch als
des Jenseits. (*Der Todesgedanke in der deutschen Dichtung vom Mittelalter
bis zur Romantik* [Halle, 1928], p. 244).

48. "Anleitung zum vergnügten und gelassenen Sterben." German originals of the subsequent quotations from *Irdisches Vergnügen
in Gott*, vol. 9 (Hamburg and Leipzig, 1748):

. . . den Tod am meisten fürchterlich und schrecklich macht.

(P. 571)

Von der ganzen Ewigkeit wird geredet. Ob du selig
Oder wirst geplaget werden,
Hängt von diesem Zeitpunct ab.

(P. 571)

"erwiesen, daß man nicht einmal wegen der Gefahr der künftigen
Seligkeit oder Verdammniß den Tod zu fürchten habe, noch daß des-
wegen die Zeit des Todes vorher zu wissen nöthig" (p. 604).

Es wär unser Tod erschrecklich, und die allerherbste Plage,
Ja selbst der Natur zuwider, wenn nach unsrer Lebenszeit,
Voll mühselger Eitelkeit,
Eine beßre nicht zu hoffen.

(P. 604)

So sey denn ruhig, wer du seyst, und unbekümmert um die
    Stunde . . .
So laßt uns denn vernünftig handeln,

Und thun, was uns zu thun gebührt; so lang wir leben, redlich
wandeln.

(Pp. 617–618)

Ich . . . uebergeb an meinem Ende
Meinen Geist in deine Hände.

(P. 624)

49. *The Last Words of Thomas Lord Pride, Taken in Short-Hand by T. S.
[,] Late Clerk to his Lordship's Brew-House* (London, 1659?); *The Last
Speech, and Confession of the Whore of Babylon, at her Place of Execution, on
the Fifth of November Last* (London, 1673); *The Last Speech and Dying
Words of the Bank of Ireland. Which was Executed at College-Green, on Sat-
urday the 9th Inst.* (Dublin, [1721]); *The Last Dying Speech and Confession
of the Late Parliament; Made on Saturday the 10th of March, before their
Execution* (London, 1722); *The Last Speech, Confession, and Dying
Words, of a Queen Ann's Guinea, Who Was Tried, and Condemned, on a
Late Act of Parliament, for Being too Light; and Executed by the Unmerciful
Hands of a Butcher, in Salisbury Market* (n.p., 1774?); *The Last Dying
Words of the Retail Shopkeepers, Who Departed this Life, on the 13th of June,
1785* (London, 1785); *The Dying Groans of Sir John Barleycorn, Being his
Grievous Complaint against the Brewers of Bad Ale* (n.p., 1789); Andrew
Merry [pseud.], *The Last Dying Words of the Eighteenth Century: A
Pindarick Ode* (London, 1800); *The Apotheosis of Bonaparte* (London,
1803); *The Last Speech & Dying Words of that Unfortunate Potatoe Mer-
chant and Mealmonger, Who Underwent the Awful Sentence of the Law, on
Wednesday the 14th of January, 1824, and his Body Hung in Chains on the
Hill of Ballengiech, for the Abominable Crime of Forstalling the Meal and
Potatoe Markets, and Thereby Raising the Price of Provisions* (Glasgow,
1824).

50. Eudo C. Mason, " 'Wir sehen uns wieder!': Zu einem Leitmotiv
des Dichtens und Denkens im 18. Jahrhundert," *Literaturwissenschaftliches Jahrbuch* n.s., 5 (1964): 79–109.

51. Especially Jörg von Uthmann, *Paris für Fortgeschrittene* (Hamburg, 1981), pp. 18–19, 80–81; Michelin Guide to Paris (London,
1982), p. 43.

52. *Derniers Moments de Louis XVI* (Paris, 1793?), p. 6. Similar word-
ings are given by G. Lenotre in *La Guillotine et les exécuteurs des arrêts
criminels pendant la Révolution* (Paris, 1893) p. 4 (Sanson); Claude

Aveline, *Les Mots de la fin* (Paris, 1957), p. 41; and Evelyne Lever, *Louis XVI* (Paris, 1985), p. 665. On Marie-Antoinette see above, p. 90, and Ch. 1, note 73. Mirabeau, who died not under the guillotine but in bed, nevertheless managed to catapult his last words into the collective consciousness of his contemporaries: "I take with me the death of the monarchy. The factious will prey upon its remains." They appeared in many "memorial prints," one of which is reproduced in Simon Schama, *Citizens* (New York, 1989), p. 544; see also pp. 543–545. Last Words are frequently reported in H. Sanson, *Mémoires des Sanson*, 6 vols. (Paris, 1862–1863), especially in vol. 5 which deals with the period of the Revolution.

53. See above all Garrett Stewart, *Death Sentences: Styles of Dying in British Fiction* (Cambridge, Mass., 1984).

54. Rehm, *Der Todesgedanke*, pp. 466–467; Karl Röttger, "In Schönheit sterben," *Die Schönheit* 1 (1903): 678–689; Philippe Ariès, *The Hour of our Death* (New York, 1982), ch. 10; J. K. Huysmans, *Against Nature* (London: Penguin, 1959), p. 199:

> The truth of the matter was that the decadence of French literature, a literature attacked by organic diseases, weakened by intellectual senility, exhausted by syntactical excesses, sensitive only to the curious whims that excite the sick, and yet eager to express itself completely in its last hours, determined to make up for all the pleasures it had missed, afflicted on its death-bed with a desire to leave behind the subtlest memories of suffering, had been embodied in Mallarmé in the most consummate and exquisite fashion.

I owe this reference to Eric Downing.

55. See H. L. Mencken on Whitman's death in the *Dreiser-Mencken Letters*, ed. Thomas P. Riggio (Philadelphia, 1986), 2:450–451. This case is, however, anecdotal; cp. *In Re Walt Whitman*, ed. Horace L. Traubel et al. (Philadelphia, 1893), p. 434: "In his last whisper [he] said [to Warren Fritzinger]: 'Warry, shift.'" An authentic example is that of George Eliot, the unexcelled master of the "satisfying" novelistic closure: "Tell them I have great pain in the left side" (J. W. Cross, *George Eliot's Life* [New York, 1965], p. 630; reprint of the 1885 edition). There is also the irony that Lytton Strachey, the biographical master of the last word, died "taking back" the significance of last words (see above, p. 23); one might at this point also wish to think of

the statements by Traven, McManners, and others on the "taking back" potential of last words, above, pp. 26–27, 153–154.

56. Last words would be prominent among such details, as is generally the case in Isaac Walton's biographies, for example, whereas E. M. Forster took the opposite position: a book could not be judged by its last page any more reliably than a life by its last word (see *Albergo Empedocle and Other Writings* [New York, 1971], p. 134). On Walton's five biographies, which invariably culminate in an exemplary Christian dying-scene, see Richard D. Altick, *Life and Letters: A History of Literary Biography in England and America* (New York, 1965), p. 210; on eighteenth and nineteenth century biography, see pp. 210–211; and on the reaction against it in the twentieth century, see pp. 367–368. See also my essay "Life from the End: Last Words in Narrative Biography," in *Reading Stories*, ed. Raymond A. Prier (Albany, N.Y., 1993).

Two approaches might be helpful in a study of biographers' use of last words: one could compare numerous biographies of the same person, published over a considerable period of time, with a view to the "mileage" they get out of—which?—last words; or one could study the procedure of leading biographers over centuries. See also above, pp. 22–26.

57. See above, pp. 29–47.

Select Bibliography

Anon. "Exit Lines." *Time* (17 January 1955): 53.

Anon. "Last Words." *Every Saturday* 2 (8 September 1866): 276–277.

Anon. "Last Words." *Musical America* (December 1954): 9.

Anon. "Last Words of Poets." *Talks and Tales Magazine* (November 1899): 30–32.

Ariès, Philippe. *L'Homme devant la mort*. Paris, 1977. Trans. *The Hour of our Death*. New York, 1982.

Arnebeck, Bob. *Proust's Last Beer: A History of Curious Demises*. Harmondsworth and New York, 1980.

Auerbach, Nina. "Death Scenes." In *Private Theatricals: The Lives of the Victorians*. Cambridge, Mass., 1990.

Aulard, Alphonse. "Derniers moments et exécution de Danton." In Aulard, *Etudes et leçons sur la Révolution française*, 9th ser., pp. 45–70. Paris, 1924.

Aveline, Claude. *Les Mots de la fin*. Paris, 1957.

Bauer, Harry C. "Shakespeare's Last Words." *Library Review* 24 (1974): 255–261.

Beaty, Nancy Lee. *The Craft of Dying*. New Haven, 1970.

Bedell, Thomas D. "The Tongues of Dying Men." *Reader's Digest* 115 (July 1979): 122–125.

Berrigan, Daniel. *We Die Before We Live: Talking with the Very Ill*. New York, 1980.

Birrell, Francis, and F. L. Lucas. *The Art of Dying: An Anthology*. London, 1930.

Böhm, Rudolf. *Wesen und Funktion der Sterberede im elisabethanischen Drama*. Hamburg, 1964.

Borst, Arno. "Zwei mittelalterliche Sterbefälle." *Merkur* 390 (November 1980): 1081–1098.

Brack, O. M., Jr. "The Death of Samuel Johnson and the Ars Moriendi Tradition." *Cithara* 20 (1980): 3–15.

Brandreth, Gyles. *The Last Word*. New York, 1979.

———. *Famous Last Words and Tombstone Humor*. New York, 1989.

Brazil, P. "A Matter of Theology." *Australian Law Journal* 34 (24 November 1960): 195–199.

Brémond, Henri. *Histoire littéraire du sentiment religieux en France*. Vol. 9. Paris, 1932.

Brim, Orville, Jr., ed. *The Dying Patient*. New York, 1970.

Burke, Kenneth. "Thanatopsis for Critics: A Brief Thesaurus of Deaths and Dying." *Essays in Criticism* 2 (1952): 369–375.

Cecil, R. "Holy Dying: Evangelical Attitudes to Death." *History Today* 32, no. 8 (August 1982): 30–34.

Chandler, Kenneth A. "Three Processes of Dying and Their Behavioral Effects." *Journal of Consulting Psychology* 29 (1965): 296–361.

Chartier, Roger. "Les Arts de mourir, 1450–1600." *Annales* (1976): 51–76.

Choron, Jacques. *Death and Western Thought*. New York, 1963.

Codd, A. P. ("Bega"). *Last Words of Famous Men*. London, 1930. Reprints. Folcroft, Pa., 1973. Philadelphia, 1977.

Comper, Frances, ed. *The Book of the Craft of Dying*. London, 1917.

Confucius. *The Analects of Confucius*. Ed. William Edward Soothill. Yokohama, 1910.

Conrad, Barnaby. *Famous Last Words*. New York, 1961.

Cunningham, Homer F. *The Presidents' Last Year*. Jefferson, N.C., 1989.

De'ath, Richard. *Died Laughing*. London and Boston, 1985.

Demiéville, Paul. *Poèmes chinois devant la mort*. Paris, 1984.

———. "Stances de la fin." In *Mélanges offerts à M. Charles Haguenauer*, pp. 11–29. Paris, 1980.

Dennis, Nigel. "Arthur from the Barge: A Study of Last Words." *Encounter* 98 (November 1961): 27–31.

Detweiler, Robert. "The Moment of Death in Modern Fiction." *Contemporary Literature* 13 (1972): 269–294.

Donaldson, Norman, and Betty Donaldson. *How Did They Die?* New York, 1980.

Eissler, K. R. *The Psychiatrist and the Dying Patient*. New York, 1955.

Enright, D. J., ed. *The Oxford Book of Death*. Oxford, 1983.

Eshelman, Byron E. *Death Row Chaplain*. Englewood Cliffs, N.J., 1962.

Fadiman, Clifton. "Some Passing Remarks on Some Passing Remarks." In Fadiman, *Party of One*, pp. 466–473. Cleveland, 1955.

Falk, Franz. *Die deutschen Sterbebücher*. Köln, 1890.

Faller, Lincoln B. *Turned to Account: The Forms and Functions of Criminal Biography in Seventeenth- and Early Eighteenth-Century England*. Cambridge, England, 1987.

Favre, Robert. *La Mort dans la littérature et la pensée françaises au siècle des lumières*. Lyon, 1978.

Feifel, Herman, ed. *The Meaning of Death*. New York, 1959.

Finkenstaedt, Thomas. "Galgenliteratur: Zur Auffassung des Todes im England des 16. und 17. Jahrhunderts." *Deutsche Vierteljahrsschrift für Literaturwissenschaft und Geistesgeschichte* 34 (1960): 527–553.

Forbes, Malcolm. *They Went That-a-Way*. New York, 1988.

Frazier, Harriet C. " 'Like a Liar Gone to Burning Hell,': Shakespeare and Dying Declarations." *Comparative Drama* 19 (1985): 166–180.

Green, Jonathon. *Famous Last Words*. London and New York, 1979.

Guthke, Karl S. "Die Faszination des letzten Worts: Gedanken zu einer Konvention in Leben und Literatur." *Schweizer Monatshefte* 72 (1992): 389–402.

———. " 'Gipsabgüsse von Leichenmasken'? Goethe und der Kult des letzten Worts." *Jahrbuch der Deutschen Schiller-Gesellschaft* 35 (1991): 73–95.

———. "Last Words: A Convention in Life, Literature and Biography." In *Fictions of Culture*, ed. Steven Taubeneck. New York, 1992.

———. "Last Words in Shakespeare's Plays: The Challenge to the *Ars moriendi* Tradition." *Jahrbuch der Deutschen Shakespeare-Gesellschaft West*. 1992:80–90.

———. "Life from the End: Last Words in Narrative Biography." In *Reading Stories*, ed. Raymond A. Prier. Albany, N.Y., 1993.

———. "Kunst und Konvention des 'letzten Worts' im Drama der Goethezeit: Notizen zu einem Thema." In *Texte, Motive und Gestalten der Goethezeit: Festschrift für Hans Reiss*, pp. 177–194. Tübingen, 1989.

———. " 'Richter' oder 'Leuchtöl'? Schillers Letzte Worte in der Biographie." *Jahrbuch des Freien Deutschen Hochstifts*. 1992.

Hendrickson, Robert. *The Literary Life and Other Curiosities*. New York, 1981.

Hertslet, William Lewis, et al. *Der Treppenwitz der Weltgeschichte: Geschichtliche Irrtümer, Entstellungen und Erfindungen*. Berlin, 1967. First published in 1882.

Hoffmann, Yoel, ed. *Japanese Death Poems, Written by Zen Monks and Haiku Poets on the Verge of Death*. Rutland, Vt., 1986.

Holubetz, Margarete. "Death-Bed Scenes in Victorian Fiction." *English Studies* 67 (1986): 14–35.

Hunter, R.C.A. "On the Experience of Nearly Dying." *American Journal of Psychiatry* 124 (1967): 84–88.

Hurst, Mary Jane. "Samuel Johnson's Dying Words." *English Language Notes* 23 (1985): 45–53.

Jay, Elizabeth. *The Religion of the Heart: Anglican Evangelicism and the Nineteenth-Century Novel*. Oxford, 1979.

Kaines, Joseph. *Last Words of Eminent Persons, Comprising, in the Majority of Instances, a Brief Account of their Last Hours*. London and New York, 1866.

Kamenetz, Rodger. "Last Words." *North American Review* 269, pt. 2 (1984): 61–63.

Kastenbaum, Robert. "Deathbed Scenes." In *Encyclopedia of Death*, ed. Robert Kastenbaum and Beatrice Kastenbaum, pp. 97–101. Phoenix, Ariz., 1989.

Kettle, Thomas M. "On Saying Good-Bye." In Kettle, *The Day's Burden*, pp. 101–105. Dublin and London, 1918.

Kübler-Ross, Elisabeth. *On Death and Dying*. New York, 1968.

Kümmel, Werner Friedrich. "Der sanfte und selige Tod." In *Leichenpredigten als Quelle historischer Wissenschaften*, ed. Rudolf Lenz, pp. 3:199–226. Marburg, 1984.

Langer, Lawrence L. *The Age of Atrocity: Death in Modern Literature*. Boston, 1978.

Langston, Beach. "Essex and the Art of Dying." *Huntington Library Quarterly* 13 (1950): 109–129.

Lauritzen, Henry. *Berømtheders sidste Ord*. Aalborg, 1967.

Le Comte, Edward. *Dictionary of Last Words*. New York, 1955.

Lenotre, G. *La Guillotine et les exécuteurs des arrêts criminels pendant la Révolution*. Paris, 1893.

Lifton, Robert Jay, et al. *Six Lives, Six Deaths*. New Haven, 1979.

Lindsay, James. "Last Words." *The Outlook* (14 April 1928): 470–471.

Lockyer, Herbert. *Last Words of Saints and Sinners*. Grand Rapids, Mich., 1983.

Lofland, Lyn H. *The Craft of Dying: The Modern Face of Death*. Beverly Hills and London, 1979.

Lucas, E. V. "Last Words." In Lucas, *Luck of the Year*, pp. 180–184. New York, 1923.

Macksey, Richard. "Last Words: The *Artes Moriendi* and a Transtextual Genre." *Genre* 16 (1983): 493–516.

McCormick, Charles T. "Dying Declarations." Chap. 28 in *McCormick on Evidence*. 3d. ed. St. Paul, Minn., 1984.

McManners, John. *Death and the Enlightenment*. Oxford, 1981.

Maillard, Firmin. *Le Requiem des gens de lettres*. Paris, 1901.

Martensen-Larsen, H. *An der Pforte des Todes*. 2d ed. Berlin, [1931].

Marvin, Frederick Rowland. *The Last Words (Real and Traditional) of Distinguished Men and Women*. New York, 1900. 2d ed. New York, 1901. Reprint. Detroit, 1970.

Mason, Eudo C. "'Wir sehen uns wieder!': Zu einem Leitmotiv des Dichtens und Denkens im 18. Jahrhundert." *Literaturwissenschaftliches Jahrbuch* n.s., 5 (1964): 79–109.

Mencken, August. *By the Neck: A Book of Hangings*. New York, 1942.

Michaelis, Rolf. "Wörterbuch des Todes." *Die Zeit* (6 January 1984): 36.

Montaigne, Michel de. *The Complete Essays of Montaigne*. Trans. Donnald Frame. Stanford, Calif., 1965.

Moore, Virginia. *Ho for Heaven! Man's Changing Attitude Toward Dying*. New York, 1946.

Morrow, Lance. "A Dying Art: The Classy Exit Line." *Time* (16 January 1984): 76.

Nette, Herbert. *Adieu les belles choses*. Düsseldorf, 1971. 2d ed. published as *"Hier kann ich doch nicht bleiben": Eine Sammlung letzter Worte*. Munich 1983.

Nettler, Gwynne. "The Quality of Crisis." *Psychology Today* (April 1985): 54–55.

Neusner, Jacob. "Death-Scenes and Farewell Stories: An Aspect of the Master-Disciple Relationship in Mark and in Some Talmudic Tales." *Harvard Theological Review* 79 (1986): 187–197.

Ohlmarks, Åke. *Sista Sucken*. Stockholm, 1970.

O'Connor, Mary Catherine. *The Art of Dying Well: The Development of the Ars Moriendi*. New York, 1942.

O'Kill, Brian. *Exit Lines: Famous (and Not-So-Famous) Last Words*. Harlow, Essex, 1986.

Paz, Octavio. "The Day of the Dead." In Paz, *The Labyrinth of Solitude*, pp. 47–64. New York, 1961.

Pickering, Samuel, Jr. "The Grave Leads But to Paths of Glory: Death-bed Scenes in American Children's Books, 1800–1860." *Dalhousie Review* 59 (1979): 452–464.

Prochnik, Leon. *Endings: Death, Glorious and Otherwise As Faced by Ten Outstanding Figures of Our Time.* New York, 1980.

Ramsay, Robert, and Randall Toye. *The Goodbye Book.* New York, 1979.

Reed, John R. *Victorian Conventions.* Athens, Ohio, 1975.

Rees, Nigel. *"Quote . . . Unquote."* London, 1978.

Rehm, Walther. *Der Todesgedanke in der deutschen Dichtung vom Mittelalter bis zur Romantik.* Halle, 1928.

Roche, D. "La Mémoire de la mort: Recherches sur la place des arts de mourir dans la librairie et la lecture en France au XVIIe et XVIIIe siècles." *Annales* (1976): 76–119.

Ronconi, A. "Exitus illustrium virorum." *Reallexikon für Antike und Christentum,* vol. 6 (1966): 1258–1268.

Rudolf, Rainer. *Ars moriendi.* Cologne and Graz, 1957.

Saldarini, Anthony J. "Last Words and Deathbed Scenes in Rabbinic Literature." *Jewish Quarterly Review* 68 (1977): 28–45.

Santayana, George. "English Death-Bed Manners." In Santayana, *Soliloquies in England and Later Soliloquies.* New York, 1922.

Schmidt, Willibald. *De ultimis morientium verbis.* Marburg, 1914.

Schubart, Christof. *Die Berichte über Luthers Tod und Begräbnis.* Weimar, 1917.

Schulz, Hans Jürgen. *Letzte Tage: Sterbegeschichten aus zwei Jahrtausenden.* Berlin, 1983.

Sharpe, J. A. " 'Last Dying Speeches': Religion, Ideology and Public Execution in Seventeenth-Century England." *Past and Present* 107 (1985): 144–167.

Slater, Scott, and Alec Solomita. *Exits: Stories of Dying Moments and Parting Words.* New York, 1980.

Smith, L. B. "English Treason Trials." *Journal of the History of Ideas* 15 (1954): 471–498.

Spencer, Herbert. "The Closing Hours." In Spencer, *Facts and Comments,* pp. 94–96. New York, 1902.

Spencer, Theodore. *Death and Elizabethan Tragedy.* Cambridge, Mass., 1936.

Stauffer, E. "Abschiedsreden." *Reallexikon für Antike und Christentum,* vol. 1 (1950): 29–35.

Stewart, Charles D. "The Art of Dying." In Stewart, *Fellow Creatures*, pp. 268–278. Boston, 1935.

Stewart, Garrett. *Death Sentences: Styles of Dying in British Fiction*. Cambridge, Mass., 1984.

Szechi, Daniel. "The Jacobite Theatre of Death." In *The Jacobite Challenge*, ed. Eveline Cruickshanks and Jeremy Black, pp. 57–73. Edinburgh, 1988.

Tenenti, Alberto. *La Vie et la mort à travers l'art du XVe siècle*. Paris, 1952.

Thurmond, Charles J. "Last Thoughts before Drowning." Clinical Supplement. *Journal of Abnormal and Social Psychology* 38 (1943): 165–184.

Tosswill, M. S. "Religious Belief in Dying Declarations." *New Law Journal* 131 (11 June 1981): 617–618.

Twain, Mark. "Last Words of Great Men." In Twain, *The Curious Republic of Gondour*, pp. 132–140. New York, 1919.

van Dülmen, Richard. *Theatre of Horror*. Oxford, 1990.

van Ingen, Ferdinandus Jacobus. *Vanitas und Memento mori in der deutschen Barocklyrik*. Groningen, 1966.

Vovelle, Michel. *La Mort et l'occident*. Paris, 1983.

Waetzoldt, Wilhelm. "Die letzten Worte." In Waetzoldt, *Schöpferische Phantasie*, pp. 84–87. Wiesbaden, 1947.

Walker, Robert G. "Public Death in the Eighteenth Century." *Research Studies of the State College of Washington* 48 (1980): 11–24.

———. "Rochester and the Issue of Deathbed Repentance in Restoration and Eighteenth-Century England." *South Atlantic Review* 47 (1982): 21–37.

Wehl, Feodor. *Der Ruhm im Sterben*. Hamburg, 1886.

Weiss, Jay. "Last Words." *The Humanist* 36, no. 6 (1976): 27–29.

Whaley, Joachim, ed. *Mirrors of Mortality: Studies in the Social History of Death*. London, 1981.

Wheeler, Michael. *Death and the Future Life in Victorian Literature and Theology*. Cambridge, England, 1990.

Zaleski, Carol. *Otherworld Journeys: Accounts of Near-Death Experience in Medieval and Modern Times*. Oxford, 1987.

Index

Abélard, Pierre, 68
Adami, Johann Samuel, 215n.17
Addison, Joseph, 24, 49, 50, 124, 154
advertising, 15
Aesculapius, 50
aesthetics of LW, 102, 144–148
Ahlwardt, Hermann, 211n.49
Aeschylus, 177
Alexander, J. H. *See* Jean Hester
    Buggs
Allen, Woody, 15
Altick, Richard D., 228n.56
Alvarez, A., 58
Amado, Jorge, 34
Amida, 219n.6
Anacreon, 177
anecdotes, 8, 25, 149, 197n.73,
    227n.55
Anne, Queen of Great Britain, 107
Annuncio, Gabriele d', 188
anthologies of LW, 17, 20, 97, 99–
    154; of criminals and traitors, 106–
    109, 111–115; of freethinkers, 109–
    110, 122–123; of model Christians,
    106, 115–121; cum *ars moriendi*,
    162–168
antiquity, 12, 24, 48, 55, 100–101,
    103, 132, 157, 164, 193n.21, 219n.6
Antler, 18, 88
apocryphal nature of LW. *See*
    authenticity
Applebee, John, 112
appropriateness of LW, 68, 90–91,
    95, 133
Archimedes, 11, 133

Argens, Jean Baptiste de Boyer, Mar-
    quis d', 122
Ariès, Philippe, 47, 53, 135, 140,
    156, 158, 188, 212n.2, 218n.2,
    222n.34
Arnebeck, Bob, 217n.23
Arnim, Bettina von, 86
Aronson, Gerald J., 61, 62
Aronson, Theo, 90
ars moriendi, 29, 36–37, 61, 98–99,
    101–102, 104–105, 117, 130, 137–
    138, 159–168; criticism of, 35–47,
    173–176, 182–183; and dying
    speeches, 171–172; and literature,
    159, 220n.11
Art of Dying Well. See *ars moriendi*
art. *See* pictorial art
artifact, LW as, 26, 54, 72, 96, 142,
    144
attention commanded by LW, 10–
    12
Auden, W. H., 14
Augustine, Saint, 159, 175, 177
Augustus, Emperor, 69
Austin, Sarah, 86
authenticity, 67–97, 142, 150–151,
    212n.58
Aveline, Claude, 149–151, 185, 186

Babington, Anthony, 108
Bacon, Francis, 101, 106, 110
Baker, Osmon C., 124
ballads, 6, 19, 30
Balzac, Honoré de, 150
Bankhead, Tallulah, 68

Barbarossa, Frederick. *See* Frederick I, Holy Roman Emperor
Barillon, Jean-Jacques de, 21
Barnes, Julian, 19
Barrès, Maurice, 188
Barrie, J. M., 32
Barry, Marie Jeanne, Countess du, 187
Barthes, Roland, 11
Bassi, Ugo, 31
Bate, Walter Jackson, 80–81
Baudelaire, Charles, 22
Baudrand, Barthélemy, 160
Bawdin. *See* Fulford, Sir Baldwin
Bayer, Hyazinth, 20
Beatty, William, 69
beautiful death, 188
Beauvoir, Simone de, 22
Becket, Thomas, 159
Beckett, Samuel, 31
Beethoven, Ludwig van, 69
Bega. *See* Codd, A. P.
Behan, Brendan, 5
Bellarmino, Roberto, 173, 178
Bengel, Johann Albrecht, 120
Benjamin, Walter, 3–4
Bennett, James Gordon, 142
Bergmann, Wenceslaus, 164–165
Bergson, Henri, 57
Bernadette, Saint, 135
Bernhard, Thomas, 89
Bernhardt, Sarah, 135
Bernstein, Leonard, 13
Berrigan, Daniel, 100
Besplas, Joseph Marie Anne Gros de, 122
Bible, 12, 38, 48, 121, 163, 164, 193n.21, 194n.36
Biedermann, Flodoard von, 86
Bierce, Ambrose, 58
Bileam, 164

biographies, 6, 9, 22–26, 51, 72–89, 95, 157, 189, 197nn.75, 76, 198n.85, 228n.56; of rogues, 111–112, 214n.14
Birrell, Francis, 138–139
Blanc, Olivier, 92
Blight, Isaac, 177
Blumenberg, Hans, 17
Böhme, Jakob, 139
Boleyn, Anne, 113, 188
Bolingbroke, Henry St. John, Viscount, 124
Bolívar, Simon, 31
Bonar, Andrew Redman, 120
book titles, 19, 21
Boswell, James, 23, 58, 75, 80, 81, 189
Boyer, Abel, 110
Brandstätter, Alois, 18
Bresson, Robert, viii, 15
broadsides, 19, 111, 170, 221n.23
Broch, Hermann, 22
Brockes, Barthold Hinrich, 182–183
Brooks, Van Wyck, 24
Browne, Sir Thomas, 60
Bruce, Rev. Robert, 118
Bruno, Giordano, 123
Buddha, 135
Buggs, Jean Hester, 121
Burnet, Gilbert, 23, 179
Burns, Jabez, 120
Burns, Robert, 32, 124, 135, 185
Burroughs, William S., 22
Butler, Joseph, 120
Butler, Samuel (d. 1902), 68, 90, 146
Byron, George Gordon, Lord, 10, 21, 123, 124, 125

Caesar, Julius, 11, 141
Cain, 178
Calvi, François de, 111

Calvin, John, 120, 164
Calvinists, 117, 160–161, 163–164, 167
Camoens, Luis Vaz de, 31
Canada, 126
Canetti, Elias, 162
Carlyle, Thomas, 130, 137, 186
Caroline, Queen of Great Britain (d. 1737), 136
Caroline, Queen of Great Britain (d. 1821), 21
cartoons, 8, 15
Casanova, Giovanni Giacomo, 71
case histories, 72–89
Cassandra, 16, 31
Cather, Willa, 9, 65, 66
Catherine the Great, 16
Catholics, 63, 160–161, 167, 178, 221n.17
Cato, Marcus Porcius, 29, 125
Cenci, Beatrice, 21
Cervantes Saavedra, Miguel de, 52
Chalier, Marie Joseph, 187
Chamberlain, Houston Stewart, 83, 84
chapbooks, 19, 170
Chaplin, Charlie, 16
Chapman, Joseph Miller, 119
Charlemagne, 50, 159, 167
Charles I, King of England, 21, 111, 184
Charles Stuart, Prince, 107
Charron, Pierre, 102–103, 134, 164
Chateaubriand, François René de, 99, 126
Châtillon, Gaspard de Coligny, Duke of, 21
Chatterton, Thomas, 30
Chekhov, Anton, 68, 69
Chesterfield, Philip Dormer Stanhope, Earl of, 68, 90, 146

children, 105
China, 157, 219n.6
Choron, Jacques, 101, 135
Christie, Agatha, 30
Cicero, 165
Citizen Kane, 15
Clark, Davis W., 124
Claudel, Paul, 188
Clemm, Maria, 74, 75
Clissold, Henry, 119
Cobbin, Ingram, 119
Cobham, Richard Temple, Viscount, 50, 184
Cockshut, A.O.J., 198n.85
Codd, A. P., 137–138, 140
collectors of LW, 16, 97, 165
Colombo, John Robert, 126
Columbus, Christopher, 50
comic strips, 15
common law, 27–28, 37–38, 169, 199n.95
competitions. *See* contests
completion of life, 49–53, 60–64, 103
conduct books, Puritan, 9
Confucius, 219n.6
Conrad, Barnaby, 143–145
Conrad, Joseph, 34–35, 53
Conrady, Karl Otto, 82
consistency. *See* completion of life
contests, 16
controversies, vii–viii, 69–71
convention. *See* "institution" of LW
Cooper, Robert, 224n.40
Cooperman, Robert, 30
Corday, Charlotte, 187
Corot, Jean Baptiste Camille, 144
Coudray, Clemens Wenzeslaus, 81–87
Covenanters, 106
Cowper, William, 49
Cranmer, Thomas, 139

Cretzer, Paul, 164
criminals. *See* anthologies
Cromwell, Oliver, 139
culture, idea of: and LW, 48
curiosity value of LW, 143
Curle, Richard, 53
Curtiz, Michael, 15
Custine, Adam Philippe, Count de, 187
Cuvier, Georges Chrétien, 133

Daiches, David, 14
Dante Alighieri, 55, 161, 178
Danton, Georges, 123, 187, 208n.13
Däubler, Theodor, 58
David, Jacques Louis, 28
David, King of Israel, 157, 167
Davies, Robertson, 18
Davis, Jim, 15
Dayrolles, Solomon, 68, 90, 146
death: circumstances of, 91–92; de-personalized, 53, 62–63, 99, 189, 204n.13, 212n.2; staging of, 9, 25, 53, 100, 144
deathbed recantation, 26, 52, 178–179
deathbed revelation, 14, 52
deathbed scenes, cult of, 9, 50, 193n.24, 201n.129
death mask, 53–54
decadence, 188, 227n.54
Defoe, Daniel, 107–111, 112
Dennis, Carl, 30
Dennis, Nigel, 93–95
Descartes, René, 16
Deslandes, André François Boureau, 109–110, 113, 122, 180
Desmoulins, Camille, 187
Desmoulins, Lucille, 187
detective thrillers, 30
diary entries, last, 92
Dickens, Charles, 29

Dickinson, Emily, 68
dictionaries of LW, 17, 132, 142
didactic tracts, 31, 159
Diderot, Denis, 5, 70, 123, 140, 207n.6
Dido, 32
Dikaiarchos, 101
Disraeli, Benjamin, 207n.5
dissenters, 106, 168
Dobree, Samuel, 123
Donaldson, Betty, 217n.23
Donaldson, Norman, 217n.23
Donne, John, 175
Doumer, Paul, 12
Doyle, Arthur Conan, 30
drama: Elizabethan, 29, 35–47, 54; Everyman plays, 29; middle-class, 29
Dreiser, Theodore, 13
Dreyfus, Alfred, 16
Dubnow, Simon, 171
Dukakis, Michael, 49
Dunn, James, 169
Dunton, Rev. John, 106, 174, 175
Dürrenmatt, Friedrich, viii, 31
Duveen, Joseph, 25
Dyherrn, George Charles de, 180
dying declarations, in law, 27–28, 37–38, 199n.95
dying speech, 19–20, 29, 32, 37, 168–172, 221n.23

East, Timothy, 118
Easter Island, 219n.6
Eckermann, Johann Peter, 89
Eco, Umberto, 18, 88
edification. *See* guidance
Edison, Thomas Alva, 30
Egbert, Walter R., 132–133
Egypt, 54, 157, 219n.6
Einstein, Albert, 16
Eissler, K. R., 61–63, 66

electric chair, 22, 197n.74
Eliot, George (Mary Ann Evans), 68, 227n.55
Eliot, John, 105, 106
Eliot, T. S., 135
Elisabeth, Queen of Romania, 25
Elizabeth I, Queen of England, 11, 188
Ellison, Ralph, 33
Ellmann, Richard, 77
encyclopedias, 18
Enlightenment, 96–97, 150, 177, 181, 224n.47
Enright, D. J., 4, 93, 95
entertainment, 98–154
Epaminondas, 25
Epictetus, 31
Erasmus, 164
Erdmann, Christoph Gottlieb, 166
Espina, Enrique Chao, 141
Essex, Robert Devereux, Earl of, 108, 113, 188
examined life, 3–4
executions, public, 19, 37, 106–109, 111, 168–172, 197n.73
existentialism, 63–64, 151
expectations, social, vii, 9, 35, 50–51, 102, 170, 192n.10, 212n.62
Ezekiel, 167

Fabert, Abraham de, 21
fable convenue. See myth
Fadiman, Clifton, 16, 143–145
Faller, Lincoln B., 214n.14
fame. *See* immortality
familiar quotations, LW as. *See* proverbial nature of LW
fascination with LW. *See* attention commanded by LW
Faust book, 178
Favre, Robert, 135
Feinler, Gottfried, 115–116

Fenwick, John, 169
Ferrand, Max, 8
films, viii, 15, 195n.45
Finucane, R. C., 56
first words, 48
Flanner, Janet, 194n.33
Flaubert, Gustave, 195n.40
Fleischer, Fritz, 82
folklore, 8, 39, 57–58, 193n.21; highbrow or literary, 4, 13, 18, 21
Fontane, Theodor, 29, 100
Foote, George William, 88, 122–123, 180
Forbes, Malcolm, 143
forgiveness, 36, 41, 44, 171
Forster, E. M., 198n.76, 228n.56
Förster-Nietzsche, Elisabeth, 92, 93
Fortis, Leone, 31
Foucault, Michel, 11
France, 112, 168. *See also* French Revolution
Francis I, Emperor of Austria, 12
Francis Ferdinand, Archduke of Austria, 90
Franco, Francisco, 54
Frazier, Harriet C., 202n.135
Frederick I, Holy Roman Emperor, 164, 176
Frederick II, King of Denmark, 163
Frederick II, King of Prussia, 21, 123, 124
Frederick William I, Elector of Brandenburg, 21
Frederick William I, King of Prussia, 5, 191n.9
freethinkers, 109–110, 122–123, 180–182
French Revolution, 15, 21, 59, 113–115, 152, 170, 185–187, 226–226n.52
Freud, Sigmund, 162
Friedell, Egon, 8

Frommann, Friedrich Johannes, 84
Fuentes, Carlos, 7
Fulford, Sir Baldwin, 30
funeral sermons, 46, 115, 156, 165, 166–167, 175–176, 187, 222n.34

Gainsborough, Thomas, 6
gallows speech. *See* dying speech
García, Frutos, 7
Gassendi, Pierre, 110
George, Stefan, 189
George I, King of Great Britain, 107
George II, King of Great Britain, 136
George V, King of Great Britain, 69–70, 207n.4
George VI, King of Great Britain, 126
Gerhardt, Paul, 208n.8
Germany, 112, 115–117, 121, 168
Gide, André, 68
Godwin, Edward, 180
Goethe, Johann Wolfgang von, 3, 5, 7, 8, 14, 51, 54, 59, 60, 61, 70, 81–89, 91, 94, 123, 145, 187
Goethe, Ottilie von, 84–85, 94
Gold, E. J., 12
Golding, William, 58
Gontaut-Biron, Armand Louis de, 187
Gorer, Geoffrey, 127
Goya y Lucientes, Francisco José de, 29
Green, Jonathon, 147–148
Greene, Graham, 31
Gregory VII, Pope, 71
Grenzerfahrung, 59, 66
Grey, Lady Jane, 50, 113
Grierson, Herbert J. C., 76
Groening, Matt, 15
Gros de Besplas. *See* Besplas, Joseph Marie Anne Gros de

Groß, Johann, 164
Grosse, Henning, 214n.13
Grosvenor, Benjamin, 173, 174
growth, in last phase of life, 62–63, 66
Gruenter, Rainer, xi
Grynaeus, Johann Jakob, 163–164
guidance, 98–154
Guitry, Sacha, 18
Gunther, John, 22

H., J. M., 131
H., M., 10
Haas, Nicolaus, 178
Hadrian, Emperor, 54
Hale, Nathan, 7, 21, 71, 208n.9
Haller, Albrecht von, vii-viii, 71, 133
Hamilton, William, 185
Harcourt, William, 169
Hardy, Thomas, 35
Hardy, Thomas Masterman, 69
Harvard University, 25
Hase, Pauline, 84
Hauer, Jean Jacques, 187
Hauptmann, Gerhart, 23, 54
Hawkins, John, 80
Hawthorne, Nathaniel, 29
Hecht, Anthony, 88
Hecker, Max, 81, 87
Heermann, Johann, 160
Heidegger, Martin, 17, 63
Heine, Heinrich, 5, 51, 70, 87
Heller, Joseph, 34
Hemingway, Ernest, 16, 18
Henckel, Erdmann Heinrich, Count, 117
Henry VIII, King of England, 78, 110, 113
Herberger, Valerius, 176
Herder, Johann Gottfried, 199n.92
hero worship, 130, 133, 137–138

Herwig, Wolfgang, 86
Hewet, John, 111
Hildebrand, Joachim, 165
Hildesheimer, Wolfgang, 9
Hill, Reginald, 30
Hilton, Conrad, 6
historiography, 100, 157
history of LW, 96–99, 127, 135–136, 139–142, 154, 155–158, 187–190, 219n.5; landmarks in, 158–189
hit songs. *See* songs
Hitler, Adolph, 14
Hobbes, Thomas, 110, 122, 123
Hofmannsthal, Hugo von, 4, 41, 50, 66, 188
Holberg, Ludwig von, 3
Homer, 32
Hooker, Richard, 173, 174
Hoole, John, 80
Horace, 118
hospice movement, 99–100, 204n.13
Houghton, Arthur A., Jr., 25
Housman, A. E., 16, 61
Howie, John, 115
Hugo, Victor, 29, 123
Hume, David, 3, 11, 123, 124, 181
Huntington, Henry, 25
Hurst, Mary Jane, 79, 80
Huss, John, 159, 164
Huston, John, 15
Hutschnecker, Arnold A., 60
Huxley, Aldous, 14
Huysmans, Joris Karl, 227n.54
Hyde, Tom, 143

Ibsen, Henrik, 4–5, 32, 147
Ice Cube, 200n.106
idioms, 7
imitatio Christi, 159–160
immortality, secular, 29, 53–56; and Christian theologians, 55

Indians, 31, 105
individualization, completed in last phase of life, 62–64
infidels vs. believers, 122–125, 128, 131, 148, 180, 224n.41
"institution" of LW, viii, 4, 6–7, 9–10, 18; criticism of, 17, 26–27, 69, 90–91, 93–95, 107–109, 152–154, 169–170, 198n.76, 213n.12, 227n.55. *See also* parody
intellectual life, breakdown of religious frameworks of. *See* secularization
Ionesco, Eugène, 31, 32
Iribarren, Manuel, 141
Isaac, 157

Jackson, Jesse, 13–14
Jackson, Thomas Jonathan ("Stonewall"), 18
Jacob, 157
James V, King of Scotland, 12
James, Alice, 66
James, William, 66
Janeway, James, 105
Japan, 7, 54, 144, 157, 219n.6
Jarry, Alfred, 90, 211n.52
Jaspers, Karl, 59, 64
Jean Paul. *See* Richter, Jean Paul Friedrich
Jeffreys, George, Lord, 106
Jerome, Saint, 163
Jesuits, 20, 109, 169
Jesus, 32, 42, 50, 57, 96, 105, 125, 138, 159, 160
Jetzer, Johann, 20, 109, 169
Joan of Arc, 114
Johnson, Edgar, 76
Johnson, Greg, 30
Johnson, Samuel, 3, 23, 58, 75, 79–81, 83, 92

jokes, 7–8, 13, 16–17, 25, 32–33
Jones, Peter, ix
Joséphine, Marie Rose, Empress of
    France, 68, 133
Judas, 23, 45, 178
Julian Apostata, Emperor, 25
Junghans, Heinrich, 221n.17

Kafka, Franz, 5, 33, 135
Kaines, Joseph, 126–131, 132, 133,
    134, 137, 153
Kamenetz, Rodger, 72–73, 74
Kane, Joseph Nathan, 18
Kant, Immanuel, 68
Karl August, Grandduke of Weimar,
    84
Karloff, Boris, 135
Kawabata, Yasunari, 219n.6
Keßler, Harry, Count, 170
Keyserling, Eduard, Count, 188
Kidder, Daniel P., 123, 128
Kierkegaard, Søren , 92
King, Martin Luther, 14
Klopstock, Friedrich Gottlieb, 125
Klopstock, Robert, 5
Knebel, Karl Ludwig von, 51
Koch, Edward, 13
Krause, Friedrich, 83, 84, 87
Kübler-Ross, Elisabeth, 100

Lalemant, Pierre, 167–168
Lamarck, Jean Baptiste de, 8
Lamartine, Alphonse de, 4
landmarks. See history
Landor, Walter Savage, 30
La Rochefoucault, Guy de, 114
last hour, significance of. See ars
    moriendi
Laubscher, Friedrich, 149
law. See common law; dying
    declarations

Lawrence, James, 7, 11
Le Brun, François, 29
Le Comte, Edward, 71, 74, 75, 88,
    141–142
Lee, Robert E., 135
legacy, LW as cultural, 152
legend. See myth
Leo X, Pope, 135
Lessing, Gotthold Ephraim, 11, 29
letters, last, 92
Levitt, Justin, xi
Lévy, Bernard-Henri, 22
Lewes, G. H., 81
Lewin, Thomas H., 132, 137
Library of Congress, 17
Lillo, George, 29
Lincoln, Abraham, 92
litany, in Catholic church, 101, 161,
    172
literature: use of LW in, 29–47, 64–
    66, 190; techniques and devices in-
    volving LW in, 32–35. See also nov-
    els; drama; poems
Lloyd, David, 104–105
Locke, John, 122
Lockhart, J. G., 75–76
Lockyer, Herbert, 63, 117, 125, 148,
    149
Logan, Robert W., 21
Lot, 16
Louis the Pious, Emperor, 167
Louis II, King of Bavaria, 21
Louis XVI, King of France, 21, 186,
    226n.52
Lucas, F. L., 138–139
Ludwig II, King of Bavaria, 21
Ludwig, Johann Christoph, 116
Luther, Martin, 50, 120, 164, 173,
    201n.130
Lutherans, 115–117, 160–161, 163–
    164, 166–167, 175, 178, 221n.17

M***. *See* Thiessé, Léon
MacCarthy, Desmond, 197n.75
McCartney, Paul, 31
McCormick, Charles T., 28
MacDonald, Arthur, 215n.21
Macdonald, Stephen, 69
McGavin, William, 115
McManners, John, 153, 180
Maeterlinck, Maurice, 188
magical power of LW, 8, 65
Mahler, Gustav, 5
Maillard, Firmin, 135
Malamud, Bernard, 32
Malesherbes, Chrétien Guillaume,
    186
Mann, Thomas, viii, 51, 59, 91, 146
Marat, Jean Paul, 187
Marie-Antoinette, Queen of France,
    21, 90, 186
Marius, Richard, 78
Marsh, William, 10
martyrs, 50, 61, 120. *See also*
    anthologies
Marut, Ret. *See* Traven, B.
Marvin, Frederick Rowland, 132
Marx, Karl, 199n.92
Mary Stuart, Queen of Scotland, 12,
    108, 113, 188
Mary II, Queen of England, 106
Mather, Cotton, 111
Maty, Matthew, 90
Maugham, W. Somerset, 32
Maupassant, Guy de, 195n.40
Maximilian, Emperor of Mexico, 15
Mazarin, Hortense de, 110
Mel, Conrad, 116
Melanchthon, Philip, 164
Melville, Herman, 59
Mencken, H. L., 13, 227n.55
Mengs, Raffael, 14
mentalités, 156, 158

Mera, Juan León, 31
Meredith, George, 30
Meredith, Owen, 30
metaphysics. *See* mystique
Mexico, 7, 10, 15, 51, 54, 170
Michelangelo, 141
Middle Ages, 56, 96–97
Mill, John Stuart, 123
Millowitsch, Willy, 31
Mirabeau, Honoré Gabriel Riqueti,
    Count de, 8, 21, 124, 226n.52
Mishima, Yukio, 54
Montagu, Lady Mary Wortley, 127
Montaigne, Michel de, 47, 98–99,
    101–103, 106, 110, 134, 164, 174,
    190
Montgomery, Bernard Law, 135
Montherlant, Henri de, 8, 192n.10
Moore, Virginia, 140–141
Moran, John J., 73–74
More, Thomas, 24, 78, 79, 108, 113,
    188
Morris, Valentine, 80
Moser, Johann Jakob, 112, 166, 179,
    215n.17
Moses, 157, 167
Mozart, Wolfgang Amadeus, 9, 16
Müller, Friedrich von, 81, 84–87
multiple sets of LW, vii–viii, 69–70,
    94, 207nn.4, 5, 6
Myers, John, 148
Mylius, Martin, 162–163, 164
mystique, 56–66, 116, 129, 148
myth, LW as, 6, 71–72, 95. *See also*
    authenticity

Nabokov, Vladimir, 33
Napoleon I, 10, 68, 125, 133, 146,
    184
Narcissus, 16
"natural history" of LW, 72

Neale, Erskine, 124
near-death experiences, 57–58, 204n.13, 205nn.23,25, 28
Nelson, Horatio, 69
Nero, Emperor, 16, 139
Nette, Herbert, 22, 151–152, 186
Nevin, Alfred, 120
New Statesman, 16
New York Times, 12, 16
New Yorker, 8, 12
Newgate, 112
Newman, John Henry, 159
newspaper accounts of LW, 12–13, 194n.34, 195nn.40,42
Newsweek, 12, 13, 14, 35, 193n.16
Nick's Mate Island, 12
Nicolson, Harold, 24
Nietzsche, Elisabeth. *See* Förster-Nietzsche, Elisabeth
Nietzsche, Friedrich, 12, 92, 94, 101
normative LW. See *ars moriendi*
novels, 9, 18–19, 29, 159

obituaries, 13, 25
Ockanickon, 31, 105
Ohlmarks, Åke, 142, 144
O'Kill, Brian, 88, 144–147, 202n.132
Olivier, Laurence, 8
Oman, Carola, 76
O'Neill, Eugene, 52
opera, 29
Ormes, Cicely, 125
Orton, Joe, 32, 77
Orwell, George, 32
Oxburgh, Henry, 106

Paine, Thomas, 123, 124, 181
panoramic vision, 57, 205n.23
parodies, 20, 32, 35, 43, 183–185, 195n.42, 199n.93, 226n.49
Pascal, Blaise, 177

Patch, Richard, 177
Pater, Walter, 188
patriots, 21, 50, 133
pattern. *See* completion of life
Paul V, Pope, 21
Paul, Jean. *See* Richter, Jean Paul Friedrich
Paz, Octavio, 51
Pearse, Edward, 160
Peretti, 31
Pericles, 139
Petrarca, Francesco, 55
phrases, 7
physiology of dying, 57, 60, 64, 120, 129, 224n.40
Picasso, Pablo, 14, 16, 31
pictorial art, 28–29, 61
Pinter, Harold, 32
Pitaval, François Gayot de, 111
Pitt, William, the Younger, 70, 91, 207n.5
Plath, Sylvia, 30
Plato, 3, 133
Playboy, 8
Plessner, Helmuth, 3
Pliny the Elder, 174, 177
Plunket, Oliver, 222n.28
Poe, Edgar Allan, 31, 72–75
poems, 30
Pohl, Gerhart, 23
polemics, 31
Pope, Alexander, 50, 93, 184
Pound, Ezra, 32
Pratz, Claire de, 70
Presbyterians, 106, 115
Pride, Thomas, Lord, 184
"primitive" cultures, 9, 157
Pritchard, M. C., 125
Pritchett, V. S., 69
professions, LW classified according to, 127, 133–135, 137, 148, 215n.21

Pronzini, Bill, 30
prophecy of dying persons, 9, 38, 40, 165, 193n.21
Proust, Marcel, 16
proverbial nature of LW, 4, 11, 50, 93
psychiatrists on death, 60–64
public dying, 53. *See also* executions
Pückler-Muskau, Hermann, Prince, 86
Puritans, 9
Pyritz, Hans, 81

Quakers, 106, 115
Quinault, Philippe, 4
Quinos, Bruno, 163
quotations, LW as familiar, 4, 6, 55, 88–89, 186, 192n.10, 196n.58

rabbinic literature, 157
Rabelais, François, 69, 70, 110
Raleigh, Walter, 113, 188
Rancé, Armand Jean le Bouthillier de, 99
Rees, Hulda A., 131
reference works, biographical, 18
Rehm, Walther, 135, 155, 224n.47
religious frameworks. *See* secularization
Renaissance, 29, 55, 96–97, 101
Reynacher, Johann Caspar, 176
Rhodes, Cecil, 5
Ribbentrop, Joachim von, 16
Richardson, Samuel, 29, 220n.11
Richebourcq, Jacobus de, 103–104, 106, 126
Richepin, Jean, 77
Richter, Jean Paul Friedrich, 142, 155, 156
Rilke, Rainer Maria, 9, 62–63, 99, 188
Rimbaud, Arthur, 16

Rochester, John Wilmot, Earl of, 23, 52, 125, 179
Rodríguez, Luis Angel, 141
Roland, Manon, 15, 59, 60, 84, 187
Roman emperors, 101, 125, 163, 164
Rommel, Erwin, 135
Roper, William, 78
Roque, Pierre de la, 117
Rosenbach, A.S.W., 25
Ross, Robert, 77
Rousseau, Jean-Jacques, 29, 124
Rubens, Peter Paul, 28
Rückert, Friedrich, 88
Ryland, John Collett, 122, 180

Sabatier, Antoine, 112–114
Sacher, Johannes Chrysostomus, 20
Sade, Donatien Alphonse François, Count de, 31
sagas, Icelandic, 32, 54, 144
St. Evremond, Charles Marguetel de Saint-Denis, 122, 174
saints, 24, 56–57, 61. *See also* anthologies of last words, of model Christians
Sand, George, 21
Sanson, Charles Henri, 186, 197n.73
Santayana, George, 152–153
Saroyan, William, 10
Sassoon, Siegfried, 69
Sastres, Francesco, 80
satire. *See* parodies
Saunders, Cicely, 99
Saxe, Moritz, Count de (Marshal), 69
Schaller, David, 160
Schama, Simon, 186
Schiller, Friedrich, 11, 35, 51, 70, 208n.6
Schmidt, Willibald, 100
Schönberg, Arnold, 5

Schüddekopf, Carl, 82–85
Schultz, Dutch, 22
Scliar, Moacyr, 65
Scobie, Stephen, 210n.49
Scorsese, Martin, 35
Scott, Robert, 92
Scott, Sir Walter, 75–76
secularization, 26, 44–47, 53–56, 96–
    97, 100, 102, 128–130, 133, 149,
    185
Seelbach, C., 124
Segal, Erich, 33
Seidler, Luise, 84
self-transcendence. *See* immortality
Seneca, 28, 163, 183
Shakespeare, William, xi, 4, 8, 16,
    27, 35–47, 53, 55, 64, 66, 102, 160,
    169, 191n.6
Shalit, Gene, 8
Sharfstein, Daniel, xi
Sharpin, E. C., 119
Shaw, S. B., 131
Shelley, Mary, 126
Shelley, Percy Bysshe, 123
Shelston, Alan, 95
Shepheard, James, 106
Silverman, Kenneth, 74
simultaneity of the nonsimultane-
    ous, 47, 181, 222n.34
sincerity of LW, 177–180
Sitwell, Edith, 6
Smiles, Samuel, 133
Smith, Alexander, 111–112
Socrates, 3, 8, 11, 25, 28, 34, 50, 139,
    141, 190
Sommer, Christoph, 165–166
songs, 31
Songs of Huexotzingo, 54–55
Sophocles, 176
Spencer, Herbert, 60, 153
Sperber, Doris, ix

Spinoza, Baruch, 122, 123
Sprung, Robert C., xi
Stalin, Joseph, 14, 135
Stanhope, James, 207n.5
Stauffer, Donald A., 197n.76
Steele, Richard, 154
Stein, Gertrude, 11, 135, 144, 146
Sternberger, Dolf, 85–87
Sterne, Laurence, 200n.111
Stevenson, Burton E., 93
Stevenson, Robert Louis, 143
Stewart, Charles D., 155
Stowe, Harriet Beecher, 69
Strachey, Lytton, 22–23, 189,
    198n.77, 227n.55
Strafford, Thomas Wentworth, Earl
    of, 20, 111
Strauß, Botho, 65, 202n.131
Strauß, David Friedrich, 123
Strindberg, August, 144
Stromberger, Christian Wilhelm, 121
stylistics of LW. *See* aesthetics
sudden death, 36, 47, 99, 101, 102,
    161, 172–177, 222n.34
suicide notes, 91–92
survival in LW, 6, 26, 29, 53

taboo of death, vii, 100, 127
Tarquinius, Emperor, 174
Tasso, Torquato, 50, 125
Taubeneck, Steven, xi
Taylor, Jeremy, 36, 180
Tecumseh, 126
Teresa, Saint, 92, 139
Tertullian, 55
Thackeray, William Makepeace, 29
theater metaphor, 52
theatricality of dying. *See* death, stag-
    ing of
thief on the cross, 37, 44, 164, 172,
    179, 223n.39

Thiessé, Léon, 114–115, 186
Thomas, Dylan, 135, 143
Thoreau, Henry David, 143, 146
titles. *See* book titles
Toklas, Alice B., 11
Tolstoy, Leo, Count, 5, 23, 53, 64
tradition (handing down of LW), 67,
71, 151, 152
traitors. *See* anthologies of last
words, of criminals and traitors
Traven, B., 26, 153
trivia calendars, 15
Trivial Pursuit, 15
Trudeau, Garry, 15
truth revealed in LW, 4, 20, 37, 49,
53–54, 61, 95, 96, 129, 166, 169–
170
Turner, Frederick Jackson, 8
Turner, Reginald, 77
Twain, Mark, 17, 26–27, 153,
199n.93
Tyburn, 112

Umberto II, King of Italy, 5
unexamined life, 3

Valerius Maximus, 177
Vallee, Rudy, 13
Van Dyck, Anthonis, 6
Verlaine, Paul, 188
Vespasian, Emperor, 15
Victoria, Queen of Great Britain, 22–
23, 70, 126, 130
Victorian ethos, 133
Vidal, Gore, 88–89
Villa, Pancho, 10, 15, 150
Virgil, 22, 32
Vitellius, Emperor, 139
Voltaire, 11, 31, 70, 123, 124, 125,
181
Vovelle, Michel, 156

Wagner, Richard, 16, 17, 90, 146
Wailing Wall, 220n.7
Waller, William, 20
Walton, Isaac, 228n.56
Warhol, Andy, 195n.42
Warton, John. *See* Wood, William
Washington, George, 21, 68
"We shall meet again," 185
Webster, Daniel, 70
Wehl, Feodor, 134–136, 138
Weil, Grete, 192n.10
Weißenborn, Wilhelm, 84
Weller, Hieronymus, 176
Wentworth, Thomas. *See* Strafford,
Thomas Wentworth, Earl of
Wertenbaker, Charles, 25
Wesley, John, 124
West, Benjamin, 29
White, Patrick, 33
Whitman, Walt, 13, 51, 153, 227n.55
Wieland, Christoph Martin, 51
Wilde, Oscar, 4, 23, 70, 76–77, 129,
135
Wille, Wilhelm, 163
William the Conqueror, King of En-
gland, 135
William III, King of England, 106
Wilson, A. N., 23
witticisms. *See* jokes
Wolf, Christa, 31
Wolfe, James, 8, 21, 29
Wolsey, Thomas, 113
Wood, William, 117
Woolf, Leonard, 138
Woolf, Virginia, 138
Worbs, Erich, 142
Wordsworth, William, 68

Yeats, John Butler, 24,
Yeats, William Butler, 24, 54
Young, Edward, 52, 61

Yourcenar, Marguérite, 204n.16

Zelter, Karl Friedrich, 86
Zielesch, Lotte, 149

Zischka (Ziska), Johann, 50
Zitzewitz, Otto von, 121
Zola, Emile, 29
Zwingli, Huldrych, 164

By the Same Author

Die Entdeckung des Ich: Studien zur Literatur, 1993

Letzte Worte: Variationen über ein Thema der Kulturgeschichte des Westens, 1990

B. Traven: Biographie eines Rätsels, 1987 Tr.: B. Traven: The Life Behind the Legends, 1991

"Das Geheimnis um B. Traven entdeckt"—und rätselvoller den je, 1984

Erkundungen: Essays zur Literatur von Milton bis Traven, 1983

Der Mythos der Neuzeit: Das Thema der Mehrheit der Welten in der Literatur- und Geistesgeschichte von der kopernikanischen Wende bis zur Science Fiction, 1983 Tr.: The Last Frontier, 1990

Das Abenteuer der Literatur: Studien zum literarischen Leben der deutschsprachigen Länder von der Aufklärung bis zum Exil, 1981

Haller im Halblicht: Vier Studien, 1981

Gotthold Ephraim Lessing, 1973 (3d ed. 1979)

Das deutsche bürgerliche Trauerspiel, 1972 (3d ed. 1980)

Die Mythologie der entgötterten Welt: Ein literarisches Thema von der Aufklärung bis zur Gegenwart, 1971

Wege zur Literatur: Studien zur deutschen Dichtungs- und Geistesgeschichte, 1967

Modern Tragicomedy, 1966. Tr.: Die moderne Tragikomödie: Theorie und Gestalt, 1968

Der Stand der Lessing-Forschung, 1965

Haller und die Literatur, 1962

Gerhart Hauptmann: Weltbild im Werk, 1961 (2d ed. 1980)

Geschichte und Poetik der deutschen Tragikomödie, 1961

Das Leid im Werke Gerhart Hauptmanns (with Hans M. Wolff), 1958

Englische Vorromantik und deutscher Sturm und Drang, 1958